The
RETIREMENT
REVOLUTION

The
RETIREMENT
REVOLUTION

A Strategic Guide to
Understanding & Investing Lump-Sum Distributions
from Qualified Retirement Plans

by Dan L. Flores

iUniverse Star
New York   Lincoln   Shanghai

The Retirement Revolution
A Strategic Guide to Understanding & Investing Lump-Sum Distributions
from Qualified Retirement Plans

iUniverse Star
an iUniverse, Inc. imprint

For information address:
iUniverse, Inc.
2021 Pine Lake Road, Suite 100
Lincoln, NE 68512
www.iuniverse.com

ISBN: 0-595-29790-0 (Pbk)
ISBN: 0-595-66053-3 (Cloth)

Printed in the United States of America

Dedication

To those who make my life worth living: Karen, my wife of twenty-three years, and to my twin daughters, Brittany and Jessica. Their birth made my life complete. I never understood how much my parents loved me until I became a father and my daughters came into my life.

Contents

Appendix

Acknowledgments

I am grateful to the research team at Stanford University whose many hours of research helped me assemble the contents of this book: John Chi, Amy Long, Christina Li, Koome Gikunda, Yoshio Osaki, Margaret Vo, and team leader Lili Wang. A special thanks to Stanford graduate Margaret Vo who helped me with editing and taught me more about English grammar than all my previous teachers and professors combined. I would also like to thank my friend and mentor Steve Lewis, a money manager in the San Francisco Bay area, whose class in financial investments I attended some twenty years ago. He is the person who opened my eyes to the world of investing and stressed that I always look for both the advantages and disadvantages of any given investment. A special thanks to Dwight Ruddell, my good friend of forty-one years, for his comments, editing, and advice. Last but not least, a personal from the bottom of my heart thank you to Ralph Saroyan, my advisor at the University of the Pacific who helped me realize my dream of a college education.

Foreword

Everyday, we seem to be faced with fresh reminders—from the media, from the government, and within the workplace—that the world of retirement is dramatically changing. The responsibility of securing financial support in retirement has mostly fallen into our own laps. Retirement, once considered by many to signal a relaxing stage of life, is now fraught with complicated questions about employee benefit plans, investment strategies, and projected cost-of-living expenses. These were just a few of the issues I worried about while planning for my own retirement. I started to wonder, "Will I be able to enjoy my retirement years?"

When I first met Dan during the early 1990s, he had just begun offering a series of retirement and financial planning seminars for employees at Lockheed (now Lockheed Martin) Missiles and Space Co. These classes were provided free of charge on the employees' own time for people who desired to learn more about their personal finances, as well as how they could tailor their future financial planning for retirement security. My colleagues and I were immediately impressed with how Dan directly addressed many of our financial retirement worries. From the outset, Dan's presentations became popular and well accepted by the employees as a valuable resource for solving the many mysteries of decision making for a sound retirement plan. To this day, many of my former Lockheed Martin associates entrust Dan on a continuing basis for their retirement and financial planning needs.

In his book *The Retirement Revolution*, Dan takes a dynamic approach to addressing the questions and problems that we all face in our day-to-day retirement planning. From his experience advising hundreds of clients, he presents essential retirement guidelines and thorough invest-ment analyses in a clear and easy to understand manner. The informa-tion included is comprehensive and will empower readers with the knowledge to plan and implement their own financially sound retire-ment plan. Dan draws upon nearly two decades of experience as a Retirement Planning Consultant to share with readers what he has shared with so many clients: a true understanding of investor concerns, informed investment decisions, and exceptional financial advice. *The Retirement Revolution* will be an excellent financial and retirement-plan-ning tool for not only the layperson, but the experienced investor as well.

The opportunity for me to write opening remarks for this book brought many memories. I have pleasantly reflected upon all the time that Dan Flores and I have spent together, his unsurpassed knowledge, his easy personality, and above all, his high ethical standards.

I sincerely believe that *The Retirement Revolution* will prove to be an invaluable addition to any investor or investment resource library. It will bring a new level of financial confidence to those making this tran-sition, allowing them to focus on more important things: enjoying retirement.

Emmett R. Taft, CM
Executive Director
Lockheed Martin Management Association
Sunnyvale, California
(Retired)

Introduction

Retirement is a profound life-cycle event. You owe it to yourself to make the most informed choices you can. These issues merit consideration not only after you retire, but also as you build up to that point in your life and strive to ensure your future financial security and well-being. Understanding the rules and regulations of lump-sum distributions, investment strategies, and the portfolio offerings of various investment firms can be vital to your financial well-being. This book is designed to help you accomplish those goals.

You may be surprised to discover that some investment firms and financial professionals deal with a limited number of investment alternatives and thus lack access to the full range of financial options that may be pertinent to your individual financial needs. For that reason, whether you make financial decisions alone or follow the advice of an investment counselor, this book will increase your ability to evaluate the many options with which you will be presented.

Moreover, if you are a retirement-planning professional—a benefits or human resource director—you will find this book to be a useful, easy-to-read resource to share with your employees.

I have divided the book into three major sections with an appendix at the end. Key terms appear in bold throughout the book and are defined in the appendix glossary. In the first section, I discuss the rules and regulations of IRA rollovers plus the procedures for handling a lump-sum distribution from a company's qualified retirement accounts. In the second section, I show you how to build a portfolio blueprint, which covers the important topics of financial planning, asset allocation, and investment product selection. The third and final section gives an analysis of various investments and portfolio strategies and walks you through the process of constructing and monitoring a sample portfolio.

While numerous books about retirement planning are available and well intended, they generally fail to deal in detail with the very specific needs of lump-sum recipients or with individuals managing IRA assets. Also, by attempting to cover everything from A to Z, they are unable to give more than superficial coverage to the important fundamentals of IRA and lump-sum planning.

The information in this book is based on real-world experiences, which can help you to avoid the costly mistakes that occur all too often to individuals before, during, and after retirement. Welcome, then, to the world of lump-sum distributions, retirement planning, and investment strategies.

Dan Flores
Vice President Investments
Retirement Planning Consultant

Part I

Understanding the Retirement Revolution

Chapter 1

The Changing World of Retirement

When I was a little kid, I remember how our family used to get together for special occasions. Everybody would be there: my parents and brothers, along with aunts, uncles, and cousins. All the kids would be outside running and playing, the mothers would be in the kitchen getting the food ready, and the fathers would be in the back yard around the barbecue pit talking about work. The interesting part of those conversations is that the dads never talked about retirement. There was no need to have those types of discussions since it was assumed that somehow everything would work out. The fathers knew they would eventually collect Social Security, get a company pension, and never have to make decisions about something called a lump-sum distribution, because back then it didn't exist. How the world has changed! Now at family gatherings, the kids are inside the house playing video games, the food is catered, both parents are working, everybody is worried about retirement, and you better add the term lump-sum distribution to your vocabulary.

Receiving a lump-sum distribution from a qualified retirement plan may represent the largest financial asset you will ever come to control. You may discover that the only other asset that comes close to your accrued retirement benefits is your home.

It is estimated that during the next five years approximately $2.7 trillion of individual investment funds could be withdrawn from company retirement plans.[1] While this number is impressive, consider that you may in fact spend more years in retirement than you did working. Furthermore, many experts estimate that during retirement you will need an income of up to 75 percent of your pre-retirement income.

The assets that will be required to fund the income needs of our nation's future retirees are staggering. Compounding this fact is that the first wave of the baby boom generation is on the verge of retirement. The sheer size of this group will most certainly strain the country's financial system; plus, the problem will be exacerbated because baby boomers (sometimes referred to as the "baby zoomers") are expected to revolutionize the meaning of retirement by pursuing the same active lifestyle they've always had. This begs the question:

If you plan to have an active retirement, will 75 percent of your working income be enough to support you as you move into this stage of your life?

This revolution in retirement lifestyle expectations is one of the driving forces behind the increased participation in retirement plans. A

---

[1] Spectrem Group "2000 Capturing IRA Rollover Study."

recent study by the Employee Benefit Research Institute (EBRI) showed that 55 million people participated in retirement plans during 1994, whereas during 1999 the number had increased to 62.7 million.[2] While the number of individuals in retirement plans is increasing, an important and life-changing national trend is emerging:

You as an individual, not your company or the U.S. government, are going to have more responsibility for funding your own future retirement benefits.

Moreover, increased life expectancies mean that you'll be dealing with the consequences of your decisions during a longer period of time. While the need for and importance of careful retirement planning is growing, unfortunately not all sectors of the population are taking the necessary financial steps to fund their eventual retirement needs.

In a mail survey, 1,285 individuals were asked where they parked the assets that came out of their company retirement plans. Approximately 38 percent of the participants had put money in IRA rollovers, 23 percent left their assets in a former employer's retirement plans, and 32 percent took the money out as a taxable distribution.[3] Unfortunately, a large percentage of the participants surveyed had not chosen to allow their money to continue growing on a tax-deferred basis. What we're seeing then is that often, when individuals receive company retirement distributions, they are not only ill-prepared to make good financial decisions, but they must often make those important decisions under time constraints and at a stressful time in their lives. All this is taking place in the context of a tidal wave of change in the retirement market.

---

[2] EBRI Employee Benefit Research Institute January 2001, vol. 22, no. 1.

[3] Spectrem Group, *Capturing IRA Rollovers* Study, 2000.

These changes are so far-reaching they are having an impact on everyone trying to make smart retirement choices.

Why is retirement planning becoming so complicated, why are you having to take more personal responsibility for your retirement-planning needs, and why have there been so many changes in company retirement plans? The genesis of the retirement changes you are being confronted with can be summed up in one word: ERISA.

ERISA

When I was preparing for my senior year in high school (quite a long time ago), I recall being worried about a variety of issues. I was preoccupied by questions like, who was I going to invite to the senior prom, how was I going to do on my SAT tests, and was I going to get enough academic scholarships to attend a good university? At that time, I had no idea that the president of the United States and the U.S. Congress were passing laws that would have such a profound effect on my future career in business.

To address the public's concern that assets in private pension plans were being mismanaged or otherwise abused, the U.S. Congress enacted the provisions of Title 1 of the Employee Retirement Income Security Act (ERISA). Before the passage of ERISA during 1974, private pension funds were often used as political tools to benefit the administrators of retirement plans, rather than the plans' recipients. While many of these original concerns have been addressed, ERISA and other legislative rulings have created an environment where the current retirement field is now awash with choices and decisions. While changes in investment cycles have always been a fact of life, the plethora of new retirement tax laws have become increasingly complex and replete with constantly changing nuances. Quite understandably, navigating ERISA and concurrent tax code changes is a task many people choose not to tackle on their own.

As you plan for retirement and review your employer's retirement plans, ask your benefits department this important question: Does your company offer **qualified** or **non-qualified** employee retirement plans? Since different companies use a variety of names for their retirement plans, it is important not to get bogged down by the "name" of your company's plan but rather to focus on the status of the plan: qualified or non-qualified.

Categories of Qualified Plans

If you are covered under a company's qualified plans, you need to dig a little deeper before you can start studying and executing your retirement plans by getting an answer to the following question:

Are you participating in a defined benefit plan, a defined contribution plan, or in both types of plans?

It is possible to participant in more than one type of qualified plan and each type of plan will have its own set of rules and regulations. We'll now look at the definition and characteristics of each type of plan.

Defined Benefit Plans

Defined benefit plans are plans that are not defined contribution plans. On the surface that may sound pretty simple, but, depending on your plan and distribution options, the differences can be a bit confusing. Here are the essentials of being a participant in a defined benefit plan:

- Fixed, defined benefits are paid out at retirement or early retirement.

- Fixed benefits are based on your age, length of service, and compensation.
- Under most circumstances, the longer you work, the higher your pay scale, then the richer your retirement package.

Although you may receive all kinds information from your employer explaining the features and benefits of your defined benefit plan, these types of calculations are often not done by the company, but by **actuaries** who specialize in this area.

Calculations by actuaries also help to highlight an important difference between **defined contribution plans** and **defined benefit plans**. With a defined benefit plan, the employer, not the employee, bears the investment risk to fund the future retirement benefit. The basic funding of a defined benefit plan is as follows:

- The employer deposits money on behalf of the employee into the defined benefit plan.
- The contributions are invested in a variety of investment alternatives.
- Typically, the company hires a professional **money manager** to invest and monitor these funds.

It's possible, depending on the results of the investments, for a defined benefit plan to become either **under-** or **over-funded**. This can have important ramifications for a company because if the plan becomes under-funded, the employer may be required to make additional contributions (which adds to company costs) to fund its employees' future retirement benefit. Conversely, if a plan becomes over-funded, its assets—based on ERISA guidelines—will be greater than what is required to fund future retirement benefits. So, on a yearly basis, smaller contributions by the employer (which gives cost savings to the company) may be required to fund its employees' future retirement benefits.

On the surface, having an over-funded company pension fund would seem to be a financial advantage. But, during the 1980s, in a perverse way, it had dire consequences for some corporations because corporate raiders often focused their hostile takeover efforts on companies with over-funded pension plans.[4] They viewed over-funded pension plans as a source of excess capital that could be stripped away once the takeover was completed. Some of the oldest, best-known companies in the United States had to make financial changes to protect themselves from these takeover predators. Among the changes were adding more debt to the underlying corporation, expanding as rapidly as possible, or taking on partners.

Regrettably, many of these corporate changes did not give the companies long-term benefits and often resulted in corporate layoffs after the defense of the takeover battle had been won. Since the number of years of service is one of the factors that determines the future amount of an employees defined benefit income, many individuals found themselves not only out of work, but also receiving smaller retirement packages than originally planned.

Although hostile takeovers are not as common today as they were during the 1980s, many current defined benefit participants realize that because of ongoing changes in company retirement plans they cannot count on accruing the same level of benefits that were accumulated by workers in the past. There was a time when generous defined benefit company pension plans were a simple fact of life. It was common for people to work at the same company their entire career; they worked

---

[4] In a hostile takeover, one company (the predator) attempts to acquire another against the wishes of the second company's shareholders, management, and board of directors.

hard, received raises from time to time, and knew that they had a yearly pension (usually a yearly, fixed-income benefit) coming to them upon their retirement. When I was young, I heard about retirees who also received a gold watch upon retirement, although I must admit I have yet to meet one of those mythical retirees wearing one of those treasured timepieces.

Unfortunately, the generous benefits of these types of plans appear to be going the way of the dinosaur. This unwelcome reality is in some measure the effect brought about by ERISA and other legislative rulings. Some of the other reasons for these dramatic changes are as follows: (1) defined benefit plans are more complicated and more expensive to administer than ever before, (2) the attitude of many companies toward their employees has become less paternal during recent years, (3) our workforce has become very mobile, and (4) the influence of labor unions has waned.

Additionally, international competition is also fueling changes on our nation's labor front. The so-called "global village" we now live in has created a tidal wave of change, which has affected employees' relationships with their employers.

While the impact of national and global changes on many organizations is great, surprisingly it has often been local employees, and not companies, who have driven many of the changes that have occurred in retirement plans. Younger and more mobile workers seem less interested in traditional defined benefit plans that will give them a fixed benefit upon retirement. Their reasoning is that the benefits of these plans may be **back-loaded,** a feature that allows older employees to accrue more valuable benefits in relation to their income than younger workers. It's no wonder that more people are now looking to participate in the less age-sensitive defined contribution plans.[5]

The number of participants in defined contribution plans, as compared to defined benefit plans, has already increased dramatically and participation is expected to accelerate. Chart 1-A demonstrates just how dramatic those changes are. During the past twenty years, the number of participants in defined benefit plans has hardly changed; yet during the same period, the number of participants in defined contribution plans has increased by almost 300 percent.

The bottom line is that now and in the future, more retirement needs will be met by the employee and not by the employer.

Chart 1-A.

Active Participation in Defined Benefit and Defined Contribution Plans (in thousands).

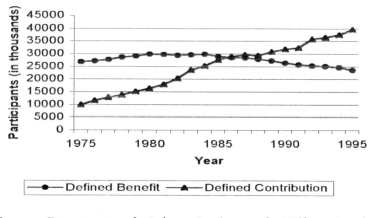

Source: Department of Labor, Pension and Welfare Benefits Administration, 1999.

---

[5] See Chapters 2 & 3 for a comparison of the advantages and disadvantages of the options you may confront when receiving a distribution from company-sponsored retirement plans.

Defined Contribution Plans

Each participant in a defined contribution plan has an individual account whose benefits are largely based on the contributions to the account. These contributions may come from (1) the employee, (2) the employer, or (3) a combination of the two.

If you decide to participate in your company's defined contribution plan, all you have to do is meet a few of your company's requirements and check a few boxes on your company's retirement plan forms. By doing this, you inform the company how much you want to contribute each year (contributions are not mandatory) and then the company, based on its retirement plan documents, may also contribute money to match part or all of your personal contributions.

While you may be in a financial situation that allows you to contribute large amounts of your income, keep in mind that both U.S. government and company guidelines strictly determine the amounts you or the company may contribute each year to these types of plans.

Once contributions are made, the next step is to decide where you will invest the money. Defined contribution plans will typically offer employees a variety of investment alternatives (it varies from company to company). Here are some examples of investment alternatives:

- Money market funds
- Bond funds
- Stock funds
- Your company's common stock

While you know what you will contribute and usually what your company's match will be, you won't know what the results of your investments will be. No one has a crystal ball for that, so although you make contributions to a defined contribution retirement plan, the success of your investment choices will vary. Depending on your plan and "your" choices, you could have income, growth, and appreciation. You could also have expenses (the cost to manage and administer the funds) and perhaps losses to the plan that will affect your total benefit and investment return.

Retirement Plan Features

Now that I've discussed some of the differences between a defined benefit plan and a defined contribution plan, we'll look at some additional features of retirement plans and how they can impact your retirement planning.

Vesting

Vesting refers to the amount of time you must work before you can earn benefits that cannot be forfeited. Once you are vested, you retain the benefit that has accrued, even if you leave the company before you reach retirement age. The benefit does not need to be paid to you at the time of your departure, but must at the very least be reserved for normal payout when you reach the company's normal retirement age.

Two key types of vesting are available to you as an employee: **cliff vesting** and **graduated vesting**. As an employee, you typically have very little to say about these choices, but understanding their features can be useful as you evaluate different companies. (It is important to note that your personal contributions are 100 percent vested at the time of your contribution and are non-forfeitable.)

Early Retirement

Early retirement refers to the age at which you can start receiving accrued retirement benefits before the normal retirement date. In a defined benefit plan, there is a reduction in retirement benefits based on the number of years you are retiring in advance of a company's stated policy. These dollar reductions will vary from company to company.

Some companies offer early retirement as a matter of policy, while others make it available only under certain conditions. During the last few years, a number of companies have also started offering early retirement "incentive" programs. One of the ways companies do this, is by utilizing a point system that calculates retirement benefits based on age and years of service. If a company wants to give its employees an incentive to take early retirement, it can, under certain guidelines, add points to the years of service or to the age requirement. These additional points allow more people to qualify for their normal retirement benefits but on an accelerated basis. Why would a company offer this benefit to its employees? It is a simple, politically correct way to thin the ranks—to decrease the number of employees at a company.

If the early retirement incentives I have just discussed don't do the trick, then another incentive employers can utilize, to increase participation in early retirement offers, is to give employees their retirement benefits in the form of a lump-sum distribution rather than as a yearly pension. This is often called a pension buyout.[6]

Qualified Domestic Relations Order (QDRO)

One final note about retirement plans: if you are married, then by law, unless your spouse agrees to another form of payment such as the lump sum, a defined benefit pension plan must be taken out as a joint income annuity. Defined contribution plans generally do not require annuity payments, but the spouse must consent to a lump-sum payout. If you should become divorced, you or your spouse may qualify for or be the subject of a **Qualified Domestic Relations Order (QDRO)**:

---

[6] See Chapter 2 for a comparison of the advantages and disadvantages of the lump sum and annuity options.

A judgment or order relating to the payment of child support, alimony, or marital property rights to a spouse, former spouse, child, or other dependent. Normally, if a spouse or former spouse receives money under a QDRO, he or she will report the income as if he or she were the primary plan participant. However, the recipient of a QDRO may be exempt from the early retirement tax penalties that would normally apply. Recently passed legislation now allows a recipient spouse to roll over (under certain guidelines) a qualified lump sum received from a QDRO into another qualified plan, such as another 401(k). If you are in a situation that might warrant a QDRO, it is advisable for you to seek legal counsel.

INCOME SOURCES IN RETIREMENT

Pensions

A yearly pension will give you a fixed benefit at retirement. This income is often paid out in the form of an annuity that will be funded by your company. Although pensions are fairly straightforward, if you are leaving a company and receiving a yearly pension, there are some important decisions you must make. You will want to choose wisely because these decisions are usually irrevocable. See the following discussion for pension alternatives, and then answer this critical question:

Do you want to receive your benefits based on single life, joint life, period certain, or life plus period certain?

Single Life

You receive a fixed amount of income for your individual single life. The benefit is based on your age, years of service, income, and actuarial tables.

+ *Advantage:* This choice usually gives the highest yearly benefit.

- *Disadvantage*: If you live for only a short time after leaving the company, these benefits will stop. The benefit will go to zero, leaving nothing to your estate and no other income to your heirs.

Joint and Survivor Life

The first **annuitant** (you, as the person receiving the income) receives a fixed amount for life. Upon your death, a second annuitant receives a fixed amount for the rest of his or her life. The amount paid to the second annuitant may be the same or different from what was paid to you. However, that payment cannot be more than 100 percent or less than 50 percent of your original payout.

+ *Advantage:* The plan guarantees both of the recipients' income for life.

- *Disadvantage:* The amount received monthly is usually less than what you might have received with a single life annuity.

Period Certain

You are offered a definite dollar amount for a specified period of time. For example, if you have a ten-year period certain, benefits will be paid out over ten years.

+ *Advantage*: The income is guaranteed for the fixed period of time, even if the original recipient dies soon after retirement.

- *Disadvantage*: The type of a program does not provide pension income for the remainder of your life beyond the period certain time frame.

Life Plus Period Certain

This option provides an income that is paid for the greater of the period certain or your life.

+ *Advantage:* Income will continue to go to the heirs even if you die before the period certain time frame.

- *Disadvantage:* The income from this type alternative is usually lower than the single life option.

401(k) Plans

Over the years, there has been a tremendous increase in the number of 401(k) plans and the assets in them. During 1990, there were approximately 153,000 401(k) plans in the United States and by the year 2000 the number of plans had surged to more than 377,000. These plans are expected to grow to 481,000 by 2005, mainly from the added participation of small and mid-sized companies.[7] Some of the advantages of these plans and reasons for this tremendous growth are as follows:

Pre-tax contributions

While your pre-tax-deferred wages are not on your 1040 (federal income tax return), they are included as wages subject to Social Security, Medicare, and federal unemployment taxes. These pre-tax contributions may lower your federal income tax liability, but the government is not going to let you avoid your tax obligations to other programs such as Medicare.

After-tax contributions

This allows for additional retirement benefit contributions above and beyond your pre-tax contributions.

---

[7] Source: Business Wire, April 26, 2001. "Stock Market Takes Toll on High Percentage of Investments in Equities."

Company matching

Of course, contribution-matching amounts vary from company to company, but if you can get matching funds from your employer, why not take advantage of this "free money"? You might be eligible to earn as much as a 20, 30, 40, or 50 percent return or more on your 401(k) contribution, even if the plan's investment alternatives earn nothing during the year of the contribution.

Tax-deferred growth

Your money grows more quickly when it is no longer under the thumb of yearly taxation. You can see in Chart 1-B how profound the differences can be. As dramatic as these differences are, this example does not take into account the company contributions, which would increase the difference between the two accounts even more.

Chart 1-B.

The Power of Tax-Deferred Savings.*

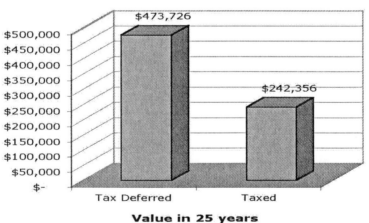

* Assumes $6,000 per year pretax savings, annually compounded 8 percent rate of return, and a 28 percent tax bracket.

The bottom line is that pre-tax contributions, after-tax contributions, pre-tax company matching, and tax-deferred growth make for a powerful combination.

Furthermore, most 401(k) plans give you the option (if guidelines are met upon termination of employment) of receiving your accrued retirement benefits either as a lump sum or a yearly income annuity. If it is economically possible, I encourage you to take advantage of these programs to the maximum amount allowed by law. Here are the new limits for 401(k) contributions, beginning from 2002.

Year	Contribution Limit
2002	$11,000
2003	$12,000
2004	$13,000
2005	$14,000
2006	$15,000

After 2006, increases will be indexed for inflation

Q: *What happens to your company's retirement account—such as a 401(k)—when another company buys your company?*

A: *The answer is "it depends."*

Example: Several years ago, PaineWebber bought out the investment firm of Kidder Peabody. Employees were given the choice of either rolling over their 401(k) assets into PaineWebber's plan or rolling over the assets into an IRA rollover. Some five years later, PaineWebber was bought out by UBS, but the employees were not given these options. So, you see, it really depends on the circumstances of the buyout, IRS regulations, and the decisions of the acquiring company.

Profit-Sharing Plans

Historically, profit-sharing plans were set up so that a business could share its profits with its employees on a tax-deferred basis. An important advantage of these plans is that employees do not make any contributions. Furthermore, profit sharing plan's profit sharing contributions were historically expressed as a percentage of compensation, not as a percentage of profits. Despite the name, profit sharing plans do not require contributions even if there are profits, and they do permit contributions even if there are losses.

Employee Stock Option Plans (ESOPs)

An ESOP is a stock bonus plan or a stock bonus and money purchase plan. It is designed to invest primarily in employer securities.

403(b) Plans

403(b) plans are typically for employees of public school systems and certain tax-exempt organizations. Investments cannot include a profit-sharing component because the contributing organizations are, by definition, non-profits. As a result, the money contributed can only be invested in mutual funds or annuities. These contributions are state and federal tax-deductible, just like 401(k)s. While 403(b) plans can be rolled over into an individual retirement account (IRA), they are not eligible for special tax treatments such as ten-year averaging, which is a very important difference between them and their close relative, the 401(k).

Keogh Plans

Keoghs generally are defined contribution plans. They're also sometimes called H.R. 10 plans. If you are self-employed, you may have both a money-purchase component and a profit-sharing component to your

Keogh plan. However, recent law changes have made it possible to eliminate the money purchase plan, yet still maximize deductions.

Non-Qualified Deferred Compensation Plans

Non-qualified deferred compensation plans are frequently offered to executives and recipients of early retirement programs and are used by state and local governments and tax-exempt organizations.

By definition, non-qualified deferred compensation plans are not qualified plans because they do not meet Internal Revenue Code (IRC) requirements for qualified money. This also makes them ineligible for any special tax treatments. In the past, they could not be rolled over into IRA accounts, but recent changes to government "457 plans" allow for rollovers under specific guidelines. If you think you qualify for these rollover exceptions, consult with your tax advisor.

Standard Individual Retirement Account (IRA)

A standard IRA is not considered a qualified plan, and depending on your circumstances, your contributions to one may or may not be tax deductible. Anyone with earned income (or alimony) can contribute to an IRA. IRA distributions are ineligible for special tax benefits associated with distributions from qualified plans such as a 401(k).

Here are the new annual IRA contribution limits. As you can see, they will gradually increase from $3,000 in the year 2002 to $5,000 in the year 2008. Contribution limits to IRAs after 2008 will be indexed for inflation. If you are 50 years of age or older, you will also be able to contribute a little more to your accounts to allow you to make up for lost time and catch up on your IRA contributions.

Year	Contribution Limit
2002-2004	$3,000
2005-2007	$4,000
2008 and after	$5,000

Social Security Benefits

Social Security is but one of many sources of income available to you if you have planned carefully for your retirement. When Social Security was created during 1935, the average life expectancy of a 65-year-old retiree was an additional 12.5 years. The U.S. Census Bureau reports that the average 65-year-old today has a life expectancy of an additional 17.5 years. During 1945, there were forty-two workers funding the Social Security Trust fund for every one retiree receiving benefits. The ratio of workers funding the trust fund compared to benefit recipients is now lower than ever before and according to the Social Security Administration, by the year 2020 there will be only 2.4 workers contributing to the system for every one person receiving benefits.[8]

With the average age of the population increasing, the strain on the system can be expected to worsen. How to repair the current system will no doubt be a topic of debate as advances in medical care and technology continue to extend life. It should be very clear then that counting on Social Security to keep you in the lifestyle to which you have become accustomed or strive to achieve would be unrealistic. Especially when you consider that according to a study by the Employee Benefit Research Institute, an individual 65 years of age or older whose post-retirement

---

[8] Source: Social Security Administration and U.S. Bureau of the Census

annual income was at least $50,000 would generally derive only 13 percent of his or her total retirement income from Social Security.[9]

As you retire or prepare for retirement, see Table 1-1 for a Social Security checklist of the benefits for which you are eligible.

Table 1-1.

Social Security Benefits, "To Do" Checklist.

When	Action
Every 1 to 3 Years	* Review accuracy of Social Security Statement
6 Months Before Retirement	* Review the following: * Certified Birth Certificates * Marriage License * Divorce Papers
3 Months Before Retirement	* File Application * Evaluate Benefit Start Date
At Retirement	* Report Earnings in Excess of Limitations

SUMMARY: Retirement Planning is an ever-growing part of our busy lives. Changing laws, changing attitudes, and changing investment markets are forcing us to take more of our retirement responsibility upon ourselves than ever before. Because many of the decisions you make will be based on the type of plan in which you are participating, educating yourself about the nuances of your retirement plan(s) is more important than ever.

---

[9] Source: Employee Benefit Research Institute (EBRI) *Estimates of the March 1999 Current Population Survey*

Chapter 2

Annuity Versus Lump Sum

I can't believe this is happening to me. I've been with this company for almost thirty years. I have always been a model employee, and yet the company now informs me that I'm being pushed out the door. My entire department is being offered an early retirement package. Yes, they're adding some incentives to make it attractive, and no, I don't have to take it. I'm just not ready for early retirement—I can't afford to retire. But, if I don't take the package, I might get a lay off notice anyway but without the incentive bonus. There are so many retirement plan decisions to make and I am so unprepared to make them.

The scenario above exemplifies the nation-wide revolution that is occurring among employers, employees, retirement plans, and individual retirement planning. For some people, receiving this kind of notice can be a positive, once in a lifetime opportunity to cash out their qualified retirement benefits and sail off into the sunset, either to seek employment elsewhere or to retire. For others, it can be one of the most traumatic events they will ever have to face. In addition to financial issues, there are health care issues (will I have adequate health coverage for my family?), and emotional issues, as so many people's identities are tied up in their work.

When you leave a company that has qualified retirement plans, you may be confronted with one of the most important financial decisions that you will ever make:

Do you want to receive your retirement plan benefits as an annuity or as a lump-sum distribution?

Before I compare the advantages and disadvantages of each alternative, it is important to review the following definitions:

Annuity
A constant stream of income for a single or joint lifetime, or for a certain period of time.

Lump-sum distribution
The distribution or payment from a qualified plan within a single tax year, of a plan participant's entire balance to the credit of the participant.

If you decide to take a distribution of your company's retirement benefits and want to qualify for a lump-sum distribution, certain provisions must be met. If you have more than one account in any category (e.g. ESOP, pension, or profit sharing), then all your account assets from the same employer or affiliated group must be distributed. In addition, before you can receive a lump-sum distribution, your company's retirement plan documents must contain certain provisions and a triggering event must occur. Some examples of triggering events are as follows:

- Separation from service (now called severance from employment)
- Attainment of age 59.5
- Disability
- Death

Even if a "triggering" event has occurred, it is still not enough to qualify you for any special tax treatments; you must have been a plan participant for five or more taxable years prior to the year of distribution and meet other IRC (Internal Revenue Code) guidelines.

Last but not least, before you can receive your lump-sum distribution, you must pay off any loans you may have against your company retirement accounts.

WHICH IS BETTER: THE ANNUITY OR THE LUMP-SUM DISTRIBUTION?

Annuity Advantages

1. *Simplicity.* Is there anything in the world simpler than getting a check in the mail and cashing it? That is what happens when you take advantage of the annuity option (direct deposit is also available).
2. *Guaranteed income.* Even if you live to be 110 years old, you know that the income from an annuity will be there. There is no need to worry about out-living your investments. That can be very comforting, especially when the volatility of the stock market rears its ugly head.

3. *No investment decisions.* With an annuity, you don't need to worry about pesky details such as deciding which bond or mutual fund to purchase. During the mid- to late 1990s, many investors convinced themselves that they had figured out the secret to making money in the stock market. However, when the stock market declined in 2000, many investors were reminded that investing in equities doesn't guarantee a large positive rate of return and that equity investments, can indeed decline in value. With an annuity, stock market changes will no longer be a portfolio concern.

Annuity Disadvantages

1. *No flexibility.* The annuity option is a simple one, but you pay for the simplicity by giving up flexibility. Once you take the yearly income annuity, it's an irrevocable choice. With the way that most plans are designed, changing your mind—"Oops, I made a mistake"—just isn't an option.
2. *Income is not indexed for inflation.* As a general rule, an annuity is not indexed for inflation and will not protect you from its ravages, which include the loss of purchasing power. It may be safe, but going broke safely is not a sensible strategy for a retirement plan. Unfortunately, this can happen more easily than you may think.

> *Example:* Let us assume that you earn $60,000 per year and you receive a fantastic early retirement package that will allow you to retire at the age of 50, with your pension for life locked in at the same $60,000. What happens to your purchasing power after five, ten, and twenty years if inflation remains constant at 3 percent per year? Here are some answers:

- In five years, you will need to earn $69,697 to give you the same purchasing power that your $60,000 gives you today.
- In ten years, you will need to earn $80,961 to give you the same purchasing power that your $60,000 gives you today.
- In twenty years, you will need to earn $109,245 to give you the same purchasing power that your $60,000 gives you today.

With the annuity option, you will still be earning $60,000 per year, even though in twenty years it will require almost $110,000 per year to buy the same amount of goods and services that you can purchase today with $60,000.

3. *No control over investments.* Over time, financial markets change and new investment opportunities can become available. Once you have taken the annuity option, you receive income, but you will not have investments to manage.
4. *No estate.* After you and the secondary annuitant die, the income stops and there is no further benefit for the estate. There are no assets to pass along to the heirs.
5. *No access to your original principal.* One of the most significant disadvantages associated with choosing the annuity option, and one worth evaluating more deeply, has to do with losing access to your original principal. What do I mean by your original principal? If you have accumulated $100,000 in your company's retirement plan, a 401(k) for example, that $100,000 represents your principal. It is the value of your account: real money you can receive as a lump-sum distribution or utilize in an emergency. If you decide to take the annuity option rather than a lump-sum distribution, the

money is turned over to an insurance company, which will then pay you a retirement income. The principal becomes theirs, not yours. You no longer have access to the $100,000 of original principal, just to the income stream it creates.

Lump-Sum Advantages

1. *Income flexibility.* With a lump-sum distribution you can create annual income. For instance, you could invest your lump-sum distribution in long-term U.S. government bonds, which are backed by the U.S. government and lock in your yield for the life of the bonds.[10]

2. *Access to principal.* Having access to your principal can be critically important especially during a financial emergency. It's your money and, unlike an annuity, doesn't belong to an insurance company.

3. *Control over investment strategies.* With a lump-sum distribution you control your investment decisions. You are free—under IRS guidelines—to decide where and how much should be placed in the investments of your choosing. Of course, with this freedom comes responsibility.

4. *Hedge Against Inflation.* Your portfolio's war against inflation makes it one of the most important financial enemies you must battle and defeat. By allocating resources into investments that give your investment portfolio growth, you increase your odds of being an investment winner in retirement. Historically, investments such as stocks have been one of the few alternatives that have given a positive, real rate of return after taxes and inflation.[11]

5. *Estate planning.* If you invest wisely, there is the possibility that you will have an estate for your heirs. Plus if you are in a situation

---

[10] See Chapters 8 and 9 in which I discuss bond investing and bond alternatives.

[11] See Chapter 6 for a comparison.

where you can afford to reinvest the growth and income of your IRA rollover rather than take distributions, you could see a substantial increase in your net worth. Consider the benefit if you were to leave your company at age 50 and earn an average of 7 percent per year in your account and reinvest the earnings. With this type of a return, your account would double in value approximately every ten years. By the time you are 60 years old, your account will have doubled—from say $100,000 to $200,000. If you can average 10 percent per year, your money will double in value every 7.2 years. This kind of estate growth is not possible with the annuity option.

6. *Income tax flexibility.* An IRA rollover will permit you to accelerate or in many cases to defer the recognition of taxable income to meet your particular income tax planning objectives.

7. *Special tax treatments.* Depending on your age and circumstances, you may qualify for special tax treatments on your distributions. You may also be able to defer taxes for an extended period of time.[12]

Lump-Sum Disadvantages

1. *Tax issues.* Depending on your distribution choice, there may or may not be any tax deferral. Additionally, depending on your age and circumstances, there could be added penalties onto your distribution.

2. *Payments not guaranteed for life.* If you take the lump-sum distribution and do not invest it wisely, your retirement assets could be depleted during your lifetime. This issue didn't seem to be much of a problem during the mid- to late 1990s when investment returns

---

[12] These special tax-treatments will be discussed in Chapter 3.

were so outstanding, but during uncertain times or market declines it becomes important.

3. *Investment and principal risk.* There is no hiding from the fact that many types of investments have principal risk.[13] Should you opt for handling your investments on your own, you will be responsible for making informed choices. It is also true that if you choose to work with a financial advisor there are no guarantees that he or she will be able to perform as competently as you might wish.

Which Alternative is Better?

In addition to reviewing the advantages and disadvantages of each distribution option, consider the following issues before making any final decisions on the annuity versus the lump-sum option:

1. *Health.* If you are terminally ill or in poor health, the lump-sum distribution may be the best choice since the capital from your lump-sum distribution can be passed on to your heirs. Should you die soon after taking the annuity income option, all income payments to your estate will be terminated. (The only exception would be if you had taken the joint-life or period-certain payment schedule.)

2. *Estate planning.* If you are concerned with a legacy and are assisting children or other loved ones, give serious thought to the lump-sum distribution.

3. *Money management.* If you have no confidence in your ability to manage money and no confidence that you will find someone to help you, the yearly guaranteed income from an annuity might be an attractive choice for you.

---

[13] See Chapter 5, where I discuss types of risk and how to manage them when confronting choices for your investment portfolio.

4. *Family issues.* Some of you will have to deal with the financial needs of family members. These types of issues can have a profound impact on your retirement distribution choices. As the father of twin girls, I must admit that it would be difficult for me to say no to their financial requests, especially if they were to start the conversation by telling me that I am a wonderful father and that they love me very much. If that happened I must admit I would probably succumb to their requests and give up graciously. Luckily they are only four years old, so I still have a few years before the serious financial requests begin.

SUMMARY: Whether you decide to take the annuity or the lump-sum distribution, it's a big decision to make. Sit down, develop your profile based on the information I offer here, review and evaluate your needs, compare the advantages and disadvantages of the alternatives, and if necessary work with competent advisors.

Chapter 3

Lump-Sum Rules & Regulations

I was talking to my co-workers the other day about retirement, and they said that there are no early retirement penalties at 59.5. But, then somebody else said it was 55, not 59.5. They can't both be right, can they? I called my bank for confirmation and they said one thing, while my credit union said something else. Does anybody know what he or she is talking about? I'm getting ready to retire—I need some help and some answers.

In the preceding chapter, I talked about the differences between taking an annuity option as opposed to taking a lump-sum distribution. Should you decide to take the lump-sum distribution, there are many rules, regulations, and alternatives you will need to evaluate before you can start assembling your investment portfolio.

Many of the lump-sum choices I will discuss will require you to meet specific guidelines and will apply only if your distribution is coming from a qualified plan. If you do not meet the guidelines, you will not be able to take advantage of some of the alternatives. The information that appears in Chart 3-A should give you a clear roadmap of the alternatives you will need to evaluate. I will then discuss their specific nuances individually and review some special situations that require further explanation.

Even if you are a shrewd investor, making the wrong lump-sum choices can have a profound negative impact on your investment portfolio, retirement plans, and estate planning.

Chart 3-A.

Lump-Sum Distribution Options.

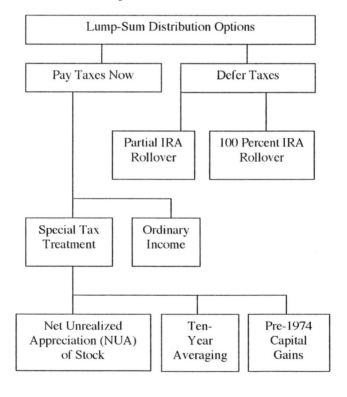

PAYING THE TAXES NOW

Are you nuts, pay more taxes to the government? Why would I want to take a lump-sum distribution from a company's qualified plan in a way that means I'll have to pay taxes up front?

If you receive a qualified distribution and decide to pay the taxes up front, your employer is normally required to withhold 20 percent of the distribution value. The amount withheld is automatically sent to the IRS, and when you file your taxes the withheld amount becomes part of the calculation that determines your total tax liability for the given year. Depending on your tax rate, it may be possible to get back (as a refund) part or all of the original amount of money withheld. It's also possible that the final tax liability could be even higher than the original 20 percent that was withheld.

Are all taxable distributions subject to the 20 percent withholding rule? Fortunately, there are some exceptions: (1) your after-tax contributions, (2) certain distributions that are part of a series of substantially equal payments, (3) required minimum distributions at age 70.5, and (4) net unrealized appreciation (NUA) on employer stock. Some of these exceptions and other special situations will be discussed in detail in the following pages and chapters.

Here are some of the reasons why you might consider paying the taxes up front.

1. *High tax bracket.* You expect to be in a higher tax bracket in the future. You believe that present tax rates are as low as they are going to get and you want to lock in your liability before they increase.
2. *Favorable tax treatments.* You may qualify for favorable tax treatments such as long-term gains or ten-year averaging.

3. *Concentrated company stock positions.* You may work for a company where you have been accumulating a large position of company stock, which has the potential to be taxed in a very favorable manner.

4. *Tax efficient earnings.* If you take the proceeds in this manner, you have the option of investing in instruments such as tax free municipal bonds that will give you tax free income or in other investments that may be taxed at long-term capital gains rates, instead of being taxed at tax-deferred ordinary income rates.

5. *Start a business.* Perhaps, you are in a situation in which you want to use the lump-sum distribution as seed money to start a business.

Ordinary Income

Some recipients of qualified lump-sum distributions do not meet the necessary requirements for special tax treatments when deciding to "pay the taxes now." If you are in that situation, the income from your distribution is added to all your other taxable income, either as a single or joint taxpayer. If you have a taxable income of $50,000 and take receipt of a taxable $100,000 lump-sum distribution but don't qualify for any special tax treatments, your federal taxable income will shoot up to $150,000. The federal tax liability for a single unmarried individual with a taxable income of $150,000 is approximately $40,000. Also, depending on your age, an additional 10 percent penalty could be imposed on your distribution.

> *Example:* If you leave a company before turning 55, you will—under most circumstances—be subject to an additional 10 percent penalty on your distribution. To clarify this, let us assume that you leave a company when you are 53, not 55, and choose to keep the money in the company

retirement plan for two years. Once you reach 55, if you then take your distribution and pay the taxes rather than roll it over, you will not avoid the 10 percent penalty. The reason is because you were 53, not 55, when you actually terminated your employment.

Q: *What happens if you leave the company in January when you are 54, receive your distribution a couple of months later and then turn 55 in November of the same year—do you avoid the 10 percent penalty?*

A: *The surprise answer is yes. The official rules for qualifying for this exemption are as follows:*

- The distribution is made after the employee separates from the service of the employer maintaining the plan.
- The separation occurs during or after the calendar year in which the employee reaches age 55.

Special Tax Treatment

Ten-Year Averaging

If you qualify, ten-year averaging can be an attractive way of taking your lump-sum distribution and "paying the taxes now." The term can be a little confusing, and often people think they can pay the tax liability over ten-years. This is not so. With ten-year averaging, you pay the tax as a one-time tax—not as a liability spread over time. It is also a stand-alone calculation that does not take into account your other income. Table 3-1 shows you what your approximate federal tax liability would be, based on the value of your lump-sum distribution.

You will note that as the distribution amount grows, the percentage of the tax liability increases as well. This eliminates some of the incentives for taking advantage of the strategy.

If you choose to take advantage of this special tax treatment, you can only use it once. Also, before you can utilize ten-year averaging, you must first meet certain qualifications.

Table 3-1.

Ten-Year Averaging Tax Liability.

Lump-sum Amount	10-year Rate (%)
$ 25,000	7.2
$ 50,000	11.8
$ 100,000	14.5
$ 200,000	18.5
$ 300,000	22.1
$ 500,000	28.7
$ 1,000,000	38.2

Qualifications:

1. Ten-year averaging is only available if you were born before January 1, 1936.[14]
2. You must have been a participant in your company's retirement plan for at least five years. If you were born before 1936 but have only been in a new company plan for 3.5 years, you will not

---

[14] Fewer and fewer people are going to be taking advantage of ten-year averaging because the number of working Americans born before 1936 is decreasing.

qualify for ten-year averaging because you will not have met the five-year participation guidelines.

3. You must receive 100 percent of the plan balance within one calendar year, and you may not roll over any part of the distribution into an IRA account.
4. Your ten-year averaging calculations will be based on the *1986* tax tables, not the current tax tables.

Net Unrealized Appreciation (NUA) Stock

Taking a lump-sum distribution could be one of the most complicated financial decisions you will ever make. If a portion or all of your qualified distribution is in your employer's company stock, the issue can become even more complex. Before you consider rolling over company stock into an IRA account, I want to explore with you the following distribution alternative known as net unrealized appreciation (NUA). Here's how NUA works:

> *Example:* Each share of company stock you receive from a qualified plan is comprised of *cost* and *appreciation.* Let us say you worked for company ABC Inc. In one of your company 's qualified retirement plans, you acquired company shares for $10 per share and you are the proud owner of a thousand shares. This gives you an acquisition cost of $10,000 ($10 x 1,000). Let us further assume that the stock is now trading for $100 per share and that you still own the original thousand shares, which gives you a new total stock value of $100,000 ($100 x 1,000). The difference between the $10 per share cost and the $100 per share market value on distribution is the NUA.

You might decide to take your distribution, pay the taxes, and not roll over your company stock into an IRA account. If so, here's what the consequences might be: if you were to take the shares as a taxable distribution, current income tax rates would be assessed on the thousand shares, but only at the $10 per share rate. You would pay ordinary income tax on only $10,000 ($10 x 1,000), not on the full value of your stock distribution.

If you later sell the stock for $100 per share, the $90 per share gain would be taxed as long-term capital gains in the year you sold it. Any gains that occur from a stock sale above the distribution price of $100 per share will be taxed as long term or short term, depending on the holding period from the date of distribution.

In this example, if you had not taken the taxable distribution and instead had *rolled over all the company stock into your IRA,* all future distributions from your IRA would be taxed as ordinary income. Remember that, as of this writing, long-term capital rates are only 20 percent, whereas the maximum federal tax rate on IRA distributions (taxed as ordinary income) can be almost 40 percent. Calculating NUA can be complicated, so I have listed this example in Table 3-2.

Table 3-2.
Calculating NUA.

Number of Shares:	1,000
Cost Basis Of Stock:	$10 per share
Market Value on Date of	
Distribution from Plan:	$100 per share
Net Unrealized	
Appreciation (NUA):	$90 per share (100 - 10)

* Ordinary income tax on $10,000 (1,000 x $10)
* Long-term gain on $90,000, (1,000 x $90) when sold
* Long- or short-term gain on amount over $100,000

Q: *Are there any early distribution penalties for taking stock in this manner?*

A: *It depends. If you are younger than 55 when you leave the company and take receipt of your lump-sum distribution, you normally would be subject to a 10 percent penalty, but only on the $10,000 taxable portion. Upon distribution, you would not have to pay any taxes or penalties on the $90 per share gain ($100 per share value minus $10 per share cost).*

Q: *Can you combine the NUA tax treatment with other favorable tax treatments, such as ten-year averaging? (Remember, ten-year averaging is taxable in the year you take the action and is an once-in-a-lifetime election.)*

A: *If you are eligible, the answer is yes.*

Here are some reasons for considering the NUA Strategy:

1. Upon your death, your heirs will be responsible for the capital gains that accumulated in your company retirement plan, although any increased appreciation after distribution will receive a stepped-up cost basis. Current law allows assets passing through an estate to report as "cost" the market value of the stock on date of death. This new cost basis is what will now be in the hands of the beneficiaries. If, alternatively, the shares were held in an IRA, their entire value could be subject to an income tax. In either situation, your shares would be subject to estate taxes. Your beneficiaries, however, might receive a tax deduction based on all or a portion of the estate tax attributed to the inherited shares.

2. If you are in a high income tax bracket and believe that you will always be in one, this strategy may be worth investigating.

3. If there is a very large difference between the cost basis of your company stock and the NUA, I again recommend careful evaluation.

4. If your stock holdings are part of a well-diversified investment portfolio, this strategy could be an attractive alternative for you.

5. If you take a taxable distribution from your IRA account before age 59.5, you may be subjected to the 10 percent penalty. But, if you are 55 or older when you leave your company and take distribution, you will not be subject to the penalty.

NUA calculations and considerations can be a complex issue. If you are considering following this course of action, it is imperative that you consult with tax and/or estate planning experts.

Pre-1974 Capital Gains

The pre-1974 capital gains tax treatment is often confused with NUA because investors associate the term "capital gains" with NUA and company stock. They are, however, not directly related. The capital gains alternative is simply another special tax treatment for those who prefer to pay their taxes up front and meet the necessary requirements. If you participated in a plan before 1974, you could qualify for the pre-1974 capital gains treatment. You can only elect the strategy once, and the pre-1974 portion is taxed at a flat rate of 20 percent.

Lump-Sum Distributions: Special Circumstances

As with most things in life, there are some exceptions to the rule that need to be understood. The following list of special circumstances is by no means complete, but they will alert you to some of these important issues.

20% Withholding Exceptions

If you receive a lump-sum distribution and the distribution is made payable to you rather than to the firm that will be handling your account, then the transaction is known as **constructive receipt**. As I discussed earlier, taking a distribution in this manner normally results in 20 percent of the distribution value being withheld. While there are standard exceptions to this withholding rule—which I reviewed earlier—there are also some "special situation" exceptions to the mandatory 20 percent withholding rule. What happens if you work for a great company, ABC Inc., and over the years the company has been putting its fabulous company stock in your retirement plan.

> *Example 1:* You will be receiving a $100,000 distribution from your company's qualified retirement plan, and the distribution is 100 percent company stock. Under these circumstances, there will be no mandatory 20 percent withholdings. Distribution-$100,000, withholdings-zero.

> *Example 2:* Your distribution is in cash and company stock: $90,000 in company stock and $10,000 in cash. The company will withhold only the $10,000 in cash and not the full 20 percent, which in this example would have been $20,000. Distribution-$100,000, withholdings-$10,000.

If you receive distributions of securities from companies other than the company for which you work, you will *not* qualify for these special exceptions. You would also be required either to sell enough securities to cover the mandatory 20 percent withholding or to contribute enough cash to cover the withholding amount.

Older Than 70.5 When You Retire

If you leave a company when you are 70.5 or older, you will not be able to roll over 100 percent of your company retirement plan into your IRA. Part of your qualified lump-sum distribution must be distributed to you in the form of a taxable distribution, which will be based on your age and on required minimum distribution (RMD) regulations.[15]

Two-Part Distribution: Same Year, Same Account

A sixty-day deadline exists between the receipt and deposit of your distribution into your IRA rollover account. What happens if you receive two distributions at different times from the same account? The IRS has ruled that your sixty-day rollover period begins on the date you receive the last part of your lump-sum distribution, as long as all portions are received within one calendar year.

> Q: *How do you prove that your deposits are still within the sixty-day deadline?*
>
> A: *Deposit the first part of your lump-sum distribution as soon as it arrives. When the balance of your distribution arrives, simply make a second deposit. Keep the dated envelopes in which your distributions arrive and file them with your records.*

Simple, easy, and neat—don't complicate your life by holding the first distribution and waiting until you receive the second part.

Two-Part Distribution: Same Year, Different Accounts

If you receive distributions from more than one type of retirement plan in the same calendar year—for example, your 401(k) in cash and your ESOP as stock—the usual procedure would be to treat each distribution

---

[15] I discuss RMD rules in detail in Chapter 4.

the same way. As a general rule, you may not roll one over and apply a ten-year average to the other.

Two Part Distribution: Different Years, Different Plans

When distributions come to you from two different plans in different years, you have more flexibility—as compared to the preceding option—on handling them. For example, you might receive a 401(k) distribution this year and an ESOP distribution next year. If you want to, you could roll over the 401(k) and then, if you qualify, you could ten-year average the ESOP.

DEFERRING THE TAXES

Here is a basic fact of human nature: most investors do not like the idea of paying taxes, particularly when they are receiving a large lump-sum distribution. If you are not receiving company stock, there are two ways to defer taxes on your lump-sum distribution: partial or 100 percent IRA rollover.

Partial IRA Rollover

If you decide to take advantage of a partial rollover, you can divide your distribution in any percentage you prefer. For example, you could roll over 50 percent of the account into an IRA—which would defer taxes—and then pay taxes on the remaining 50 percent that you do not roll over.

While this may appear to be an attractive option to ten-year averaging, there is a caveat with partial rollovers: you cannot take advantage of favorable tax treatments (such as ten-year averaging) with the taxable portion you don't roll over into the IRA—even if you are old enough to qualify for the benefit. The money you haven't rolled over will be taxed as ordinary income, and it will be added to your other taxable income. Also, if age requirements are not met, penalties may apply. Before implementing a partial rollover, make sure that you have performed a thorough analysis of the tax consequences associated with this course of action.

100-Percent IRA Rollover

If you are planning to roll over your lump-sum distribution into an IRA, you have a sixty-day deadline to complete the transaction. Failure to do so might not only disallow your ability to put your distribution into an IRA, but it could also end up costing you a tremendous amount in taxes and potential penalties. (I will discuss this issue in detail later in the chapter and provide guidelines that will help you to avoid this pitfall.)

Having your money grow on a tax-deferred basis is one of the most compelling advantages of the IRA rollover. In Chart 3-B, you can see how dramatic the difference in account appreciation and growth can be between a taxable account and a tax-deferred account such as an IRA rollover. The example assumes that you are starting with a $200,000 lump-sum distribution and that the accounts are compounding on a monthly basis during a ten-year period. The pre-tax IRA rate of return is 10 percent per year; the non-IRA alternative qualifies for ten-year averaging and earns a 7.2 percent after-tax equivalent, which assumes a 28 percent bracket.[16]

---

[16] If you withdraw the entire IRA balance at the end of ten years of tax-deferred growth and pay taxes at a rate of 31 percent, $373,572 will remain.

Chart 3-B.

The Rollover Advantage.

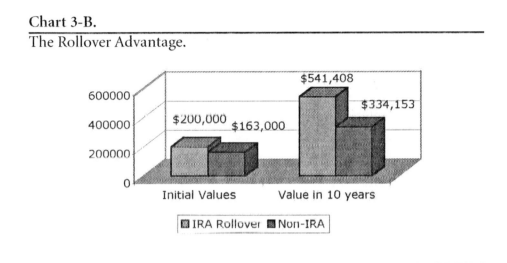

I realize that you may not be in a financial situation where you can reinvest all of your IRA assets for ten years, as in the example in Chart 3-B. However, observe the impact reinvesting can have on your net worth. If you decide to start taking income from your accounts after ten years, your IRA account will have grown to $541,408. Compare that to the non-IRA account, which will have a market value of $334,153. Given the choice, it's easy to see which account you'd rather have after ten years.

Q   Which parts of a qualified distribution are eligible to be rolled over?

A: Employer before-tax contributions, employee before-tax contributions, earnings, dividends, and growth. Beginning in 2002, employee after-tax contributions can be rolled over as well—under certain conditions.

SETTING UP YOUR IRA ROLLOVER

During 1999, assets in IRAs reached almost $2.5 trillion—more than a 20 percent increase compared to 1998 assets. IRA assets have become so large that during 1998 they surpassed the assets in private defined benefit plans as well as defined contribution plans.[17] You can see from Chart 3-C how the assets of IRAs have grown. One of the interesting aspects of this unprecedented growth is that the increases are coming from rollovers of qualified retirement accounts and market appreciation, rather than from regular IRA contributions.

The importance of IRAs to retirement is not only growing, but also the sheer size of the assets involved is influencing financial trends and the management of securities in the equity and bond markets. When that much money is being invested in individual accounts, it's no wonder that all kinds of financial institutions are now marketing their services to this segment of the population.

Chart 3-C.

IRA Assets, Private-Trusted Pension Assets, 1997-1999.

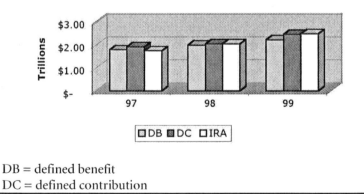

DB = defined benefit
DC = defined contribution

---

[17] Source: Employee Benefit Research Institute, *Pension Investment Report*, 2nd *Quarter 2000* (Washington, D.C.: Employee Benefit Research Institute, December 2000); and Craig Copeland, "IRA Assets Continue To Grow," *EBRI Notes*, no. 1 (Employee Benefit Research Institute, January 2001), p. 1-8.

Where Are Investors Placing Their IRA Assets?

During 1981, banks and thrift deposits held some 73 percent of IRA assets, while mutual funds had a paltry 8.1 percent. However, during 1999, the amount handled by banks had dwindled to less than 10 percent, while the assets controlled by mutual funds had climbed to more than 49 percent and brokerage self-directed accounts grew to almost 32 percent.[18] The numbers become even more significant than just the percentage changes when you consider how much money was being invested during 1999 as compared to 1981. The size and sheer bulk of IRA account assets suggest that setting up your accounts properly is paramount. To make a mistake on a $1,000 account is one thing, but to make the same mistake on a $100,000, $500,000, or $1 million account is a very different problem.

From Company Plan To IRA Rollover

Your employer is normally required to give you written notice prior to the distribution of your company's retirement accounts. This written explanation will cover the company's options and distribution policy.

There was a time when large companies regularly had on-site retirement representatives whose job it was to assist you in this transition. The process was fairly straightforward: you made an appointment with this competent company retirement or benefits advisor and filled out the required forms. If you had any questions, you could ask them at your meeting or later telephone the person designated to follow your progress. My, how the world has changed!

Many companies no longer have local retirement representatives and many of the company's retirement services are consolidated at a central

---

[18] See the Investment Company Institute, *Mutual Fund Factbook* (Washington, D.C.: Investment Company Institute, 2000); and Paul Yakoboski, "IRA Assets Total More than 2 Trillion" EBRI Notes, no. 5 (Employee Benefit Research Institute, May 2000): p. 1-3

facility. You may receive your "help" and retirement or termination information packet in the mail, along with an "800" number you can call if you have additional questions. After your company has "helped" you wade through all the options and retirement paperwork and you have correctly submitted the forms, you will be paid your lump-sum distribution.

Distributions from company plans are usually sent out within a few weeks after your final date of employment. However, assume nothing: be sure you understand your employer's lump-sum distribution policies and what the normal time frame is for processing a distribution.

After your former employer sends you your distribution, a notice called a **1099R** will be sent to the IRS. This notice lets the IRS know that a certain amount of cash or assets have been sent out to you from your company's qualified retirement plan.

To avoid complications and possible tax withholdings, have the lump-sum distribution check made out in the name of the **trustee** that will be handling your account. When your distribution is handled in this manner, nothing is withheld. Your check will be deposited, and the trustee of your IRA rollover will send a notice to the IRS. This notice by your trustee lets the IRS know how much was deposited into your IRA account.

Strict adherence to IRS distribution deadlines is an absolute necessity. Let me repeat the warning from earlier in the book: when you receive your lump-sum distribution, you have sixty days to deposit it in your IRA account. If you fail to deposit your distribution within the allotted time, or if the distribution is not handled correctly, you could find yourself owing a sizeable amount of money in taxes and/or penalties.

> *Example*: If your $100,000 lump-sum distribution is made out to you and not to the trustee of your IRA, 20 percent of the value of the distribution (under most conditions) will be

withheld and automatically sent to the IRS. Remember that even if 20 percent is withheld, you still have only sixty days to deposit the remaining balance ($100,000–$20,000) in your IRA rollover before the entire amount is considered taxable income.

If you only deposit 80 percent of the distribution (given that 20 percent was withheld), it will be considered a partial rollover; the withheld portion will be considered taxable income, and penalties may apply. If you find yourself in this situation, you can make up the 20 percent shortfall by tapping into other assets to bring the total of your deposit back to the original value of your distribution.

Once you've made up the 20 percent shortfall and deposited the entire amount, you will have qualified for a 100 percent rollover contribution. Unfortunately, even if you're able to make up this shortfall and deposit the full amount, you'll still need to wait until tax season before you can apply for a refund of the 20 percent originally withheld by your employer.

Conduit IRA

A conduit IRA is the name given to separate IRA accounts established for assets rolled over from qualified plans. Before January 1, 2002, conduit IRAs that were not mixed with other regular contributory IRAs could be moved back into a company-qualified plan such as a 401(k). (A requirement was that the new company plan had no restrictions on such transfers.)

The passage of the Economic Growth and Tax Relief Reconciliation Act of 2001 (EGTRRA 2001) created a host of new rules that can impact IRA transfers and companies' retirement plans. These changes have decreased the significance of the term conduit IRA, and have increased rollover alternatives. Whether it's under the old rules that still apply or

under the new rules that began in 2002, there are important IRA qualifications, restrictions, and alternatives that you will want to understand.

> Q: *Can you take qualified money from two different qual-
> ified company plans, consolidate them in one IRA
> rollover, and then in the future transfer the assets back
> to a qualified plan?*
>
> A: *Yes, you can.*
>
> Q: *Do you have to transfer 100 percent of your IRA back
> into a qualified plan or can you transfer only a part of
> the account?*
>
> A: *You are not required to move 100 percent of the account.
> You have the option of moving just a portion of your IRA
> back into another qualified plan.*
>
> Q: *Can you consolidate all of your regular IRA accounts
> with your rollover IRA accounts and then, at a future
> time, move the consolidated account back into a com-
> pany's qualified plan such as a 401(k)?*
>
> A: *You can transfer or roll over all taxable (eligible) assets
> into your new 401(k). Although you may have after-
> tax money in your IRA, you cannot move it into the
> new 401(k), nor can you move nondeductible IRA con-
> tributions.*

There are both disadvantages and advantages to moving your IRA
rollover back into a 401(k). Company retirement plans certainly don't
give you all the investment options you would have in an IRA and they
can be more restrictive. But, depending on your age, there could be tax
advantages to transferring back to a 401(k) and then taking a new
lump-sum distribution sometime in the future.

A word of caution is in order here. If you consolidate certain types
of IRA accounts, and then move back into a company-qualified plan,

you may lose the ability to ten-year average or apply other favorable tax treatments to those accounts. You can see that the new "simplification" rules have made it more complicated than ever. Consult your tax advisor before you make any final decisions about the co-mingling of your IRA assets.

Financial Institution Alternatives

Prior to handing in your retirement or termination paperwork and receiving your lump-sum distribution, your employer may require you to have an established IRA account with a qualified trustee. If this is the procedure at your company, you need to verify that the receiving trustee of your new IRA rollover is capable of handling the types of investments that are appropriate to your particular needs. Here are some of the trustees that can set up your IRA rollover accounts:

- Full-service brokerage firms
- Discount brokerage firms
- Credit unions
- Banks
- Insurance companies
- Mutual fund companies

While there are several trustee alternatives, each institution has its own particular range of products and offerings. The institution that is best for you will depend on your investment goals and financial needs. In the good old days—although I'm not really sure when that was—there were clear divisions in the world of money. If you wanted insurance, you went to an insurance agent. If you wanted CDs (certificates of deposit) or savings accounts, you went to a bank or a Savings and Loan. If you wanted to buy stocks, you went to a brokerage firm.

Over the last several years, as a result of market conditions and changes in the law, the trend has been toward "financial supermarkets." The idea behind this development is that the financial supermarket can handle any transaction you need, so long as it involves your money. Today, your bank can offer you mutual funds and your local stockbroker is a financial advisor and an asset manager who can get you CDs as well as stocks, bonds, and mutual funds.

But while national advertising from a variety of firms may attempt to downplay the differences among financial institutions, there are some important distinctions worth investigating. You'll want to compare their range of services and get answers to some of the following questions:

- Do they offer financial planning?
- Can they prepare asset-allocation models?
- Do they offer estate planning?
- Do they offer research on individual stocks?
- Do they handle individual bonds or just bond funds?
- How many different mutual funds do they offer?
- As your assets and investment needs change, can you transition to different investment alternatives?
- With whom will you be working and what are their qualifications and experience?
- How will the ongoing management of your account be handled?
- What are the firm's fees and commissions and how are they calculated?

These types of issues need to be thoroughly investigated before deciding where your lump-sum distribution will be transferred.

Your Beneficiaries

Recently implemented changes in the law regarding beneficiaries make it more important than ever for you to decide who or what is going to be the beneficiary of your IRA rollover account. Because of these sweeping legislative changes, I will discuss these issues in detail in Chapter 4.

SUMMARY: So many choices, so little time. If you are receiving a lump-sum distribution from a qualified retirement plan, the first question you must ask yourself is "Do I want to pay the taxes now or defer them?" If you pay the taxes up front, then of course you will need to evaluate whether you qualify for any special tax treatments. If you decide to defer the taxes, you can utilize either a partial or a 100 percent rollover.

If you plan to take advantage of an IRA rollover, remember that while recently enacted regulations give IRA holders more flexibility than ever before, it is fraught with potential pitfalls:

- *Don't sign IRA paperwork or co-mingle your accounts until you are certain of the consequences of your actions.*
- *Confirm that the trustee handling your account can offer you the full range of investments and services you need.*
- *Be sure that the individual working with you to set up your account is a real professional and not just a clerk assigned to handle paperwork for new IRA rollover recipients.*

For more information about the tax code and lump-sum distributions, visit the Department of the Treasury's web page (www.ustreas.gov/) and review IRS publication no. 575.

Chapter 4

Taking Money Out of Your IRA

My whole life, I've been working and paying more than my fair share of taxes. In spite of the yearly tax bite, I've been able to build up a nice nest egg for retirement. Now, you're telling me that when I take money out, I'm not only going to pay more taxes, but I might also be socked with an additional 10 percent penalty! Plus, if I don't set up my beneficiaries correctly, the whole account might need to be liquidated within five years.

When you start taking distributions from your IRA accounts, it can be in the form of cash and or securities.

Example: You decide that you need a distribution of $4,000. If you have cash in the account it is simple procedure to have the money distributed to you. On the other hand, you might also own 100 shares of a stock valued at $40 per share and decide to take the stock rather than the cash. If you distribute this stock from your IRA, you will have a taxable distribution of $4,000 (100 x $40) just as you would have had with the cash distribution. Your new cost basis for this stock outside of your IRA will then be $40 per share.

Your IRA distributions will be taxed as ordinary income and you will not be able to take advantage of favorable tax treatments such as ten-year averaging or long-term capital gains, which are only available if you meet certain qualifications and if the distributions are coming from qualified accounts such as a 401(k).

Depending on your circumstances, you can pay your tax liability when you file your taxes or on a pay as you go basis. It is a simple process; most investment firms can, upon your request, withhold your state and federal tax liabilities from your distributions and send them to the respective government agencies. (This service can be of particular importance to those individuals making quarterly estimated tax payments.)

How much you take out of your accounts, as well as the taxes and/or penalties you pay, will be governed by your personal circumstances and by your age. Based on IRS regulations, there are three major age groups with which you need to concern yourself.

MAJOR AGE CATEGORIES

In the year 2001, the IRS made some sweeping changes regarding the way that mandatory distributions are handled at age 70.5 and, perhaps more importantly, how distributions are to be handled for your beneficiaries, which I will discuss in detail later in the chapter. For now, I will review the three major age groups that impact distributions from your IRA accounts during your lifetime.

Under 59.5

If you are younger than 59.5 years of age and take distributions out of your IRA accounts, you will pay ordinary income tax on the distributions and can expect to be subject to an additional 10 percent penalty. There are, however, some important exceptions to the penalty:

- First time homebuyer
- Qualified higher education expenses
- Disability
- Medical expenses
- Medical insurance premiums
- 72(t) substantial equal periodic payments
- Death

If you think you qualify for one of the above exceptions, consult your tax advisor.

First-Time Homebuyer

When the IRC describes someone as a first-time homebuyer, it doesn't necessarily mean what you think. It is actually referring to first-time homebuyers and "not so recent" homebuyers.

To meet IRC guidelines for first-time homebuyers, you may not have had any ownership in a principal residence for *two years* ending on the date of the new acquisition. If you are married, both you and your spouse must not have owned a principal residence within two years.

There is also a lifetime $10,000 *distribution limit* per taxpayer. Thus, if you take $6,000 out now and decide that you want to do it again in a few years, you will only be able to take out an additional $4,000 and still qualify for the 10 percent exemption.

Moreover, you must use the money you take out to acquire or construct your principal residence in which you, your spouse, you or your spouse's children, grandchildren, and parents or other ancestors will be living. You cannot, for example, take money out of your IRA and use it to buy rental property and avoid the 10 percent penalty.

Qualified Higher Education Expenses

Expenses for higher education may qualify if you are either the owner of the IRA or the spouse, child, or grandchild of the owner. The distribution that is not subject to the 10 percent penalty is generally the amount that is not more than the qualified higher education expenses. Last but not least, the education, which the IRA funds are paying for, must be at an accredited educational institution.

Disability

To qualify for disability, you must furnish proof that you are incapable of doing any substantial activity because of your physical or mental condition. A physician must evaluate and determine that your condition can be expected to result in death or is of long, continued, or perhaps indefinite duration.

Medical Expenses

Medical expenses paid for with IRA funds must be for you, your spouse, or your dependents. This can be a complicated calculation to follow and to understand. If you think that you qualify for this exception you should consult with a tax planning specialist, CPA, or estate attorney.

Medical Insurance Premiums

You can only use the distributions from your IRA to pay for health insurance premiums for you, your spouse, or your dependents provided that you have received unemployment benefits for at least twelve weeks and have not been re-employed for at least sixty days.

Death

If you die before reaching the age of 59.5, the assets in your IRA rollover can be distributed to your beneficiaries without their having to pay the 10 percent penalty. The distributions will be considered taxable income, and while certain estate taxes might apply, there would be no 10 percent early distribution penalty.

72(t) Substantial Equal Periodic Payments

The 72(t) calculation allows you to take IRA distributions and avoid the 10 percent penalty if you are younger than 59.5 years of age and do not meet any of the other qualifying exceptions. The calculations can be a little tricky, and there are several calculation alternatives that I discuss in detail later in the chapter.

59.5 to 70.5

If you take distributions from your IRA account and are between the ages of 59.5 and 70.5, you will usually not be subject to any penalties. However, any income you receive will still be taxed as ordinary income. You can change your distribution amounts at any time: you can increase distributions, decrease distributions, stop distributions, and then restart distributions. You have almost total control over your distribution schedule, with the single exception that, if you had started distributions based on a 72(t) calculation before 59.5, you may be obligated to continue distributions beyond the age of 59.5 to avoid penalties.

Over 70.5

I will discuss this in greater detail later on in this chapter, but here are the basics. When you reach the age of 70.5, the IRS mandates that you must start taking distributions from your IRA accounts, even if you don't want or need the money. At 70.5, you have what the IRS calls a

Required Beginning Date (RBD), by which you must distribute what the IRS calls your **Required Mandatory Distributions** (RMD).

Your RBD must begin no later than April 1 of the calendar year following the year during which you, as the owner of the IRA, turn 70.5. After the first distribution, you must complete all subsequent distributions by December 31 of each given year. If you put off your first distribution until April 1 of the following year, you will be required to take a second distribution by December 31 of the same year.

> Q: *What happens if you own several different IRAs at different institutions? Are you required to take distributions from each of the accounts?*
>
> A: *The answer is no. The IRS calculation simply requires that a certain total amount must be distributed. Where the IRA distribution amount comes from is of little consequence. It is the total distribution that counts.*

If the withdrawal of your mandatory distribution isn't taken out by its required distribution date deadline, you risk having a 50 percent penalty (this is not a misprint, it is 50 percent) imposed on you, based on the amount you should have taken out.

72 (t): AVOIDING THE 10% PENALTY

The 72(t) calculation is part of the IRC. It is often referred to as substantial equal payments. Here are the criteria you must meet and the issues to evaluate before implementing a 72(t):

- You are younger than 59.5.
- You have money or assets in a qualifying retirement account.

- You want to start taking distributions from your account and avoid the 10 percent early distribution penalty that normally would apply.
- You do not meet any other qualifying exceptions.

The Calculation

Understanding this calculation is important because more people than ever before are leaving companies when they are younger than the age of 59.5 and finding that they need to tap into their IRA accounts to fund their cash flow needs.

The concept of 72(t) can be a little confusing and there are a number of ways to do the calculation. To help you understand the basics of 72(t), I offer this analogy involving the purchase of a house. Let us assume the following data:

- The loan on the house is $300,000.
- You take out a thirty-year loan.
- The interest rate on your home loan is 7 percent.
- Your monthly payment will be approximately $2,000 per month

Example: If you are a good citizen and make your monthly payments for thirty years, you will gradually amortize the loan, in other words, pay off the balance. In this analogy, the amount of the loan ($300,000) represents the value of the IRA. The period of the loan (thirty years in our example) is equivalent to the life expectancy of the IRA holder. The interest rate on the loan (7 percent) represents the rate of return based on U.S. government index guidelines. Finally, the monthly loan payment (approximately $2,000 per month) is analogous to the monthly distribution from the IRA account. If you understand this analogy, then you understand the basic concept of calculating 72(t) with the amortization method.

Calculation Alternatives

Besides the amortization method, there are two other ways to calculate 72(t): life expectancy, and annuitization. But, before you begin your 72(t) calculation, you will need to gather the following information:

- Current value of your account
- Your life expectancy
- The current reasonable rate of return

Current value of your account. Don't confuse this calculation with the requirement of using the closing value of your IRA account from the previous year, which you need when calculating required minimum distribution amounts (RMDs) at age 70.5.

Your life expectancy. Your life expectancy is based on either single or joint life-expectancy actuarial tables. To get a copy of the tables, you can go to the IRS website and retrieve a copy of publication 590. (See Appendix C.)

The current reasonable rate of return. You must assign an interest rate to the calculation that meets government guidelines.

What then is a reasonable rate of return that meets government guidelines? Well, during the late 1990s, "reasonable" might have seemed to many investors to be 15 percent per year. During the year 2001, which saw tremendous volatility in the stock market, earning just a few percentage points might have been reasonable. So, once again, what is a reasonable rate of return? In a private letter ruling, the IRS accepted the long-term applicable federal rate as a reasonable rate of return. However, there is no official index or rate that is required to be used for this purpose.

Once you have determined the reasonable rate of return for your 72(t) calculation, it is important to note that the earnings on your account might be completely different than the interest rate you have chosen—the actual investment returns could be larger or smaller. If you use 6 percent for your 72(t) calculation and are a stock-picking genius earning 30 percent a year, your account will continue to grow even though you are taking distributions. On the other hand, if you use 6 percent for your 72(t) calculation and make some poor investment choices that earn nothing, the value of your account will decrease yearly

Which of the methods for calculating 72(t)—life expectancy, amortization, or annuitization—is best for you? It will depend on your personal and income needs. See the calculations in Table 4-1 for examples of how the numbers would work. In this example, I will make the following assumptions:

- The owner of the IRA is 55 years old.
- The beneficiary of the account is the spouse, who is 54 years old.
- The value of the IRA is $400,000.
- The reasonable rate of return assumption, based on government tables, is 6 percent.

Table 4-1.

Calculating 72(t).

Life-Expectancy Method. The amount distributed will depend on whether you chose the single or joint life tables.
Single: $13,514/year
Joint: $11,080/year

Amortization Method. The amount distributed will depend on single versus joint life tables.
Single: $29,205/year
Joint: $27,336/year

Annuitization Method. Only single life is available.
Single: $32,781/year

The advantage of a 72(t) calculation is that you will not be subject to the 10 percent penalty. Although you avoid the penalty, you certainly don't avoid being taxed—distributions will be taxed as ordinary income. Before I conclude my discussion on 72(t), I want to make the following critical point: in order to avoid penalties, you must maintain the yearly distributions for at least five years, or until you are age 59.5.

> *Example:* If you are age 57 when you start your distributions, you must continue them until you are 62, not until you are 59.5, which is only 2.5 years. If, for example, you are 52 when you begin 72(t) distributions, you must maintain them until you are 59.5, which is 7.5 years.

Taking income based on 72(t) calculations and then arbitrarily changing your yearly distributions before the required passage of time will make you subject to a 10 percent penalty, which would be applied *retroactively* to all of that account's distributions.

Because of the requirements and restrictions of this calculation, a 72(t) may or may not be appropriate for your particular needs. Be very clear about your income needs before you begin 72(t) distributions from your IRA accounts.

Special Situations

Cost-of-Living Increases

Most 72(t) calculations result in a fixed yearly distribution. You can however, during your initial calculations, apply a cost-of-living factor to your distributions. If you utilize this methodology, you must maintain it as the strategy for the duration of the payments. For example, if you applied a 3 percent cost-of-living increase to your distributions and received distributions for five years, you would be required to apply the 3 percent cost-of-living increase strategy each year for the full five-year period.[19]

Splitting an IRA Account and Implementing a 72(t)

You can follow a strategy in which you break up an IRA into different accounts and implement a 72(t) with only one of them.

> *Example:* What are your options if you receive a $400,000 distribution and place it in an IRA rollover account, but have income needs that can be met with a $200,000 IRA account. In that case, after opening the original $400,000 IRA, you could split off $200,000 into a second IRA account and apply the 72(t) calculation to only a portion of your original $400,000 distribution.

---

[19] Before implementing a 72(t) cost-of-living increase calculation, review the information with your tax specialist.

RMDs & BENEFICIARIES

In the past, when people set out to manage their IRA rollover accounts, no area was more confusing than the rules and regulations that impacted beneficiaries and the required minimum distributions that began when an IRA owner turned 70.5. The old rules and regulations were so puzzling that not only did most people not understand them, but they also baffled many retirement professionals. To resolve the confusion, the IRS recently released new rules and regulations that will have a sweeping impact on IRA beneficiaries and required mandatory distributions.

You've heard it said: "There's no such thing as a free lunch." Well, the new simplicity comes with a price. The price the government has extracted is compliance, with a capital "C." Specifically, all financial firms and custodians will have an increased responsibility to report clients' required minimum distributions. Your failure to take out the required minimum distributions can result in a substantial penalty.

To help you avoid these types of problems, I will first present a brief overview of the most significant changes, and then to clarify the new reality, I will discuss the new rules and regulations for the following two scenarios: (1) the owner of the IRA is living, hits the magic age of 70.5, and (2) the owner of the IRA dies and IRA assets are distributed to his or her beneficiaries.

New Rules and Regulations

Here are some of the critical highlights of the changes in regulations that took effect on January 1, 2002:

1. You will be given a "fresh start," even if you had made distribution decisions upon turning 70.5 under the old IRS guidelines.

2. The new uniform distribution schedule for 70.5 or older mandatory distributions, utilizes a uniform life-expectancy table with a distribution factor that never goes below 1.9 years. The significance of this is that you are never required to deplete the assets in your IRA. (See Table 4-3.)

3. You have more flexibility in naming and changing your IRA beneficiaries and in undoing certain decisions that were once irrevocable.

4. Once you turn 70.5, you will have the option of reducing your required distributions, with the result being that your assets can remain in your IRA and continue to grow on a tax deferred basis.

The Calculation

To calculate your new required minimum distributions during your lifetime, you will need the following information:

- Age of the IRA owner
- IRA balance at the end of the prior year
- IRA beneficiary

Your IRA beneficiary is assumed to be ten years younger (there is one exception: if your spouse is more than ten years younger than you). It doesn't matter if in reality the non-spouse beneficiary is older, the same age, or thirty years younger, the calculation will assume a ten-year age gap and a uniform calculation will be used. (See Table 4-2.)

To obtain the current year's RMD, divide the account balance at the end of the prior year by the uniform life-expectancy factor found to the right of your age.

Example: If you are 75 years old and your account balance at the end of the previous year was $300,000, then your RMD is $13,100 ($300,000 ÷ 22.9).

Table 4-2.

Uniform Life Expectancy Table.

Age	Factor	Age	Factor
70	27.4	93	9.6
71	26.5	94	9.1
72	25.6	95	8.6
73	24.7	96	8.1
74	23.8	97	7.6
75	22.9	98	7.1
76	22.0	99	6.7
77	21.2	100	6.3
78	20.3	101	5.9
79	19.5	102	5.5
80	18.7	103	5.2
81	17.9	104	4.9
82	17.1	105	4.5
83	16.3	106	4.2
84	15.5	107	3.9
85	14.8	108	3.7
86	14.1	109	3.4
87	13.4	110	3.1
88	12.7	111	2.9
89	12.0	112	2.6
90	11.4	113	2.4
91	10.8	114	2.1
92	10.2	115 & older	1.9

Distributions to Beneficiaries

Payout Schedules

You now have until September 30 of the year following the death of the IRA owner to determine the length of the IRA payout and who or what will be the IRA beneficiary. (These rules and regulations can be a little confusing and I agree this may sound a bit strange—changing or determining the beneficiary and the corresponding payout after the owner of the IRA has died.) Although the final beneficiaries can be determined after death, the IRA owner must name all beneficiaries while he or she is still alive.

Some of the new distribution options allow beneficiaries to *disclaim* their interest in the IRA in favor of another beneficiary or to *cash out* their interest in an IRA. (The IRA owner must designate all the primary or contingent beneficiaries prior to his or her death for the disclaimer or cash-out strategy to be viable.)

> *Example 1:* The owner of an IRA dies and leaves his or her spouse 50 percent of the account and the other 50 percent to their only child. The surviving spouse could remove his or her name and immediately pass along 100 percent of the IRA assets to the child. This option might be attractive if the spouse doesn't need the assets and the child does— especially if, based on the estate plans, the child will eventually receive the estate anyway.

> *Example 2:* Perhaps, the original owner of the IRA dies, and the IRA assets go to the two children in the following manner: 50 percent is going to a child who is thirty years old, and the remaining 50 percent to a child who is forty. (I know that when you are thirty and forty you are no longer

a child, but that's often the way your parents see it.) The older child in this example has more pressing financial needs and wants to cash out his or her portion of the account. If that happens, the younger child can either cash out his or her portion or decide to take distributions during an extended period of time, based on his or her longer life expectancy.

Such financial decisions are very personal, and every family situation is different. The important point is that the new regulations now give you this kind of flexibility. You need to remember that this type of transaction in itself does not remove the estate from the income tax liabilities of the original IRA account.

TYPES OF BENEFICIARIES

Due to the recent changes in the IRC, beneficiaries are now broken into two major groups: (1) **designated beneficiaries**, who are either single or joint individuals, or certain qualifying trusts; and (2) **non-designated beneficiaries**, which are charities, universities, foundations, and other non-living beneficiaries such as your estate. The rules and regulations governing them are dramatically different.

Designated Beneficiary

Following the death of the owner of the IRA, designated beneficiaries are normally required to take minimum annual distributions based on their single life expectancy. The age of the beneficiary is based on his or her age in the calendar year immediately following the year of the IRA owner's death. For purposes of life expectancy, the age of the beneficiary is then reduced each year. If the distributions are not taken by the required date, the beneficiary may be subject to penalties. There can be a waiver for these penalties, but only when the entire amount is withdrawn within five years following the IRA owner's death.[20]

If you have more than one designated beneficiary (for example three children), the life expectancy of the oldest beneficiary will normally be used for the younger beneficiaries as well. Therefore, if you have more than one beneficiary and the age difference between them is large, you may want to consider setting up two or more IRAs and have one person be the sole beneficiary of each account. If you decide to do this, then the obvious question is as follows: can an IRA account be split up in this manner at any time? No! It can be done before time of death, or until the end of the year following the original IRA owner's death. Please note that all designated beneficiaries must be determined by September 30 of the year following the IRA owner's death, which seems to be inconsistent with splitting the IRA by the end of the year following the IRA owner's death. To avoid any problems, splitting up accounts so that each designated beneficiary can use their own life expectancy for required distributions should be done by September 30 of the year following the original IRA owner's death.

> *Example:* You decide to leave 50 percent of your IRA account to your son and 50 percent to his son—your grandson—who is, of course, significantly younger. At time of death, let us assume that you are 69, your son is 49, and your grandson is 21. When you die, each of your beneficiaries would receive his corresponding 50 percent benefit. However, if the IRA account is not split up in any manner, the required minimum distribution schedule from the IRA will be based on the life expectancy of your 49-year-old son. Your grandson would be forced to take the minimum

---

[20] The five-year waiver rule is available only if the original owner of the IRA was under 70.5 at time of death and had not started required mandatory distributions.

distribution—based on the life expectancy of your son, his father—whether he needed that amount of money or not.

Contrast the above example with a scenario where the IRA had been split up by the required date following the death of the original IRA owner, and one person had been named as the sole beneficiary to each respective IRA. If that had occurred, then each beneficiary could have used his own life expectancy for the required minimum distributions. Your grandson, at 21, would have had the option of extending the minimum distributions for a longer period of time, based on his longer life expectancy.

Q: *If you split up your IRA before you die, should all the accounts be managed in exactly the same way, or should one account, for example, be the stock account and the other a bond account?*

A: *Different investment strategies can give dramatically different investment results. Imagine the ensuing chaos if your intentions were to give each beneficiary an equal portion, only to discover that the stock account had dramatically outperformed the bond account. The consequence would be that one beneficiary might receive significantly more money upon your death. You'll want do a thorough analysis before you embark on these types of alternatives.*

Spouse: Special Status

The spouse is the only beneficiary who can receive distributions upon the original IRA owner's death and roll them over into his or her own IRA account. Even though the spouse has special privileges, the penalties, rules, and regulations that can impact a spousal beneficiary are neither simple nor straightforward. They can vary, depending on the age of the IRA owner at time of death and on the age of the spousal beneficiary.

In some instances, the spouse is subject to a 10 percent penalty, whereas in other instances the spouse is exempt. I will review some scenarios that should help you to understand this new "simplification." In these examples, the owner of the IRA rollover will be the husband, who I'll call Charlie. With even less imagination in play, I'll call the wife Mary-Sue.

Here is a little side note to our IRA couple: When Charlie and Mary-Sue exchanged wedding vows they decided that they wanted a long and happy marriage. So, they set down some guidelines to govern their union. They decided that Charlie would make all the big decisions in their lives and Mary-Sue would handle all the little ones. Mary-Sue happily reports that so far, after several decades of marriage, there haven't been any big decisions for Charlie to make. There you have it, the key to a happy marriage.

Now, for those of you who find this to be a cute story but are wondering what in the world it has to do with IRA rollovers, beneficiaries, and the special status of the spouse, the answer is everything. This story brings us to the important topic of how married couples make financial decisions.

There are three basic ways married couples handle investment decisions: (1) the husband makes them, (2) the wife makes them, or (3) there is some kind of a team effort, husband and wife making joint decisions. So, which one is the best? I believe that generally the third option is the best, for all the obvious reasons. The worst, in my opinion, is when the husband makes all the financial decisions. Gentlemen, before you get all worked up, let me explain that my opinion on this matter has nothing to do with your ability to make good or bad investments, or with your knowing more or less than your wives. It has to do with something called "life expectancy."

It is a cold statistical fact of life that women live longer than men. Further compounding the problem, many men are married to women who are younger than they are. If the husband makes all the investment decisions and is a lousy manager of money, of course the consequences would be terrible for the wife. If the husband is an investment genius, the spouse (your wife) still needs to be involved, because there is a good possibility that she will outlive him and eventually have to start making investment decisions on her own.

One of the worst financial scenarios is when a husband who has made all the financial decisions for a family dies before his spouse, and leaves her unprepared for financial responsibilities. Make it a team effort from the beginning. Now, I'll discuss the basic options that a spousal beneficiary (Mary-Sue in this example) has if the IRA owner (Charlie in this example) dies first.

1. She can leave Charlie's IRA account intact then take a partial or full distribution.
2. She can roll over his assets into her IRA account (only the spouse has this option).
3. She can disclaim her portion.
4. She can cash out her financial interest and pass along the remaining assets to an already named contingent beneficiary— in this case, their children.

In choosing the third or fourth option, Mary-Sue gives her children the option of spreading out their distributions based on their longer life expectancy. Because those options will always be available regardless of when Charlie dies, I won't discuss them in the following, age-of-death scenarios. (Again, you'll want to review estate and tax consequences with your estate advisor before implementing any of these strategies.)[21]

---

[21] Note: Under previous regulations, a surviving spouse who was the beneficiary of a qualified plan could roll over assets from the deceased owner into his or her IRA rollover account. However, at a future date, the spousal beneficiary could not move those assets back to a company-qualified plan such as a 401(k). Only the original owner of the account had this option. Recently enacted IRS rulings now permit these types of transfers for a spouse—under certain conditions.

Both Younger Than 59.5

In this first scenario I've chosen, Charlie and Mary-Sue are both younger than 59.5 when Charlie dies and leaves his assets to his wife. Some of Mary-Sue's options are as follows:

1. She can leave Charlie's IRA account intact and take distributions from it, in which case the income would be taxable. Fortunately she wouldn't be subject to the 10 percent early distribution penalty because death is one of the qualifying exceptions.[22]

2. Mary-Sue can leave Charlie's IRA account intact and delay the required minimum distributions until the end of the calendar year, when Charlie (the original IRA owner) would have become 70.5 (the date distributions from Charlie's account would have commenced had he lived). Mary-Sue would then use *her* age to calculate the yearly required minimum distributions.

3. Mary-Sue can roll over Charlie's IRA account into her IRA account. If she then takes distributions from her new IRA, that income will be taxable and she may be subject to a 10 percent penalty because in this example she is younger than 59.5.

You will recall that death is listed as an exception to the 10 percent penalty. However, the exception applies only if the spousal beneficiary leaves the IRA assets in the original account. Thus, Mary-Sue would need to leave Charlie's account intact and take distributions from his account for her benefit. Once she rolled over the assets, the death exception would no longer apply and she would need to implement a 72(t) calculation or meet one of the other qualifying exceptions to avoid the 10 percent early distribution penalty.

---

[22] See Chapter 4 to review this topic.

Q: *If Charlie had started 72(t) distributions before his death, what would Mary-Sue's options be?*

A: Typically, a 72(t) calculation must be maintained for at least five years. In this example, if Charlie had started the distributions when he was 58, he would have needed to continue them until he was 63. Under the circumstance of death, the spouse would no longer be required to continue the 72(t) mandatory distributions. She could stop the distributions or change the distribution amounts, and not be subject to the 10 percent retroactive penalty.

Charlie Older Than 70.5, Mary-Sue Younger Than 59.5

In this second scenario, Charlie is older than 70.5 when he dies. Mary-Sue, the beneficiary, is younger than 59.5. Some of her options are as follows:

1.   Mary-Sue can leave Charlie's IRA intact. Charlie would have begun mandatory distributions and Mary-Sue will have to continue them. During the year of his death, she would have to take out Charlie's normal distribution. From that point on, however, distributions out of his account will be based on her single life expectancy. Although she is younger than 59.5, she wouldn't be subject to a 10 percent penalty because the distributions would be coming out of the original owner's IRA account.

2.   Mary-Sue can roll over Charlie's IRA to her IRA account. She will not, however, be able to roll over 100 percent of the account. Instead, she must take out the mandatory distribution that would have come out to Charlie, had he not passed away. Starting the year after Charlie's death, she will no longer be required to take mandatory distributions because she is younger

than 70.5. There is, however, an important issue that bears repeating here: if Mary-Sue, as the spouse, rolls the money over into her account and takes distributions from it, she may be subject to a 10 percent early distribution penalty because she is younger than 59.5. To avoid the penalty, she will need to qualify for one of the 10 percent early distribution exemptions.

"Wait a minute," you say. "Isn't death one of the exemptions?" Well, that depends. It normally is an exemption, but if Mary-Sue, the wife, rolls the money into her account, that exemption no longer applies. The death exemption can only be used when the money is left in the original owner's account and distributions are taken out of it. I repeat this point because it is often misunderstood—to the spouse's dismay.

Charlie Older Than 70.5, Mary-Sue Between 59.5 and 70.5

In this third scenario, Charlie is older than 70.5 and Mary-Sue is older than 59.5, but younger than 70.5 at the time of his death.

1. Again, Mary-Sue can leave Charlie's IRA intact. However, just as with our second scenario, she'd be required to start required minimum distributions as a designated beneficiary, but based on her single life expectancy.
2. Mary-Sue can roll over Charlie's IRA to her IRA account and take distributions without paying a 10 percent penalty because she is older than 59.5. Just as with our second scenario, Mary-Sue must take out the mandatory distribution for that year, which would normally have been distributed from Charlie's account, had he not passed away.
3. Once she rolled the account over, Mary-Sue wouldn't be required to take her required minimum distributions until she turned 70.5.

Charlie and Mary-Sue Older Than 70.5 When Charlie Dies

In our final scenario, after many years of marriage, Charlie passes away when both he and Mary-Sue are older than 70.5.

1. Mary-Sue can leave her husband's account intact, but she'd have to continue the mandatory minimum distributions from her deceased husband's IRA, based, however, on her single life calculation.
2. Mary-Sue can roll over Charlie's IRA into her IRA account, but then she would have to start her own mandatory distributions based on actuarial tables. The IRS suggests that if the surviving spouse has also reached the age of mandatory distributions and wishes to roll over the assets and start a new life-expectancy period based on his or her age, it should be done within one year after the death of the original IRA owner.

I have introduced you here to some of the basic ways a spousal beneficiary can be impacted following the death of an IRA owner. Because the alternatives represent many twists and turns, review the alternatives open to you with your CPA, tax advisor, or estate attorney.

Living Trusts

Under the old regulations, when a trust met certain provisions, it qualified for a "look through" rule, in which the trust's individual beneficiaries—for example, the spouse or children—were considered to be the IRA's designated beneficiaries. Under the new regulations, a **testamentary trust** may also qualify for look-through treatment. The key provision is that the trust has to meet certain requirements to be considered a designated beneficiary. It must be valid and irrevocable or it will, by its terms, become irrevocable upon the death of the owner of the account. Trust owners must be identifiable, and you must make a copy of the trust document available to the proper individuals and institutions. If you are considering having a **living trust** as your primary beneficiary, it is imperative that you meet with your estate or tax-planning specialist before implementing this course of action.

Non-Designated Beneficiary

The required minimum distribution schedule for a non-designated beneficiary will depend on the age at which the original IRA owner died. If the original owner of the IRA was 70.5 years of age or older and the required minimum distributions had started, the minimum required distributions would continue based on his or her life expectancy. If the original owner of the IRA had been younger than 70.5 at the time of death, then the required minimum distributions would not have started, and the **five-year rule** would apply.

The five-year rule states that all the IRA account's assets must be distributed before the end of the fifth year following the death of the owner of the IRA. With the exception of certain trusts, if any of the primary beneficiaries are non-living entities, such as a charity or university, the IRA will be treated as having a non-designated IRA beneficiary, even if some of the other beneficiaries normally would qualify as designated beneficiaries.

This is an important issue because having non-designated beneficiary status can impact others that normally would have been considered designated beneficiaries. Let me give you an example to clarify this, using our friend Charlie.

> *Example:* Charlie, the owner of the IRA, names Stanford University (that is, a non-designated beneficiary) and his son as equal (50/50) beneficiaries. Usually, Charlie's son would be considered a designated beneficiary, but, under these conditions, he is viewed as being a non-designated

beneficiary. Is there any way for Charlie's son to reclaim his status as a designated beneficiary? Yes, if Stanford University cashes out its 50 percent portion in one lump sum by the required deadline of the year following Charlie's death, then Charlie's son, under the new regulations, would be able to achieve the status of designated beneficiary on his 50 percent.

SUMMARY: The year 2001 brought sweeping changes to the laws that govern retirement plans profoundly impacting required minimum distributions and IRA beneficiaries. Although the guidelines and laws have been "simplified," the calculations, terminology, and payout schedules have been changed. To handle your IRA distributions correctly, you will need to understand the differences between a designated and a non-designated beneficiary and how various ages can have an impact on distributions to you and your beneficiaries.

Part II

How to Build Your Portfolio Blueprint

Chapter 5

Financial Planning

I carefully planned my high school curriculum so I could get into a quality university. In college, I planned my classes so that I'd have the background and training that the job market demanded. When I started working, I planned my career path to maximize my opportunities in the company. All of a sudden, the years have gone by and I'm ready for retirement. It hit me like a ton of bricks. I've been a "planner" my whole life and yet I never had a formal plan for retirement. I don't even know what financial planning really means.

The first assignment in developing a portfolio blueprint or plan of action involves *financial fact-finding* and *goal setting*—both personal and financial. It is through this initial exercise in financial planning that you will learn who you are, what you have, where you want to go, and what you'll need to do to complete the journey.

Begin by thoroughly evaluating your family's personal needs and wants, in conjunction with your family's assets and liabilities. This exercise will produce a statement of your net worth. It is only after completing these tasks that you will be prepared to evaluate asset-allocation models, investment product alternatives, and investment selection. If you were living in a perfect world for financial planning, the following process is the one you could adhere to while playing out you complicated life. (I discuss asset allocation, investment product alternatives, and investment selection in subsequent chapters.)

Fact Finding

When you begin gathering your financial data, remember that your needs as a retiree will be very different from what they were when you were in the workforce or transitioning to other employment. If you are a retiree, you will discover that the fact-finding process involves more than just figuring out your consolidated balance sheet. You must also understand how to structure a portfolio so that it replaces the income you were earning while employed. If you're not retiring and expect to have several years ahead in which to invest for your retirement, your fact-finding undertaking will involve more analysis about retirement contributions and an appreciation of growth models that will allow you to fund your future retirement needs.

Regardless of your circumstances, every great structure begins with a plan. Be prepared to file and track your important financial and personal documents. I suggest that you get yourself a three-ring binder, some paper to fill it, some Post-its in various sizes ("stickies"), and a pen or pencil. I have listed some of the key items that you will want to track and file in your "Retirement Profile and Balance Sheet":

- Current age
- Anticipated retirement age
- Assets
- Debts
- Income sources
- Wills

- Trusts
- Health and insurance documents

If you need help assembling a retirement profile and balance sheet, many investment firms can supply you with a workbook that organizes and simplifies the process.[23]

Once you have gathered and organized your personal and financial data, you'll need to determine your personal and financial goals. I will focus here on those individuals who are retiring, receiving a lump-sum distribution, and then trying to figure out what they will be doing with the rest of their lives.

Goal Setting

Based on the hundreds, if not thousands of meetings that I have had with individuals during the years, I have the following recommendations:

Personal Goals

In retirement, your personal goals should allow you to keep the blood flowing, the muscles strong, and the brain sharp. To achieve this, you might want to evaluate some of the following issues and take advantage of some of the following tried-and-true components of the "good life" in retirement.

Lifelong learning. You might want to study a foreign language, which will challenge your brain and impress your buddies at the company retirement club meetings. (It also makes ordering food in certain restaurants a lot easier.)

Volunteering. If you are willing to donate your time, there are many groups that will welcome your assistance. Can there be anything more

---

[23] See Appendix A for a sample worksheet.

rewarding than helping a disadvantaged child learn to read or discover the wonders of math and science? Looking back on your life and knowing that you were a positive influence on other individuals can bring a warm glow to your heart.

Developing hobbies. When it's time to start enjoying your hobbies, you're likely to spend your time doing what you love. However, developing new hobbies can be both rewarding and stimulating. If you love gardening, why not do something different this year and enter your vegetables in a local fair? Nothing tastes better than a fresh, juicy, ripe, homegrown tomato that has a blue ribbon attached to it.

Traveling. If you enjoy traveling, there really is no limit to what you can see and where you can go. How many people do you know who have been to every state in the union?

Work, work, and more work. Some folks just can't do without it. If you plan to work, at least you can strive to find a situation in which you're working because you want to be employed, not because the state of your finances requires it. That reminds me of the $10 million lottery winner who told his friends that he would continue working. The only difference, he told them, was that he would have a whole new attitude about it.

Where you will live. Whether to stay in one's current home or leave the area is a question with which many retirees struggle. Often, people have a naïve recollection of the "good old days," become fed up with the changes surrounding them, and get convinced that the grass is greener on the other side of the fence. They're encouraged by advertisements for retirement living at locations where the sun always shines and other people anxiously await their arrival. Choose wisely before buying into this marketing hype. Selling your house and moving on can be very stressful, and once you make the decision it can be hard to reverse it.

Your home as an asset. You may have built up considerable net worth in your primary residence. I suggest that you not view this asset as capital to generate income unless you decide to sell your house and move to a less expensive community. I'm not a fan of borrowing against the equity in your house, especially when it's to invest the capital. Don't fall into the trap of taking money out of your home to take advantage of some hot "can't-miss" opportunity. Your home has value. The equity in it is available, but think of it as your capital of last resort.

Financial Goals

Now that you've put together your family's financial data and chosen your personal goals, it's time to start analyzing the data and formulating some financial goals for yourself. One of the comments I hear most often expressed by retirees is: "I'm looking forward to retirement, but I don't want to be a financial burden to my family." That concern brings you to the important topics of financial goals, your life expectancy, and not outliving your assets.

To get a handle on these critical issues, you must prepare a retirement cash-flow analysis. The results of this calculation will give you direction and determine whether your wants and expectations are viable.

Let us look at an example of why this analysis is so important. In this analysis, the retiree, in addition to Social Security benefits, has capital and sources of income outside of the IRA rollover account. However, additional income is going to be needed, and it will be funded by the retiree's IRA rollover. Based on the following information, will this individual live the life of luxury in retirement or consume his or her IRA's principal and die broke?

For simplicity's sake, I will assume that the interest earned is simple interest, the income taken out of the account will be distributed at the end of the year, and the individual does not have to pay a 10 percent early distribution penalty since he meets one of the qualifying exceptions discussed in Chapter 4.

- Retiree is 55 years old.
- IRA rollover is valued at $500,000.
- Retiree is in a 30 percent combined state and federal tax bracket.
- Retiree needs $30,000 per year in after-tax income.
- The account earns 9 percent per year.
- A rate of inflation of 3 percent per year is assumed (income needs will increase at 3 percent per year to buy the same goods and services).

On the surface, it appears that the needs of the retiree will easily be met by the IRA account. Or will it? After all, $500,000 is a pretty good-sized chunk of money. For the answer, see Table 5-1.

Table 5-1.

Retirement Cash Flow Analysis.

Year	Value of Account (in $)	Yearly Earnings (in $)	Pre-tax Distribution Amount (in $)	Desired After-tax Income (in $)
1	500,000	$45,000	$ 42,857	$ 30,000
2	502,143	$45,193	$ 44,143	$ 30,900
3	503,193	$45,287	$ 45,467	$ 31,827
4	503,013	$45,271	$ 46,831	$ 32,782
5	501,453	$45,131	$ 48,236	$ 33,765
6	498,348	$44,851	$ 49,683	$ 34,778
7	493,516	$44,416	$ 51,174	$ 35,822
8	486,759	$43,808	$ 52,709	$ 36,896
9	477,858	$43,007	$ 54,290	$ 38,003
10	466,575	$41,992	$ 55,919	$ 39,143
11	452,648	$40,738	$ 57,596	$ 40,317
12	435,790	$39,221	$ 59,324	$ 41,527
13	415,687	$37,412	$ 61,104	$ 42,773
14	391,995	$35,280	$ 62,937	$ 44,056
15	364,337	$32,790	$ 64,825	$ 45,378
16	332,302	$29,907	$ 66,770	$ 46,739
17	295,439	$26,590	$ 68,773	$ 48,141
18	253,255	$22,793	$ 70,836	$ 49,585
19	205,212	$18,469	$ 72,961	$ 51,073
20	150,720	$13,565	$ 75,150	$ 52,605
21	89,134	$ 8,022	$ 77,405	$ 54,183
22	19,752	$ 1,778	?	?

From the analysis in Table 5-1, you can see that our retiree has more than enough money to fund additional cash-flow needs, as long as he or she *dies* within twenty-two years. If our retiree lives longer than twenty-two years, then the $500,000 rollover will be gone, totally depleted because of the ravages of inflation. Don't forget to consider inflation and purchasing power risk as you plan for retirement and evaluate your cash flow needs.

You've collected your financial data, formulated some personal and financial goals, and done a cash-flow analysis—but you're still not ready to start making investments. You now need to review some of the investment principles that should direct your asset-allocation models and investment decisions: (1) preservation of capital, (2) risk, (3) income, (4) liquidity, (5) growth, and (6) taxes.

Investment Principles

Preservation of capital

The three most important words for a real estate investor are location, location, and location. The same concept can be applied to the investments in your retirement accounts, except that those three most important words are safety, safety, and safety. Without a doubt, the safety of your principal and your capital—your retirement nest egg—should be the guiding light of your investment strategy. It doesn't matter how wonderful something appears now; in retirement, you won't have the same time horizon that you had earlier in life or the ability to accept the risks that you did when you were in your 30s or 40s. Preservation of capital is at the top of your retirement pyramid, but there are other investment principles as well.

Risk

I want to be very clear about the word "risk" and what I mean by it in a financial discussion. You cannot avoid financial risk. Let me say that again: *you cannot avoid financial risk.* Right now, you might be saying to yourself, "Of course I can avoid financial risk, I'll just put everything into U.S. government-guaranteed investments like U.S. Treasuries. The full faith and credit of the U.S. government will back my investments, risk free." I'm afraid this strategy is not risk-free, because there are different kinds of investment risks: (1) **market risk** (changes to your principal), (2) **interest rate risk** (an impact on fixed income investments), (3) **purchasing power risk** (a result of inflation), and (4) **credit risk** (a change in value due to a change in the credit rating of a security, although credit risk does not apply to U.S. Treasuries).

Purchasing power or inflation risk is the most insidious of the different risks because it eats away relentlessly at your portfolio. In Table 5-2, you can see the dramatic impact inflation can have on your purchasing power. Also, don't forget that medical technology is increasing life expectancies. The result being that you may spend more years in retirement than you did working.

Table 5-2.

The Impact of Inflation.

	1970 Price	1990 price	2010 projected
Median income	$8,734	$29,943	$102,654
One dozen eggs (large)	$ 0.61	$ 1.00	$ 1.64
One pound bacon	$ 0.95	$ 2.28	$ 5.47
1/2 gallon milk	$ 0.66	$ 1.39	$ 2.93
One pound coffee	$ 0.91	$ 2.94	$ 9.50

Source: U.S. Department of Commerce

Because you can't avoid all the different types of risk with a single investment, one of your financial planning goals is to manage your risks consistent with your particular needs and risk tolerances.[24]

Income

As I discussed at the beginning of this book, retirement income can come from several sources. If some or all of your income will come from an investment portfolio, you must strive to create a diversified portfolio with the capacity to increase your income over time in order to fight inflation.

Liquidity

The bulk of your investments should be liquid, by which I mean the investments can be converted to cash on a timely basis. Keep in mind that while a conversion to cash with liquid investments may be simple and easy, it does not mean that it will be free. Depending on your investments and the institutions you are dealing with, some penalties or charges may apply. Here are some examples of liquid investments:

- Publicly traded stocks
- Mutual funds
- Money market accounts
- Bonds
- CDs (certificates of deposit)

You'll want to avoid maintaining too large a percentage of your investments in instruments that cannot easily be sold or converted to cash. Keep your distance from illiquid investments such as real estate partnerships and oil and gas partnerships that have long holding periods and do not permit timely divesting. Even if you are a long-term

---

[24] See strategies for risk management in Chapter 6.

investor, you need to maintain the flexibility that comes with owning liquid investments.

Growth

If you accept the fact that you need some growth in your portfolio, the question becomes "How much growth is required?" The rule of thumb used to be that the percentage of money you should be putting into cash and bonds should equal your age, with the balance being invested in growth alternatives.

> *Example 1:* If you are 65, then 65 percent of your portfolio should go into cash and bonds and the remaining 35 percent into growth.

> *Example 2:* If you are 40, then 40 percent of your portfolio should go into cash and bonds, and the remaining 60 percent into growth.

The idea behind this concept is that the younger you are, the more growth you should have. The older you become, the more conservative you become, and thus the amount that should be in "safe" investments increases. It is a simple concept, but these general guidelines may no longer be valid for all investors. While you do need to be more conservative when you are 60 than when you were 30, growth and maintaining purchasing power are becoming more important than ever as life expectancy increases.

Taxes

Having to pay income taxes on ordinary income as well as on your short-term and long-term capital gains can have a major impact on your portfolio decisions and investment returns. Their impact isn't important while your investments are in an IRA rollover account or a company retirement plan because the returns in those types of accounts are tax-deferred (no tax liability is due until you start your distributions). Taxes in investments outside retirement accounts are a different matter.[25]

SUMMARY: One of the most important features of financial planning is that it forces you to get organized. It jump-starts the process of creating a road map for you to follow as you journey toward building your investment portfolio. It is the invaluable reference that will keep you on track of your personal and financial goals and serve as a reminder of the investment principles you need to follow. It is not just the first step in your financial journey. It is something that you need to do before, during, and after you receive your lump-sum distribution. It is a process you should follow for the rest of your life.

---

[25] See Chapter 14 for a discussion of investment strategies you may want to employ outside of tax-deferred accounts such as an IRA rollover.

Chapter 6

Asset Allocation & Diversification

Look, I'm not asking for much, my needs are pretty simple. I want the best return possible on my investments and I want to do it with the least amount of risk possible. Plus, what is all this mumbo jumbo about diversifying my accounts. It seems to me that the best way to make money is to be in the best sector of the market at any period of time. Shouldn't we just buy things when they are low and sell them when they are high? That strategy seems like a pretty reasonable request doesn't it?

Once you have completed your financial fact-finding mission, formulated your personal and financial goals, and prepared a cash-flow analysis, you're ready for the next stage in creating a portfolio blueprint: developing your personal asset-allocation model.[26]

---

[26] In its simplest terms, asset allocation involves dividing your investments among different asset classes, such as cash, bonds, and equities.

A word of caution is due here: it's easy to stumble and not appreciate the value of properly diversifying your investments when you begin constructing your asset-allocation model. Rising financial markets can mask an incorrect or inappropriate portfolio mix that will become all too apparent when investment markets take a downturn—as they always do. Correct asset allocation is vital to your financial health; yet it is often **market timing** and other strategies that get press and airtime on financial news shows, even though they are responsible for only a small part of investment and portfolio returns.

You can see from Chart 6-A how important asset allocation is in determining your investment returns. According to this analysis, more than 90 percent of an investor's investment returns are based on asset allocation—that is, being in a given financial market or asset class for a given period of time.

Chart 6-A.

Asset Allocation and Investment Returns.

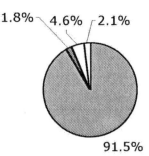

Source: *Financial Analyst Journal, May-June 1991*

To further illustrate the importance of asset allocation in determining your investment returns, I offer some observations about the San Francisco Bay Area, which has some of the most expensive residential property in the United States. If you had come to the Bay Area thirty years ago and gone to work for Hewlett Packard, there's a good chance you would have purchased a home in Palo Alto, HP's corporate headquarters. This asset (your home) has by now probably appreciated in value by perhaps twenty-fold, if not more. Now, I'd like you to fill in the end of the following statement.

You've seen a tremendous increase in the value of your house in Palo Alto because of which reason:

- You were a tough negotiator.
- You had done extensive market research and analysis.
- You knew when the market was hot and when it was not.
- You were lucky enough to have bought a home close to where you worked, which just happened to be in Palo Alto.

You may not want to complete the statement honestly when your spouse is around, but you do need to be honest with yourself. Proper asset allocation (being in a given market or asset class) is often the key to an investor's long-term financial success. So, if you accept the importance of asset allocation, what is the next step? The next step is easy to understand: structure a portfolio that will give you the best return possible with the least amount of risk. Unfortunately, the actual implementation of this can be significantly more difficult than you may imagine.

During the 1950s, Professor Harry Markowitz at the University of Chicago won a Nobel Prize in economics for his work on what is now know as **Modern Portfolio Theory.** One important feature of his work is the concept of the **Efficient Frontier,** which demonstrates how a properly diversified portfolio can achieve higher returns at any given level of risk than an improperly diversified or non-diversified portfolio. The Efficient Frontier is a mathematical attempt to address the statement investors typically make: "I want the best return possible with the least amount of risk."

Chart 6-B shows a sample of the Efficient Frontier in action and how you can use it to your benefit.[27] Building a portfolio in this fashion attempts to create the optimal portfolio (least amount of risk for a given rate of return), also referred to in financial circles as **Portfolio Optimization.**

It is interesting to note that in this example, a portfolio of 100 percent bonds had the worst return and yet the volatility of this type of portfolio was about the same as a portfolio of 30 percent stocks and 70 percent bonds—which earned a far superior return. Which portfolio would you prefer: the one with the lower return, or the one with the similar level of risk and higher rate of return? The obvious choice is the latter portfolio, as shown in Chart 6-B.

Chart 6-B.

Sample Portfolio Optimization: Domestic Stocks & Bonds.

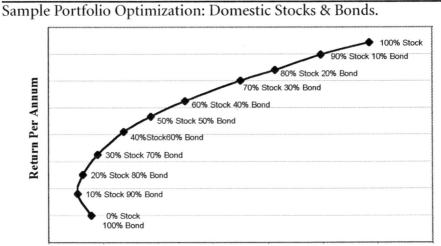

In addition to a mathematical analysis such as what we see in the Efficient Frontier and portfolio optimization, there are some additional issues you should evaluate before determining how much money you should have in each of the asset categories (cash, bonds and equities). Here are a few questions to consider:

- What is your age?
- What is your investment time horizon?
- What are your overall finances?
- How much liquidity do you need?
- Are there any personal issues?
- What are your risk tolerances?
- What are your financial goals?
- What are your income needs?
- Do you need portfolio growth?

Investment firms can usually make questionnaires available to you to help with your analysis and portfolio selection. An asset-allocation model will be generated based on your answers, and it will help you create your individual portfolio strategy.[28] An added benefit of preparing a personalized analysis is that it forces you to confront reality. It's what I like to call the "rubber meets the road" analysis.

> *Example:* "My wife and I are looking for a portfolio that will average about 10 to 12 percent per year. We also want income. But, the number one item of importance to us is that we have safety and little or no risk in our portfolio."

---

[28] See Appendix C for information on some companies that offer these types of services.

An asset-allocation analysis and a review of the Efficient Frontier would reveal that what this couple wants is probably not achievable. Something has to give. Either they must live with lower investment expectations or accept the fact that they will need to increase the volatility and risk to their portfolio before they can have a chance of achieving the returns that they want.

An interesting sideline to this type of an analysis is that very little financial advertising addresses how critical asset allocation and the Efficient Frontier are, and how they can impact your financial results. Instead, many of the advertising dollars spent on television and newsprint focus on the cost savings of trading, trading, and trading some more with a given firm, rather than its competition. The sad part of this style of portfolio management is that *overtrading*—the aggressive buying and selling of a portfolio—is a surefire recipe for disaster, whereas proper asset allocation of your investment portfolio has proven financial benefits.

ASSET CLASSES

If you accept the fact that proper asset allocation should be an important part of your investment game plan, you are now confronted with choosing from among the thousands of investment opportunities available to you. Be advised, investment firms are constantly dreaming up ways for you to invest your money. Between those new investment vehicles, the evening financial news networks, the cable channels, magazines, newsletters, and the Internet, it's easy to develop a headache trying to evaluate asset classes and alternatives.

To help you combat this information overload, I will limit my discussion of asset classes to what I call the "Big 3": (1) cash (cash equivalents), (2) bonds, and (3) equities (stocks).

CASH (CASH EQUIVALENTS)

If you're asked: "Do you have any cash?" your answer will likely be "Of course I do," as you pull out a crisp greenback with President Jackson's face on it. But, when your financial advisor is discussing your portfolio and says: "You should increase your cash or cash equivalents," he or she isn't suggesting that you rush to an ATM to make a withdrawal. In the world of investment planning, "cash" has a specific meaning:[29]

> Instruments or investments of such high liquidity and safety that they are virtually as good as cash. Examples are a money market fund and a Treasury Bill. The Financial Accounting Standards Board (FASB) defines cash equivalents for financial reporting purposes as, "Any highly liquid security with a known market value and maturity, when acquired, of less than three months."

Some well-known examples of cash investments include short-term **certificates of deposit** (CDs), short-term **U.S. Treasuries,** and **money market** accounts. Over the years, money market accounts have become very popular and for many investors are the cash investment of choice. Money market accounts are available in a variety of "flavors," including taxable and tax-free alternatives.

I haven't mentioned short-term bond funds as a cash alternative, because I generally don't like using them as a cash substitute. I discuss bond mutual funds in detail in Chapter 10, but for now, suffice it to say that there are some potential risks with these types of investments.

---

[29] *Barron's Financial and Investment Handbook* 4th ed. (Hauppauge, N.Y.:1995) p. 224

Why Have Cash Investments?

One of the most important reasons for having cash investments is that cash gives you **liquidity** (quick access to your money), which is crucial in a financial emergency. Imagine what would happen if your daughter was getting married and you suddenly discovered that the reception would cost several thousand dollars more than the original estimate. You couldn't just cancel the affair and use lack of liquidity as an excuse. You'd need to reach into one of your cash accounts to take care of the crisis.

Some experts claim that individuals should have cash amounts equal to at least three to six months' worth of living expenses.

> *Example:* Living expenses of $4,000 per month x 3 to 6 months = cash reserves of $12,000 to $24,000.

Of course, this will vary depending on your overall finances and place in the life cycle—not to mention how many daughters you have who are getting married.

Cash investments also provide you with short-term savings. They're a good holding tank while you're waiting to invest in other asset categories, such as when the stock market is showing some weakness and has declined in value.

After an initial review and analysis of your portfolio, you may be saying to yourself, "Cash investments seem pretty wonderful. They're safe, secure, liquid, and usually very inexpensive. My principal appears to be guaranteed, so all I have to worry about is whether the interest rate paid to me may change." What's the point of taking risks with investments like stocks, bonds, and mutual funds?

Caveats with Cash

While there are many advantages to cash investments—yes, they should be part of any well-rounded portfolio—there are indeed some major disadvantages you'll want to consider:

1. Over time, you'll run the risk of not keeping up with inflation. Losing purchasing power and going broke because your investments were "safe" is not a strategy for a rational individual.
2. Cash investments like a money market account pay investors a floating interest rate. It doesn't lock in a guaranteed yield for any extended period of time. The interest rate can change monthly, weekly, or even daily. The consequence is that if interest rates drop, the earnings paid to you on your money market accounts will also decline.
3. Another concern with some cash accounts has to do with *safety*. During recent years, many firms have engaged in money market price-yield wars to win the bragging rights to advertise: "My money market pays more than your money market." The goal of firms employing this type of advertising is to attract a large influx of money to their particular money market funds from their competitors' money market funds.

We live in a world where many investors spend an inordinate amount of time trying to squeeze every last penny of yield from their cash accounts, which is how investors are drawn into these yield wars. The problem with this strategy is that some money market fund managers—without investors fully understanding what is happening—have increased the risk profile of their so-called "safe" money market portfolios by investing in lower quality securities. This lowering of quality has introduced potential principal loss to the investor. Be very careful, then, not to make cash investments based solely on yield.

A final thought about cash investments: maybe you're thinking that you can leave your investments in a safe, cash investment like a money market account and then, as rates decline, move that money to riskier investment alternatives such as stocks and bonds.

Of course, you might also convince yourself that you'll only do this when the time is right or "when things have settled down." Let me be brutally honest here. If you accept and admit that no one can consistently predict and time the stock market, why fool yourself into believing that somehow it's easier to predict interest rates and determine "when things have settled down." Watching financial news channels and going on the Internet will not magically bring you special financial insight that the rest of the investment world has missed.

BONDS

The second major asset class to consider is bonds. The amount of money invested in the bond market is significantly larger than the amount of money invested in the stock market. The bond market is vast; and yet its workings remain a mystery to all but the most astute individual investors.

When you invest in a bond, you're putting your money into a **debt instrument,** an IOU. That is, you give an institution your money, they pay you an interest rate, and they promise to redeem—that is, pay back—your bond investment on a stated date. A variety of entities and institutions can issue bonds: municipalities, corporations, the U.S. Treasury Department, and various other government agencies.

Q: *Why do institutions issue bonds?*
A: *Bonds are issued to raise capital for a particular enterprise.*

Let us use General Electric as an example. There are a variety of ways that GE could fund its capital needs: it could tap into its own cash reserves, issue more of its stock, or simply go to a bank and borrow the money. Or, GE could sell—to the investing public or other institutions—corporate bonds. After close evaluation, you as an investor may decide that those GE bonds pay a good interest rate and that you're comfortable with the corporation's **credit quality**. So, you contact the investment firm or firms handling the underwriting of the bond, place an order, and there you have it: you're the proud owner of a GE corporate bond.

You have in essence, loaned GE, one of the world's largest corporations, your money. GE, in turn, will pay you a stated interest rate and eventually pay off (redeem) the bond at its stated maturity value. This is how, in its most basic form, you would invest in a new bond. Besides newly issued bonds, there is also a very large and active market for bonds in what is called the **secondary market**.[30]

Bond Basics

It is said that, "You must learn to crawl before you can walk, and you must learn to walk before you can run." In keeping with that astute observation, in this section I will introduce you to the basics of the bond market—the crawling phase, so to speak. In later chapters, I will introduce you to some key concepts and the mathematics of bonds—the walking phase. Then I will conclude with bond alternatives and strategies—the running phase—that you'll need to understand before you can become a savvy bond investor, whether in bond funds or individual bonds. With that in mind, here are some of the reasons why you may want to include bonds in your portfolio: (1) correlation, (2) income, and (3) safety.

---

[30] See Chapter 10 for a description of the secondary market.

Correlation

Correlation between different asset classes such as stocks and bonds is a statistical measurement of the degree to which the movements of different investment classes are related. If two different investment categories go up and down in tandem to any financial news that occurs, the two categories have *positive correlation*. One of the most important advantages of adding bonds to your portfolio is that they don't correlate well with other investment categories, such as stocks. At times they can have what is called *negative correlation*: you zig, I zag; you go up, I go down.

In the stock market crash of 1987, The Dow Jones average went down 508 points in a single day, a 22.62 percent drop. Yet while stocks were going down, the values of U.S. Treasury bonds were going up because investors were cashing in their stock portfolios and moving to the safety and security of Treasuries. This is but one simple example of negative correlation.

One of the goals of informed asset allocation is to show you the value of not having all your investment eggs in the same basket. You should strive to create a pool of diversified investments that will react differently to a given set of financial circumstances and decrease the volatility of your portfolio.

Income from Bonds

Another benefit of bonds is that they can pay you a high interest rate, as compared to other income-producing instruments such as money market accounts and CDs. If you invest in a savings account, a money market, or a bank CD, it's an easy enough transaction: you walk into your local bank or savings & loan, ask to see a clerk and ask how much you will earn on your investment. You really don't even need to ask about interest rates, as they typically will be posted, practically shouting what each investment is paying.

With bonds, however, you need to evaluate different types of interest rates. And, finding out a bond's yield or interest rate isn't as simple as asking, "How much are they paying?"

Most bonds will pay you a **fixed rate** of return, but some of them will pay a variable **floating rate**. The yield paid on floating-rate bonds will vary, based on a variety of market conditions. For now, it's enough to know that when you hear the terms **coupon yield, current yield, yield to maturity, yield to call,** and **yield to average life,** they are referring to bonds.[31]

While bonds do generate an income stream, consider that many bonds pay their interest only every six months. If you need monthly income from your bond portfolio, here are some of the ways it can be done:

1. Invest in different bonds with different six-month interest payment cycles. You could, therefore, invest in a bond that pays interest in the January and July cycle, while other bonds in your portfolio pay their interest in different six-month cycles, such as February and August.
2. Another strategy would be to invest in bonds such as Ginnie Maes (Government National Mortgage Association), which pay investors income monthly rather than every six months.[32]
3. Last but not least, you could invest in a bond fund, which I'll discuss in detail in Chapter 10.

A final note on bond interest: if you invest in individual bonds, you will encounter a type of interest that you need to understand called **accrued interest.** Accrued interest is neither a cost to you the investor, nor free money that you are accidentally paid. Here is an example of

---

[31] See Chapter 8 for a detailed analysis of these types of yields.

[32] See Chapter 9 for more about Ginnie Maes.

how accrued interest works. In June you invest $10,000 in a five-year corporate bond that pays 6 percent interest per year—or $600 per year in interest. You may recall that many bonds pay their interest every six months, so you will receive $300 twice a year for a grand total of $600 per year on the January/July cycle. Now, you purchased the bond at the beginning of June—not in January, February, March, April, or May, but in June. When the July payment date quickly rolls around, your bond is going to pay a full six-months' worth of interest, $300. You've only owned the bond for about a month. How can you be entitled to six months of interest? Here's how: when you purchased the bond in June, you paid $10,000, the price of the bond. But, you also paid for the accrued interest (that's the interest that had been accumulating since the January interest-rate payment five months earlier). Whoever had owned the bond since January deserves the interest that had been accruing until its sale in June. So, when buying an individual bond, don't be concerned about the accrued-interest charge. You'll receive the full six-month interest payment when the next payment cycle comes your way—even if you've owned the bond for fewer than six months.

Bond Safety

Bonds are considered to be safe investments and have historically been less volatile than stocks. For ultimate safety, you can turn to U.S. government Treasuries, while at the other end of the spectrum are high yielding junk bonds. Between the two extremes is a vast sector of the bond market with a wide range of ratings and characteristics. If you decide to invest in this middle area of the bond market (between Treasuries and junk), the most important issue to evaluate is the credit quality of the bonds you are reviewing.

If you do not feel qualified to do your own analysis or to evaluate what a given bond's rating should be you have lots of company. It is a complex undertaking that requires a tremendous amount of expertise. Very few individuals and even fewer firms do it.

Two of the best-known bond-rating agencies are Moody's Investor Services Inc. and Standard and Poor's. You can see from Table 6-1 that a wide range of ratings is available to investors (bond ratings can be broken down even further by adding pluses or minuses, e.g., A+ or A-). At the very top are the triple-A rated bonds, which are judged to be of the best quality. They carry the smallest degree of risk and are generally referred to as "gilt edged." At the other extreme are the single C-rated bonds, which are regarded as having very poor prospects for ever attaining any investment standing.

As a general rule, I am more comfortable with bonds rated single A or better. Additionally, the longer the term to maturity of your bonds, the more important credit quality becomes. If you plan to invest in longer-term bonds, you may want to consider only those rated double A or better.

Table 6-1.

Rating Bonds.

Rating	S&P	Moody's
Highest quality	AAA	Aaa
High quality	AA	Aa
Upper medium quality	A	A
Medium grade	BBB	Baa
Somewhat speculative	BB	Ba
Low grade, speculative	B	B
Low grade, default possible	CCC	Caa
Low grade, partial recovery possible	CC	Ca
Default, recovery unlikely	C	C

Although I have listed some examples of corporate bonds in each of the ratings categories, over time the rating of bonds can change. The following ratings are as of September 2002.

AAA-rated corporate bonds
- General Electric Co. AAA-Aaa
- Johnson & Johnson AAA-Aaa

AA-rated bonds
- Wal-Mart Stores Inc. AA2-Aa
- Abbott Laboratories AA3-Aa

A-rated bonds
- Wells Fargo & Company AA3-A
- Coca Cola Company AA3-A+

Changing Bond Values

When you invest in a high-quality bond, (1) it helps you to diversify your portfolio, (2) it pays you income, and (3) you can assume that upon maturity, the issuer of the bond will have the resources to pay it off at full face value. But, between a bond's purchase date and final maturity date, its value can fluctuate for a variety of reasons.

Interest Rate Changes

The values of bonds and interest rates have what is called an *inverse relationship*. (See Chart 6-C.) If you own bonds and interest rates go up, the value of your bonds will go down. If interest rates go down, the value of your bonds will go up. If you have ever sat on a seesaw or a "teeter-totter," you understand the relationship between interest rates and the value of bonds. As one side goes up, the other side goes down.

Chart 6-C.

An Inverse Relationship.

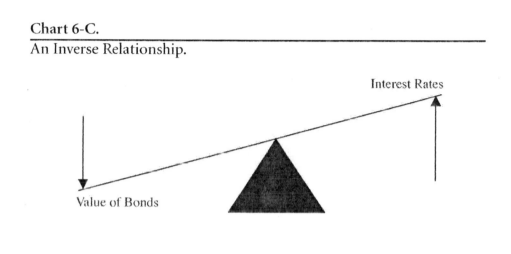

An important exception to these changes comes about when you hold your bonds to maturity. On maturity, bonds will pay off at face value regardless of the interest rates at that point in time. Because bonds pay off at maturity, shorter-term bonds are more stable in the face of interest-rate changes than are longer-term bonds. In Table 6-2, you can see what happens to the value of bonds of varying maturities when interest rates increase.

> *Example:* In the example in Table 6-2, I am assuming that you invest in a five-, ten-, and thirty-year non-callable, triple-A rated bond. To illustrate this concept as simply as possible, I am also assuming that you are investing an even $10,000 in each bond (**par**), and that each of the bonds is paying you a 6 percent **coupon**.

After the purchase of your bonds, what would happen to their values if interest rates were to increase to 7 percent, 8 percent, or 9 percent yield to maturity, and your bonds were now priced to have those same yields to maturity?[33]

Table 6-2.

New Bond Values: If Rates Increase to 7, 8, or 9 Percent.

Maturity	to 7.0%	to 8.0%	to 9.0%
5 yrs	$9,584.20	$9,188.90	$8,813.10
10 yrs	$9,289.40	$8,641.00	$8,048.80
30 yrs	$8,752.80	$7,737.70	$6,904.30

From the information in Table 6-2, you can see how much more price volatility there is with the thirty-year bond as compared to the shorter-term five-year bond when interest rates change. When interest rates increased from 6 to 9 percent, the five-year bond dropped in value to $8,813.10, while the thirty-year bond dropped in value to $6,904.30.

The quality of an underlying bond can also have an impact on how much a bond's value will fluctuate when interest rates change. If you are investing in an environment with dramatically increasing interest rates, you might witness what is called a *flight to quality*. Not only would investors be concerned with the change in interest rates and the corresponding change in their bond values, they might also be concerned about the overall economy and what the future will bring, and move out of low-rated bonds and into high-rated bonds.

Credit Rating Changes

If the rating of a bond is increased to a higher-quality rating, there can be a corresponding increase in its value. Conversely, if its rating

---

[33] I will discuss non-callable, coupon yield and yield to maturity in Chapters 8 & 9.

decreases, there can be a corresponding decrease in its value. Here's a somewhat exaggerated example to illustrate the point.

> *Example:* Perhaps, you have in your possession a $10,000 bond that matures in five years and is triple-A rated. All of a sudden, bad economic news about the corporation that issued your bond starts coming out. Sales plummet, earnings are down, lawsuits are filed, and—oh my goodness—it is alleged that the CEO and his cronies have been cooking the books and stealing money from the company that issued the bond. Your triple-A rated bond drops to double A, then to single A, then to triple B, and then to double B. When will it stop? Do you think that you could now sell your bond for the full $10,000? Not a chance. Someone might buy your bond, but maybe for 90 cents on the dollar and maybe even only 75 cents on the dollar, or less. When your bond's rating changes, so too can its price.

EQUITIES (STOCKS)

The third major asset class I will review is equities (stocks). Equity means "ownership." You can participate in equity or ownership, in a number of ways: (1) you can own property, such as your home or a property you rent out, (2) you can own a business, or (3) you can invest in publicly traded stocks.[34] Examples of publicly traded stocks are Ford Motor Company, International Business Machines Corporation (IBM),

---

[34] Throughout the rest of this book, when I use "equity" in a discussion of investment portfolios I will be referring to the ownership of stock, such as individual stocks, stock unit trusts, stock mutual funds, and stock money managers. I will not be referring to investment vehicles such as owning a business or property.

and Microsoft Corporation. If you own a hundred shares of Microsoft, you are the proud equity owner of part of that company—a minority owner, but an owner nonetheless.

The single largest advantage of equity investments is **capital appreciation**. The single largest disadvantage of equity investments is **capital loss**. The dilemma that faces most investors is whether stocks (equity investments) are worth the risk. After all, most cash investments are safe. High-quality bonds are not only safe but can also pay you a high locked-in interest rate. So, do you really want to bother with stock (equity) investments? I think the answer is yes. Over time, equities have demonstrated a far superior investment return than either cash or bonds. History has shown us that maintaining purchasing power after taxes and inflation has not come about from cash investments, but from such investment alternatives as stocks (see Chart 6-D).

Domestic vs. International Stocks

No discussion of equity investments would be complete without touching on the topic of domestic versus international stocks. International investments have always been an important component of any diversified portfolio, and the influence of the international markets continues to grow (see Chart 6-E).

Chart 6-D.

Average Annual Compound Rates of Return, 1950-2000.

12.75%	Large-company stocks
6.16%	Long-term corporate bonds
5.44%	Long-term U.S. government bonds
5.12%	U.S. Treasury bills
3.96%	Inflation

Large-company stocks are represented by the Standard & Poor's 500 Stock Index, an unmanaged, commonly used measure of common stock total return performance. Corporate bonds reflect performance of the Salomon Brothers Corporate Bond Index. U.S. government bonds reflect performance of the Lehman Brothers Long-Term Government Bond Index. Inflation is measured by the Consumer Price Index as reported by the U.S. Bureau of Labor Statistics. It is not possible to invest directly in an index. Results represent past performance with dividends, and capital gains reinvested and are not meant to imply future performance.

Source: Thomas Financial.

Chart 6-E.

Changes in the World Equity Market, (% of Equity Investment Opportunity Outside the U.S.).

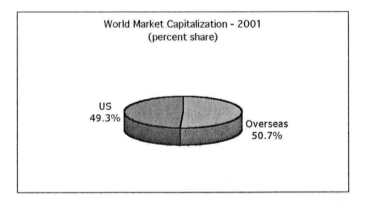

Source: Morgan Stanley Capital International, World Perspective as of

Over the last thirty plus years, the value of the U.S. equity markets has increased dramatically. Yet at the same time, the market share of the U.S. equity markets compared to the rest of the world has decreased.

Also complicating matters is the fact that we now live and work in a "global economy."

Consider this about some well-known U.S. companies: in the year 2000, only 30 percent of the Coca-Cola Company's earnings came from North America, 30 percent of Exxon's earnings came from outside the United States, and 37 percent of General Motors' earnings originated outside the country. Some other Dow Jones Industrial Average stocks that derive a large part of their earnings from outside the United States are Caterpillar Inc., The Procter & Gamble Company, McDonalds Corporation, and the list goes on and on.[35]

Having the correct amount of international exposure in an investment portfolio is important, but it can be a complicated undertaking. On the surface, it might appear that investors could get all the international exposure they need simply by investing in large U.S. multinational firms. However, there are issues to consider other than just sales by country or region, which include currency risks and exchange rates. Carefully evaluate all of these variables before making any final investment decisions.

DIVERSIFICATION

Diversification is not the same as asset allocation. Asset allocation gives you a big-picture view of your portfolio. It's a global perspective of where and in what asset classes your money is invested. Diversity, on the other hand, is more of a down to earth "local" issue. The differences between asset allocation and diversity can also depend on who you are and on what your perspective is. The confusion is rooted in more than just semantics.

---

[35] The Dow Jones Industrial Average (DJIA) is one of the most followed stock indices in the world. It is comprised of thirty "blue chip" stocks that represent some of the best-known companies in the country and the world.

Example 1: Let us assume that you own a variety of bonds in your portfolio—quality municipal bonds, corporate bonds, and U. S. government bonds—that will mature in different years (a **laddered portfolio**). Can you say that your portfolio is diversified? The answer will depend on your perspective. As a bond investor, the answer certainly would be yes. But, from an asset-allocation point of view, the answer would be a resounding no because you have all your money in a single asset class: bonds.

Example 2: Here's a more complicated example. Perhaps you have 20 percent of your money in cash, 30 percent in bonds, and 50 percent in stocks. Is your portfolio diversified? Again, that depends on your perspective and on the nuances in your portfolio. Yes, your portfolio is diversified based on some asset-allocation models because it contains cash, bonds, and equities. However, if your entire bond portfolio is in one bond, and if your entire equity portfolio is in one stock, then no, you wouldn't own a diversified portfolio.

Diversify for Stability

Correct asset allocation by asset class does not automatically give you the portfolio stability you may be trying to achieve. Only by adding diversity to an asset-allocation model do you have a fighting chance of achieving the goal of stability and consistency over time. The reason portfolio consistency is so important is that you can't know when negative investment returns will occur.

Here's an example of how important diversity and consistency can be to your financial well-being. We'll review two different investors and evaluate which investor has the better investment return.[36]

Table 6-3.

Simple Interest Rate of Return.

	Investor #1 % Return	Investor #2 % Return
Year 1	12	19
Year 2	12	20
Year 3	12	21
Year 4	12	22
Year 5	12	-17
Total	**60%**	**65%**

Example: The first portfolio in Table 6-3 will give you a simple interest rate of return of 60 percent (12 percent per year for five years), while the second portfolio gives you a simple interest rate of 65 percent (19 + 20 + 21 + 22 − 17 = 65). The latter is better because it gives you a superior return, or does it? Follow the value of the two portfolios in Table 6-4; the answer may surprise you.

---

[36] I am assuming net returns and no tax liability in these calculations. This information is for illustrative purposes only.

Table 6-4.

Compounded Yearly Rate of Return.

Investor #1

	Starting Value($)	% Return per year	$ Earned	Closing Value($)
Year 1	10,000	12	1,200	11,200
Year 2	11,200	12	1,344	12,544
Year 3	12,544	12	1,505	14,049
Year 4	14,049	12	1,686	15,735
Year 5	15,735	12	1,888	17,623

Closing account value   **$17,623**

Investor #2

	Starting Value($)	% Return per year	$ Earned	Closing Value($)
Year 1	10,000	19	1,900	11,900
Year 2	11,900	20	2,380	14,280
Year 3	14,280	21	2,999	17,207
Year 4	17,207	22	3,786	20,993
Year 5	20,993	-17	3,569	17,424

Closing account value   **$17,424**

You can see from this analysis that the investor with the 65 percent return actually has the inferior investment results. Calculating your investment returns and future retirement needs on a simple rate of return will give you very different results than applying a "real world" compounded rate of return.

As you build toward or move into retirement, consistency of investment returns and the stability of your portfolio will become more important than ever.

These examples demonstrate the importance of using the proper asset-allocation model and a diversified portfolio to bring consistency to your investment returns over time. Even with this kind of portfolio structure, you still need to have a long-term perspective and patience with your investments. Don't make the mistake of thinking that you constantly need to do something in your account.

While I realize that being consistent may seem boring and not as glamorous as bragging to your friends about the hot stock picks you've been trading, you may discover that your "hot stock trading" is feeding your ego rather than your wallet. Although they're not always mutually exclusive, consistency will feed your wallet.

SUMMARY: As you begin to formulate your investment portfolio, the first step is to decide on the proper asset-allocation model—the percentages in each asset class—based on your particular needs and risk tolerances. Your portfolio's asset allocation will determine how conservative or aggressive you are being with your portfolio. It will have more of an impact on your total return than your ability to time the market or pick brilliant invest-ments. Once you have completed that task you will be ready to evaluate ways to further diversify your accounts for consistency and stability.

Chapter 7

Investment Product Selection

In this day and age, there are so many ways to invest. Initially, I thought that buying mutual funds seemed boring and old fashioned, while investing with a money manager seemed new and glamorous. And, of course, everybody knows that investing in individual stocks offers big returns with minimal effort. You could borrow money against your house, open a brokerage account, find a few hot stock tips on the Internet, buy some stocks, and watch them go up in value. Before long, you would have enough money to pay off all the loans and retire young. But, you know what? I'm living proof that there's no such thing as a free lunch. Maybe boring and old fashioned isn't such a bad way to invest after all.

Now that you have a blueprint to guide you on a course of action, in this chapter I will introduce you to the next challenge you must resolve before you can assemble your investment portfolio: **investment product selection**. The alternatives for your stock and/or bond investments are as follows:

- Individual securities
- Money managers
- Packaged products (e.g. mutual funds and unit trusts)
- A combination of these alternatives

Because each investment product alternative offers investors its own unique set of advantages and disadvantages, it would be a mistake to assume that a given investment product alternative is best for your investment needs until you have analyzed their respective features. For example, after careful evaluation you might conclude that *equity* mutual funds offer you the best way to participate in the stock market. Simultaneously, you may decide that *bond* mutual funds are not appropriate for you and decide instead to invest in individual bonds for income and safety.

Investment product selection is one of the most significant financial decisions an investor can make.

It can have a profound impact on your taxes, the diversification of your investments, and the fees you will pay for the management of your portfolio, yet it is an area that receives very little attention and analysis.

Many years ago, actor Paul Newman starred in an Academy Award-winning film called *Cool Hand Luke* that introduced one of the most memorable lines to come out of Hollywood: "What we've got here is failure to communicate." With thousands of financial sources at our disposal, why do the major financial media outlets suffer from a "failure to communicate" on the important topic of investment product selection? Here are some of the reasons:

Lack of expertise or access. Most investors are unaware that many investment firms don't have access to or expertise in all the different security categories that are available. Some investment firms handle bond funds but don't have similar access to individual bonds. Other firms may recommend stock mutual funds, but have little or no access to individual stocks, equity research, or equity money managers.

Specialization. Some financial advisors and organizations specialize in specific investment products, which means that they will bring along their own set of biases when making recommendations. Ask yourself this basic question: if an organization only handles mutual funds, which investment product will they recommend? The answer is clear.

In all fairness, it must be noted that if an advisor has investment product biases, it does not imply that he or she is a scoundrel. Rather, it illustrates the potential conflict of interest some advisors may have with their recommendations. That's why you need to be informed about different investment product alternatives before evaluating the merits of the professional recommendations you receive. Furthermore, you should bring this same informed wariness to other sources of financial information.

While I believe that most investment advisors, stock brokers, financial planners, financial writers, and radio and television personalities have professional integrity, for purposes of your financial health, I advise you not to accept any one piece of financial advice as gospel, despite the credentials of its source. Expose yourself to many investment and financial sources before making any final decisions about your portfolio.

In Chapter 14, I will build a sample portfolio using some of the various investment product alternatives. For now, let us get started by reviewing the advantages and disadvantages of individual securities.

INDIVIDUAL SECURITIES

Some examples of individual securities would be stock in General Electric, Procter & Gamble, and a two-year U. S. Treasury note. Some investors believe that with all of the investment alternatives that are now available, investing in individual securities is no longer the best way to build a portfolio. I, on the other hand, believe that even if you don't invest in individual securities, understanding them has the potential to make you a smarter investor. Why do I believe this? Owning or analyzing individual securities won't make you an investment expert, but understanding their particular nuances will increase your ability to evaluate other investment alternatives such as money managers, mutual funds, and unit trusts.

Since I will discuss individual bonds at length in Chapters 8 and 9, in this section I will focus on the advantages and disadvantages of individual stocks.

Advantages

1. *Cost effectiveness.* Investing in individual stocks can be very cost-effective, especially if you don't do much *trading* (the buying and selling of stocks) in your portfolio. Certainly there can be a cost to buy or sell a stock, but, under most circumstances, you won't have to pay a fee or commission while you are holding it. This buy-and-hold strategy can be particularly attractive if you're investing in very solid long-term buy-and-hold stocks with little or no turnover.

2. *Upside potential.* It's exciting to buy a stock at $10 per share and watch it go to $50 per share in a short time. Although it happens

only rarely, this kind of upside return is possible with individual stocks but next to impossible in the short term with a mutual fund or money manager. This kind of investment appreciation can be an intoxicating incentive to individual stock market investors. However, you shouldn't need me to point out that those types of investment returns are less common than a flawless diamond. So, whatever you do, be sure to review the section in this book on the disadvantages of owning individual stocks.

3. *Personal expertise.* Some people prefer to invest in what they know. Perhaps, you work in the computer industry. You may feel that there are advantages to investing in companies that you deal with on a regular basis. Mind you, this strategy doesn't guarantee success, but it can bring some emotional comfort.

4. *Following the market.* Some people live and breathe the financial markets. If they can't talk about the "market," they have nothing to discuss. If that's you, then one of the best ways to get involved with the equity markets is by owning individual stocks, which will give you easy access to annual reports, quarterly reports, and shareholder meetings.

5. *What you see is what you get.* Is there anyone in the world who needs an introduction to a company named Coca-Cola? You may not understand all of Coca-Cola's corporate nuances and departments, but you know that Coca-Cola sells bottled sugar water and is not in the business of drilling for oil. Of course, a company like Coca-Cola can change its overall direction by spinning off divisions, adding product lines, and transforming its look and mission over time. Therefore, ongoing analysis of your holdings (even those with brand name recognition) will be required.

6. *Public information.* With a publicly traded stock (like Coca-Cola), you will have access to a tremendous amount of public information, which enables you to monitor and gauge changes as they occur. This kind of information can be more difficult to gather

when evaluating investment product alternatives such as unit trusts, money managers, or mutual funds. If you buy a mutual fund based on its name, you may discover the investment strategies of the mutual fund are not at all in line with the printed description. For example, you might have invested in a "growth mutual fund," only to discover that its managers had invested a large part of the portfolio in bonds. Now, buying bonds may be a prudent strategy, but not if it's inconsistent with your investment needs. Performing an analysis of individual securities allows you to alter your holdings easily, especially if the activities of the companies in which you are invested are no longer consistent with your financial needs.

7. *Understanding how markets work.* When you own individual securities, the potential exists for you to develop a better understanding of how the financial markets work. For instance, a savvy individual bond investor will have an easier time evaluating bond mutual funds than an uneducated bond mutual fund investor will have evaluating individual bonds. Many bond mutual fund investors have no idea how the bond markets work and if asked to explain what their bond mutual fund actually does, would be at a loss to give either a coherent explanation of its strategies or a good reason for why they picked the bond fund in the first place.[37]

8. *Controlling taxes.* With individual stocks, you can exert a tremendous amount of control over your taxes. There are no income taxes or capital gains taxes on individual stocks until the securities are sold. This type of control is typically not available to you when investing in mutual funds or with money managers. Keep in mind that if all your equity investments were in accounts such as IRAs, all tax liabilities would be deferred until distributions from the accounts began.

---

[37] For a book that covers individual bonds in depth, see *The Bond Book* 2nd ed. by Annette Thau (New York: McGraw Hill, 2001).

Disadvantages

1. *Cost.* There is a cost associated with buying and selling stocks. If there is a significant amount of buying and selling in your portfolio, the costs could rapidly make it a more expensive investment than an alternative like a mutual fund.

2. *Downside risks.* Individual stocks can go *down* in value. That would have been a shocking statement toward the end of the 1990s, until market changes in 2000 woke many investors from their catatonic euphoria of an ever-upward stock market spiral. The caveat here is that if you pin your financial hopes and dreams on a very narrow, non-diversified stock portfolio, you may be setting yourself up for financial disaster. No one purposely concentrates stock positions expecting that his or her portfolio will drop by 30, 40, 50 percent or even more. Unfortunately, it happens all too often. One need look no further than the Enron debacle to see the danger of concentrating your portfolio in a "guaranteed" can't miss winner.

3. *Your time is precious.* If you don't have the time to manage an individual stock portfolio, you should either not invest in individual stocks or consider working with competent advisors. There's nothing wrong with a buy-and-hold strategy, but it's the rare individual stock that's a good investment forever. The reality is that owning individual stocks requires time, effort, and ongoing management.

4. *Portfolio under-management.* Little or no portfolio trading may be inexpensive, but it can result in the under-management of your portfolio. Under-management occurs for a number of reasons. Here are the two most common: difficulty selling losers and difficulty parting with winners.

> *Example 1:* The hope that somehow a stock loser will come back to its original value or exceed it dies hard. If you own $10,000 worth of stock that has decreased in value to

$5,000, you have had a 50 percent drop in your portfolio. The percentage increase you now need to get back to the original $10,000 value is not, however, the 50 percent you lost. If your $5,000 stock position goes up 50 percent, you will only be up to a value of $7,500—a long way from the original $10,000. Your original investment dropped 50 percent, but now you're going to need a 100 percent increase to get back to the original $10,000. The bottom line is that to move from 10 to 5 takes a 50 percent drop, while to move from 5 back to 10 takes a 100 percent increase.

Example 2: It can be as hard to take profits and sell your winners, as it is to sell your losers. After all, if a stock is doing well and going up in value, won't it go up forever? I'm not suggesting that you should sell part or all of your winners and reallocate the money into other investments like clockwork. You do, however, need to evaluate your winners—particularly your big winners—especially when they appreciate to the point where they dominate your portfolio.

5.   *International stocks.* Doing research on foreign companies can be difficult at best and nearly impossible at worst. As a rule, I'd leave the international investing to the pros, unless, of course, you're investing in a truly global company that trades on an American exchange. Some examples of well-known international companies that trade on American exchanges are Nestlé SA (Nestlé's Chocolate); Nokia Corporation, ADR (the cellular phone giant); and DaimlerChrysler (Mercedes Benz). (Driving a Mercedes and chatting on the phone while eating a Nestlé's chocolate bar—now that's an investment strategy you can sink your teeth into.)

6.   *Lack of diversity.* Throughout this book, I have stressed that diversity is one of the most important guiding principles for any investment

portfolio. It simply takes more money to achieve diversity with individual stocks than it does with alternatives like mutual funds. No matter how good a company looks, putting all of your investment eggs in a few stocks can be a recipe for a disaster.

> Q: *How much money does it take to build an individual stock portfolio?*
>
> A: *There are no set rules or guidelines for how much money you need to start investing in individual stocks. However, putting together a well-diversified portfolio normally requires about $100,000 to $150,000. Naturally, the dollar amount will vary by investor, the type of account, and your other assets.*

7. *Difficulty in investing small amounts regularly.* If you want to add small amounts of money to your equity investments on a regular basis, you can do so more easily with mutual funds. Trying to do this with individual stock trades can be expensive.

8. *Dividend reinvestment.* Dividend reinvestment is a primary disadvantage of individual stocks, compared to other investment product alternatives. Some companies get around this issue by allowing direct common-stock dividend reinvestment. In this type of program, your dividends are paid or credited to your account either as whole or partial shares. The restrictions and/or charges on this kind of program vary by company. I have found, however, that the procedure can bring its own set of problems as well as create a potential accounting nightmare. When instituting a dividend reinvestment program, here are some key issues you will want to know and understand: (1) the cost basis of all the partial shares you may have accumulated during the years, (2) whether, if you chose to sell the shares, you would be able to do so at the company that issued them or if you'd first need the certificates sent to you, and (3) the

procedures and time requirements for taking possession of your shares.

Owning individual stocks—whether you make investment decisions by yourself or work with an advisor—can be financially rewarding, but it also can be time consuming. One way to address this problem is to deal with a private or professional money manager, our second investment product alternative.

PROFESSIONAL MONEY MANAGERS

When I use the term "professional money manager," I am referring to an investment manager who makes investments in individual securities in your personal account on your behalf and not to a mutual fund manager. Here is one official definition of a money manager, also known as a portfolio manager:[38]

> Professional responsible for the securities portfolio of an individual or institutional investor. Also called a money manger or, especially when personalized service is involved, an investment counsel. A portfolio manager may work for a mutual fund, pension fund, profit-sharing plan, bank trust department, or insurance company. In return for a fee, the manager has the fiduciary responsibility to manage the assets prudently and choose whether stocks, bonds, cash equivalents, real estate, or some other assets present the best opportunities for profit at any particular time.

---

[38] *Barron's Finance & Investment Handbook*, 4th ed. (Hauppauge, New York: 1995) p.501

This type of account is a relatively new alternative for the general investing public. In order to understand this sector of portfolio management, a number of key items need to be analyzed: (1) its history, (2) where it stands today, (3) what a portfolio of money managers might look like, and (4) the advantages and disadvantages of this investment product alternative.

In the Past

There was a time when only large institutions or the very wealthy had access to the types of investment managers I am about to discuss. If you wanted your money managed in this way, you first had to figure out how to contact the right money manager. Furthermore, once you'd found one, you had to evaluate the services offered and confirm that the manager's investment style was consistent with your needs. Then, of course, you needed to qualify for the minimum account size, which could mean an investment of a million dollars or more. If you qualified for the million-dollar minimum, opened an account, and started dealing with the money manager, you were still responsible for monitoring the investment returns and the manager's risk profile on an ongoing basis. After all was said and done, you might indeed have your money managed by a real professional, but much work and **due diligence** was required.

Today's Environment

Brokerage and investment firms have come to realize that people other than those with several million dollars may be interested in a professional money manager's services. As a result, most of the leading brokerage firms now give clients access to these types of institutional money managers with accounts as small as $100,000. The investment firms screen the managers, performs due diligence on them, and based on your needs, recommends an appropriate manager or mix of managers.

Plus, the service does not stop there. The firms continue to monitor and evaluate the manager's firm, style of management, and investment performance. If a manager is found to be under-performing or no longer meets the firm's due diligence criteria, he or she can be replaced.

As you can see, there are many attractive reasons for retaining the services of a money manager. However, a word of caution is in order. Don't fall into the trap of blindly relying on a money manager because of the cachet their title conveys. Unfortunately, to some people it is a thing of substance to be able to say that their money is invested with a money manager. Although I will concede that it tends to beat bragging about the free toaster you received by opening up a checking account at the local Savings & Loan, feeding your ego is a lousy reason to pick an investment.

Types of Managers

Bond Managers

I believe that bond money managers are best suited for institutional clients or very large individual accounts. They can be an expensive alternative for many individuals, compared to no-load bond funds or the buy-and-hold strategy of individual bonds. For that reason, I will mention them only briefly.

If a bond money manager is charging you 1 percent per year to manage a bond portfolio, and if tax-free bonds are paying 5 percent, then right off the top 20 percent of your return is going to fees. A bond manager has to outperform the market by a substantial amount just to make up for the yearly fee. If you are interested in investing with a bond money manager, be sure to compare the fees against the category alternatives I've discussed so far and evaluate the services you'll receive for the yearly charges.

Equity Managers

As with the other investment product alternatives, money managers can be broken down by style (growth or value) and by market capitalization: large cap, mid cap, and small cap. (See Chapter 11 for analyses and definitions of these terms.) In developing your money manager portfolio, be sure to select managers with different management styles. Each manager should have expertise in a specific market sector and be able to articulate his or her style of investing clearly.

> *Example:* At our money management firm we look for companies that are growing their earnings by 10 percent or more per year, are number one or two in their respective markets, and have a market value of at least $500 million and a book value of XYZ.

Compare that presentation with the ambiguity of the manager who says: "We look for companies that have lots of upside potential and earnings growth and will invest wherever that criteria leads us."

When investing with a money manager, you'll also want to know the manager's benchmark.[39] It's a critical piece of information because you can't evaluate performance unless you have a point of reference. If the value sector of the stock market is down 10 percent and your value manager is down only 5 percent, you could very well have a long-term winning value manager in your portfolio. Your value money manager would have outperformed his or her benchmark. On the other hand, if most growth managers are up 20 percent and your growth manager is only up 10 percent, a serious evaluation is in order,

---

[39] A standard by which something can be measured or compared

since your manager would have dramatically under-performed compared to his or her peer group.

Once you have done an initial analysis and found some money managers with whom you may want to invest, it's important to perform a blended analysis of the managers. If you don't, you could end up with two or three managers who look great individually, but who are investing in the same sectors of the market. This would defeat some of the goals of investing with money managers, which is to achieve portfolio and style diversification.

Chart 7-A is a sample analysis that shows how to assemble a money manager portfolio.

Chart 7-A.

Sample Money Manager Blended Analysis.

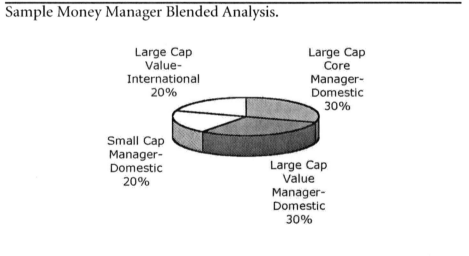

Once your sample portfolio has been put together, there is some additional information that needs to be evaluated before moving forward with your investments. You will want a blended analysis of the following information.[40]

- Historical return
- Standard deviation
- Beta
- Alpha
- R-SQR

This blended analysis will help to confirm that your portfolio is consistent with your needs and risk tolerance.

After you have assembled your money manager portfolio, you will need to monitor it on a regular basis. As good as your beginning portfolio may be, the financial reality is that you may need to replace a manager from time to time—but not for the reasons you might think. While performance is important, the raw numbers may not be the critical issue. As I said earlier, it is important to measure the performance as well as the volatility (over time) of your manager against their benchmark as well as their peer group. Remember that different sectors of the stock market go up and down at different times in their performance cycle. Having a positive return does not necessarily mean that you are dealing with a winning money manager; conversely, having a temporary negative return with a particular manager doesn't mean that you need to replace the manager.

Another important yet subtle reason that might cause you to replace a manager is if the money manager changes his or her style of management. While the investment returns might still be attractive, changes in management style can lead to over-concentration and over weighting in certain sectors of your portfolio. Remember, it is the

---

[40] These terms are defined in Appendix B.

overall blended portfolio that is important when putting together a portfolio of money managers.

At this point, you should have a working knowledge of this investment product alternative. Let us now move on to some of the advantages and disadvantages of investing with a money manager:

Advantages

1. *Professional management.* The uncertainty and volatility of today's market are powerful reasons for utilizing a full-time manager to make buy-and-sell decisions on your investment accounts.

2. *Single flat management fee.* One of the reasons to pay a single, flat management fee on a money manage account is to remove the potential conflict of interest associated with people who make a living from commission trading. Some exceptions exist, but generally no commission is charged to your account when the money manager buys or sells securities. You pay only the flat yearly management fee based on the value of your account.

3. *Individual account.* Working with a money manager will give you a personalized profile that drives the investments in your account. The profile will be tailored closely to your needs and risk tolerances. This type of control differs from investing in a mutual fund where your money is in a pooled account and you have no say over how it is invested.

4. *Account growth and percentage cost.* While the cost of a money manager account can vary, as your account grows, the percentage cost will generally come down. For example, the yearly percentage cost of a $100,000 account might be very different from the percentage cost of a $250,000 account.

Disadvantages

1. *Minimum account size.* Although account minimums have decreased substantially, it still takes a large amount of capital to qualify for a money manager account. Many money managers, even through the major brokerage firms, have minimums of $100,000 per account. Some investment experts believe that diversity requires exposure to large-cap, mid-cap, small-cap, and perhaps international investments. This kind of diversity could require as much as $400,000 to achieve ($100,000 per manager x 4 managers).

2. *Lots of paperwork.* A money manager account requires more paperwork than an individual stock or mutual fund account. If you have several money managers with different styles of management, you could end up having many different accounts and be required to sign multiple account forms. Another cumbersome feature of these accounts is that you will receive a confirmation for each trade made in each of your accounts. With several managers buying and selling stocks for you, you could get a good workout just hauling all the paperwork and confirmations that you'll be receiving.

3. *Difficulty tracking your manager.* If you are investing in a mutual fund or in an individual stock, it's pretty easy to locate information about your investment. The same cannot be said about money managers. The information about them is out there, but it can be more difficult to find and sometimes more expensive to track down.

4. *Costs.* With these types of accounts, you will normally pay a quarterly fee based on the assets under management. The cost can vary, but it is common to see charges in equity accounts of 1.25 percent to 3.0 percent per year with charges in bond accounts being lower. The charges usually will cover all trading costs and management within the portfolio. When reviewing cost, compare these fees

against the level of service and management you are receiving against alternatives such as individual securities, as well as our next investment product alternative: packaged products.

PACKAGED PRODUCTS

Two concerns commonly come to mind when an investor begins to assemble a portfolio: (1) do I have enough money to diversify my accounts, and (2) do I have the time and expertise to monitor my investments? In the mid- to late 1930s (during the peak of the Great Depression) the U.S. Congress shared those concerns and they were among the driving forces behind the passage of the Investment Act of 1940.

Among its accomplishments, the Act created several "packaged" investment alternatives. Perhaps, the most significant of the new investment alternatives is the open-end mutual fund, which is now governed by the **Securities and Exchange Commission (SEC)**.

Open-End Mutual Funds

A company that has met specific SEC regulations can legally call and market itself as a mutual fund. What are the basic ingredients of a mutual fund?

1. Investors send money to the fund, which creates a pool of assets.
2. Investors, in turn, are issued shares on a prorated basis, based on the fund's total assets.
3. Those assets, or pooled money, are invested.
4. As more money and investors come into the mutual fund and the pool of money grows, the mutual fund issues more shares.
5. If investors take money out of the mutual fund—that is, redeem their shares—they do so by cashing them in based on something

called the shares' **net asset value (NAV)**, which is the shares value represented by the prorated ownership of the underlying securities in the mutual fund, less any fees, commissions, or charges.

The investment management companies, which issue and redeem mutual fund shares on an ongoing basis, are called **open-end mutual funds.** Investors never own the mutual fund; what they own are its assets.

Growth of the Industry

This simple concept has been one of the great business success stories of the twentieth century. It would be hard to name another industry that has achieved a similar level of sustained growth. To give you some perspective on the dimensions of that growth, consider that at the end of 1990, mutual fund assets totaled about $1.065 trillion and by the end of 2000, assets had ballooned to $6.965 trillion.[41]

The number of mutual funds has also grown from a few hundred to several thousand, so that there are now more mutual funds than there are stocks on the New York Stock Exchange. Even more significant than the sheer number of funds is their role as an investment vehicle for many Americans. Consider that at the end of 2000, almost eighty-eight million individuals owned mutual funds.[42]

Why Mutual Funds?

One of the reasons that billions and billions of dollars have poured into mutual funds is the effectiveness of advertising that shows you how much money can be made in a professionally managed fund.

---

[41] Investment Company Institute, *Mutual Fund Fact Book,* 2001 p.43

[42] Investment Company Institute, *Mutual Fund Fact Book,* 2001 p.43

Why would you want to invest in a savings account at 3, 4, or 5 percent interest when advertising reminds you daily how rich you can become with a small investment in mutual funds?

Throughout the 1990s and particularly the late 1990s, people seemed to forget that the tremendous capital gains being advertised would not last forever and might actually turn into capital losses. Therefore, before you decide to invest in a mutual fund—especially one that has fantastic historical investment returns—consider the significance of the following statement:

Past performance is no indication of future results.

That's right, past performance is no indication of future results and yet sadly that is how many investors make their mutual fund buying decisions.

Last Year's Winners

We live in a culture that likes to see things ranked: the hundred best athletes of all times and the highest-grossing movies of all time are two simple examples of this cultural phenomenon. It is so pervasive in our society that it's difficult to find something that has not been ranked in some manner. Unfortunately, we're also often willing to use a "biggest" and "best" strategy—like a "Top 10 list"—to choose mutual fund investments. If you don't agree, the next time you go to a bookstore take a look at the headlines of the financial magazines. They practically overflow with articles proclaiming the secret to "The Best Mutual Funds for Today's Environment" or "The Year's Twenty Best Funds."

While catchy headlines are no doubt a great boon for magazine sales, it's less clear how good the superstar funds touted in articles are for your investment returns. These articles are usually well researched and can be good sources of information, but you don't want to rely on them as the last or only word when choosing a fund. Because magazine articles tend to focus purely on a fund's performance, it's easy to overlook the fact that a fund can have a fantastic performance because of good timing and luck, rather than solid investment strategies.

Funds that endure and generate solid returns over time are invariably based on more than just good luck. A promising mutual fund must rest on a foundation of solid management and investment principles. Paradoxically, media attention lavished on trendy funds can lead to a decline in their management quality—one reason being due to over-popularity.

As a mutual fund's reputation spreads, more and more money often pours into it. This creates an environment where, potentially, the port-folio manager is faced with the unpleasant task of investing new assets in a hyped sector of the market that may already be nearing its peak. In another scenario, the manager who has invested in and produced those remarkable returns may be lured away by an attractive offer from another investment firm aware of his or her management expertise. By the time the public jumps on the bandwagon, the very driving forces behind the fund's performance may be long gone. Insofar as there are so many variables behind a fund's success, this year's winning mutual fund sector typically will not have a repeat performance the following year. From Chart 7-B, you can see that it does however, occasionally occur.

Chart 7-B.

Mutual Fund Category with Best Performance.

Year	Mutual Fund Category	12-Month Performance %	Next Year's Performance %
2001	Gold Oriented Funds	18.78	To be determined
2000	Health/Biotechnology	55.1	12.64
1999	Science & Technology	134.2	-32.91
1998	Science & Technology	52.04	134.2
1997	Financial Services	45.82	6.35
1996	Emerging Markets Debt	38.51	12.03

Source: Lipper Analytical Services, Inc.

During 1998 and 1999, the Science & Technology mutual fund category was the winning sector. As fantastic as those returns were, I suspect that many investors who owned those types of funds didn't get in on the ground floor in the beginning of 1998, but rather invested after the numbers had been advertised and the hype had begun. That being the case, how many investors actually earned those phenomenal returns during 1998 and 1999—and then got out of that sector at the top of the market, before the technology implosion of 2000?

Trials of the Mutual Fund Manager

Because we operate in an information society and because of the flexibility mutual fund investors now have, portfolio management has become, perversely, more difficult for mutual fund managers. Investors have more choices and higher expectations than ever before, and are placing those demands on mutual funds and their managers. Because of that, two difficult issues that mutual fund managers may be forced to contend with are as follows:

Forced to Invest. I mentioned this earlier, but it is worth repeating. When a fund manager does a good job of investing, the outstanding returns are advertised, and money, money, and more money can start pouring in. The fund manager is then often given the task of investing the new cash even though he or she may not have the same enthusiasm for the portfolio's current stock holdings

Naturally, mutual fund managers are not forced to invest the new infusions of cash and there's nothing wrong with a manager building up cash reserves. Many investors, however, may feel that implementing a cash strategy is something that they can do themselves without having to pay a mutual fund manager. Investors, who send money to an outstanding wealth-creating mutual fund, want the manager to invest in more of the winning stocks he or she had been picking. So, you see, "Too much of a good thing" can have haunting consequences for a winning mutual fund manager.

Forced to Liquidate. There are scenarios in which the manager may be forced to liquidate holdings at inappropriate times. You have the same manager as in the preceding example and he or she feels that now is a great time to be investing in stocks. There are bargains galore, but alas, because of various market and financial concerns, clients are calling, faxing, and e-mailing the manager to withdraw their money. Investors may be screaming "Get me out, I can't stand this market any more." Therefore, despite it being a great time to make stock investments, the mutual fund manager may be forced to sell stock positions into a declining market to generate cash to meet clients' requests.

Now that you know how mutual funds are created and have an understanding of some of the issues that the fund managers must deal with, it is important for us to now move on to some of their specific advantages and disadvantages with which you should acquaint yourself.

Advantages

1. *Professional management.* An advantage of investing in a mutual fund is that you are hiring a professional manager who will make all daily buy and sell decisions for you—someone whose purpose in life is to make money for you, the shareholder. Also, you will receive this royal treatment whether you have $1,000 or $100,000 invested.

2. *Diversification.* I'm a huge fan of diversification and in a mutual fund a small investment of only a few hundred dollars will start you on your way to holding a diversified portfolio. While this simple method for diversification is important, it becomes critical when investing in certain sectors or areas of the market associated with added risk or volatility. Another mechanism for achieving diversity in a mutual fund is investing in a fund that is part of a large family of funds. Many mutual fund families allow you to transfer part or all of your assets to their various mutual funds with little or no cost to you, the investor. Of course, depending on the mutual fund family, some restrictions may apply.

3. *Simplicity, ease, and liquidity.* Mutual funds have created an environment in which it is easy and convenient to invest via the mail, wire transfers, or automatic payroll deductions. If you decide to take money out of a fund, you are usually only an "800" telephone number away. Once you make the call and give your instructions, like magic your money is available to you in a matter of days.

So far so good, but we know that there is no such thing as a perfect investment. Here are some of the disadvantages inherent in investing in mutual funds:

Disadvantages

1. *Professional management.* You probably feel the same way I did twenty years ago when a friend of mine (Steve Lewis, a money manager in the San Francisco Bay Area) informed me that mutual fund management could be both an advantage and a disadvantage. That's right—investing in a professionally managed mutual fund does not guarantee financial success. One of the little secrets of the mutual fund industry is that really bad funds can be merged, closed out, and magically made to disappear, giving the appearance that a given mutual fund family has only good funds that perform well for its investors. Good investment results are never assured, not even if the mutual fund manager holds three master's degrees and at least two PhDs. It's possible for a manager to make all the mistakes that individual investors make, like buying or selling at the wrong time and constantly turning over the portfolio in the hope of finding a hot stock pick. The constant turnover of a portfolio seldom produces good results and can also be very expensive for shareholders.

2. *Diversification.* Diversification in itself is not automatically an advantage. What matters is *how* you are diversified. Some mutual fund investors implement too much diversity. How can that be? If you have exposure to every stock in every sector of every market you can dilute your portfolio to the point that you may be unable to capture a large percentage of a given market's appreciation. Another common portfolio ailment comes about when investors think they are diversified, only to discover that they instead have very concentrated portfolios. Misplaced diversification can occur when you own several funds that are in the same sector of the market, creating the illusion of diversity. An example would be owning ten different growth funds, all of which—unknown to you—have Microsoft Corporation, Cisco Systems, EMC Corporation, AOL

Time Warner, and Intel Corporation as their biggest positions (largest holdings). In a scenario like this, you might not be any better off or any more diversified than just owning one or two of the different funds.[43]

3. *Liquidity and convenience.* With all the technology now available, it's easy to make changes in your mutual fund portfolio. The downside of this simplicity is often portfolio over-management. You can see it every day in homes and offices across America: people are looking up their portfolios, listening to what the chairman of the Federal Reserve has to say, and watching the latest updates on MSNBC. People have been seduced by information and delude themselves into believing that somehow they can get the data, analyze it, and make changes in their portfolios before the rest of humanity gets around to it. If you are in the practice of making ongoing changes in your mutual funds, answer this question: isn't the purpose of hiring a professional manager to let him or her utilize their necessary investment expertise? Yes, managers need to be monitored, but trying to outguess the managers defeats one of the tenets of investing in mutual funds: Let the manager that you have hired do his or her job. I'm not suggesting that after buying a mutual fund you stay in it, rain or shine, for the next fifty years. However, moving large percentages of your accounts around every few days, every few months, or even every quarter is excessive.

4. *Size of the fund.* If a mutual fund is too small, the portfolio could be expensive to manage—which might impact total returns—or lack the investment-research resources of large funds. If a mutual fund is too big, the expression "It's like turning a battleship around in a bathtub," might apply; because of their sheer size, some of the largest mutual funds in the country can have difficulty increasing or decreasing certain stock positions. Managers can be forced to

---

[43] I will discuss how to avoid those pitfalls in Chapter 12.

invest large percentages of the portfolio in the biggest, most liquid stocks, which may not offer the best investment opportunities. While I wouldn't avoid a mutual fund based on its size, it's sensible to be aware of these realities before investing.

5. *Tax issues.* Consider this investment scenario: you invest some money in a mutual fund, your investment drops in value, and yet you still owe taxes on the mutual fund's capital gains. Yes, it is possible to owe taxes on something that has dropped in value. It is one of the potential disadvantages of investing in mutual funds outside of tax-deferred accounts such as IRAs or 401(k)s. Here is one example of how it can occur.

> *Example:* Suppose that a few years ago, a mutual fund manager invested in a company named Mighty Widgets Inc. at $5 per share. The company has done very well, and the stock—which the fund still owns—is now worth $105 per share. You come along as an investor and put your money into this fine mutual fund. Shortly after you invest, the stock market starts to drop, investors start sending in sell orders, cash must be generated for the client redemptions, and the manager decides to sell the one stock—Mighty Widgets Inc.—that has not yet dropped in value.
>
> The value of your mutual fund investment may be dropping, but you will be stuck with some capital gains taxes because of the embedded capital gains from the sale of the Mighty Widgets stock, which has a **cost basis** of $5 but is sold by the manager for $105. It doesn't seem fair, but that's the way it works. Of course, if you had invested in a tax-deferred account such as an IRA rollover, you would be unaffected by such a scenario.

6. *Changing objectives.* How would you like to invest in a growth mutual fund advertised as being nicely diversified across a broad sector of the market, only to discover that shortly after you invested, most of the portfolio was moved into a handful of "hot stocks"? This can happen when a fund changes objectives or when a manager feels compelled to maximize returns and does so by over-concentrating the portfolio. To demonstrate how insidious this problem can become, consider how many mutual fund managers felt compelled to mimic and to beat the performance of the Standard and Poor (S&P) 500 during the late 1990s.[44] They did so by throwing diversification out the window and concentrating their portfolios in select hot growth stocks, which subsequently came crashing down to earth when the technology sector of the market imploded. Investing in mutual funds can create a diversified portfolio, but only if you ensure on an ongoing basis that your portfolio is still in sync with your investment needs and has not been corrupted by internal changes or over-concentration by its managers.

Enormous sums of money are invested in mutual funds and yes, there are many advantages associated with this investment alternative. But, it's clearly not a perfect investment vehicle. Depending on your needs, mutual funds may or may not be appropriate for your portfolio. With that in mind, here are some of the other packaged products that are available.

---

[44] The S&P 500 index is made up of 500 stocks. It is one of the most widely followed benchmarks of U.S. equity performance. It is a market-value-weighted index, which means that each stock's weight in the index is proportionate to its market value.

Unit Investment Trusts (UITs)

The unit investment trust is another packaged product that owes its existence to the Investment Company Act of 1940. It was created to offer investors some unique characteristics that could not be found in alternatives such as open-end mutual funds: (1) they are unmanaged portfolios, and (2) they have a finite life. The maturity of equity unit trusts is usually between zero to five years, while for bond unit trusts it can be as long as thirty years or more. Of course, these types of securities are liquid—that is they can be sold—but if they are not sold, the unit trust will eventually mature.

Equity Unit Investment Trusts

The best way to get a handle on this sector of the market is to review some examples. Here is the basic concept: (1) an investment firm gathers up several different securities, (2) puts them into a package, and (3) then sells off pieces of the package to the investing public. In the following example of equity (stock) UITs in action, we will assume that each of the stocks represents 10 percent of the portfolio:

- General Electric Co.
- Coca-Cola Company
- Pepsico Inc.
- Anheuser-Busch Companies Inc.
- Hormel Foods Corporation
- Exxon Mobil Corporation
- Microsoft Corporation
- Sun Microsystems
- Home Depot Inc.
- The Procter & Gamble Co.

One of the advantages of a unit investment trust is that it delivers diversity with a relatively small investment. With as little as $1,000 (and sometimes even less), you can participate in the ownership of these companies.

Another advantage of unit investment trusts is that what you see is what you get. UITs are fixed portfolios, so you know exactly what you are investing in, and you don't have to worry about the portfolio changes that can occur with a mutual fund. This simple strategy was so popular during the early to mid 1990s that one UIT was universally recognized in financial circles as "The Dogs of The Dow." Here is the recipe that was used to put together the portfolio: (1) take the thirty stocks in the Dow Jones Industrial Average, (2) rank them from top to bottom based on percent dividend yield, (3) take the top ten yielding stocks and place them in a unit trust portfolio, (4) at the end of one year, reevaluate the portfolio, (5) remove those stocks that no longer qualify under the criteria and replace them with those that do, and (6) start the new year with a new portfolio of the ten highest-dividend-yielding Dow stocks. Not only did this strategy deliver very good investment results, it was and is oh so simple.

Those advantages, however, were also its greatest weakness. The Dogs of The Dow fell from favor when more aggressively *managed* mutual funds began to give investors superior returns. It made many investors rethink the strategy of putting their hard-earned money into an investment that is fixed and doesn't have a professional manager making ongoing buy-and-sell decisions. Plus, remember that since UITs have a finite life, it's possible for your UIT to mature and liquidate during a low point in the market—perhaps just when the market is ready for a rebound.

Bond Unit Investment Trusts

Typically, you can invest in a bond UIT with as little as $250. Another advantage is that they are made up of fixed portfolios (like the equity

UITs) that remain constant throughout the life of the trust. Just as with individual bonds, they have the advantage of having a final maturity. Remember, bonds can change in value as interest rates change, but if you sit tight and do nothing, you will collect interest on them and, at maturity, the bonds will come due at face value.

A key disadvantage of bond UITs is that there is no active management (although this can be an advantage under some conditions). If the ratings of the bonds in the UIT start to be downgraded, there won't be any changes in the portfolio, which is very different than what can occur in a bond mutual fund. UITs also carry sales charges and administrative fees, which can be significantly higher than an investment in individual bonds—especially when investing in government bonds.

As with all investments, UITs have a unique set of advantages and disadvantages. For the right investor, they are a viable "packaged product" alternative to the open-end mutual fund, as is our next packaged product: closed-end funds.

Closed-End Funds

The third major product introduced by the Investment Act of 1940 was the closed-end fund. Even though these funds are often referred to as mutual funds, they are very different from their cousin, the open-end mutual fund.

The key difference between the two is that while open-end mutual funds constantly issue and redeem their shares, closed-end funds have a finite or fixed number of shares. In that sense, the latter resembles individual stocks that trade on an exchange. If you want to buy a closed end fund, someone has to sell some of his or her shares. This is no different from when an investor wants to buy shares of a publicly traded stock such as GE. You don't contact GE, you contact your broker who purchases the shares on an exchange. As you are buying, someone else is selling.

Another unique aspect of closed-end funds is the price per share they sell for, compared to their net asset value (**NAV**). As an individual buys and sells closed-end funds, the price of the shares may be very different from the value, or NAV, of the investments the fund holds. This can occur for a number of reasons, but I must admit that I have yet to come across a solid reason for this market aberration. However, many analysts and closed-end fund experts believe that this type of analysis is an important part of closed-end fund investing and often make their buy and sell recommendations based on the **spread** (the difference between market price and NAV) against historical norms.

For example, if international closed-end funds historically traded at a 10 percent discount to the NAV and were now trading at a 15 percent discount, it might be time to invest in those funds, since it could represent a buying opportunity of an undervalued asset.

A wide variety of closed-end funds is available: bond funds, equity funds, sector funds, international funds, country funds, regional funds—and just about anything else you can think of. Unfortunately, very few important investment firms dedicate much time analyzing closed-end funds, so they don't get nearly as much press as open-end funds.

Exchange-Traded Funds (ETFs)

It's a stock, it's a mutual fund, it's a unit investment trust—no it's an exchange-traded fund (ETF). The American Stock Exchange introduced ETFs during the early 1990s. They were created in an attempt to combine all the best attributes of individual stocks, open-end mutual funds, and index funds into a single investment. At the time, they didn't attract much fanfare, but starting during the late 1990s a sea change took place in investor's attitudes towards this sector of the market and investors began moving billions of dollars into ETFs.

ETFs offer investors a number of advantages: (1) liquidity (you can trade them minute by minute on an exchange, just as with individual stocks), (2) instant diversification (just as with a mutual fund), and (3) freedom from worry over getting a bad portfolio manager (ETFs are spread out over a specific basket of stocks, like an index fund).

I suspect that investors are going to be hearing more and more about exchange-traded funds, in part because of the proliferation of new ETFs hitting the market on what seems to be a daily basis. They now cover just about every major sector of the stock market.[45]

Although there are hundreds of different ETFs on the market, a few have been able to distinguish themselves and separate themselves from the pack. The Big 3 of this sector (the top dogs), are affectionately known as Spiders, Diamonds, and Qubes. I also suspect that within a very short period of time, the Big 3 will expand to the Big 4, with increased market awareness about Vipers.

1. *Spiders (stock symbol SPY).* This ETF is one of the simplest ways possible to invest in the S&P 500 index. Holdings in Spiders mirror the holdings in this widely followed index.
2. *Diamonds (stock symbol DIA).* This ETF tracks the Dow Jones Industrial Average. If you want to participate in the Dow Jones Industrial Average, but don't want the hassle of buying all thirty of its stocks, DIA is a simple alternative.
3. *Qubes (stock symbol QQQ).* QQQ tracks the Nasdaq-100 and as such it tends to be more volatile than either SPY or DIA. Because of this volatility, it is one of the most heavily traded securities on any exchange.
4. *Vipers (stock symbol VTI).* VTI was brought to market by The Vanguard Group, which is known for its open-end index mutual

---

[45] See Appendix C for sources of information on ETFs.

funds. This ETF covers the **Wilshire 5000** index and is therefore a much broader based investment than QQQ, SPY, or DIA.

Because of the many advantages offered by ETFs, they seem almost too good to be true.

> *Q:* *What concerns should you have with this investment*
> *alternative?*
> *A:* *Two of the important concerns have to do with over-con-*
> *centration and inaccurate labeling.*

As you evaluate the holdings, you may be surprised to discover that often the top several positions in a particular ETF will represent 20, 30, or 40 percent or more of your investment—not exactly the type of diversity one would hope for when investing in this manner. Also, some of the companies in an ETF may not cleanly match the ETF's sector name. For example, Wal-Mart Stores Inc. (the largest retailer in the world) and Delta Air Lines are both in the Select Spider Cyclical/Transportation ETF. I'm not sure what makes them so closely related that they would show up in the same ETF index—unless it's because Wal-Mart sells peanuts in all of their stores and Delta Air Lines "gives out" peanuts to their passengers.

Another disadvantage of ETFs, which they share with closed-end funds, is that there is not a lot of information or research on them. There are very few books, newsletters, or web pages devoted to their analysis. In Table 7-1 and Table 7-2, I have listed some commonly followed ETFs and their symbols.

Table 7-1.

ETF: iSHARES Sector Funds.

Symbol	Name
ICF	Cohen & Steers Major Realty Index Fund
IYM	Dow Jones US Basic Materials Sector
IYD	Dow Jones US Chemical Sector Index Fund
IYC	Dow Jones US Consumer Cyclical Sector Index Fund
IYK	Dow Jones US Consumer Non-Cyclical Sector Index Fund
IYE	Dow Jones US Energy Sector Index Fund
IYF	Dow Jones US Financial Sector Index Fund
IYG	Dow Jones US Financial Services Sector Index Fund
IYH	Dow Jones US Healthcare Sector Index Fund
IYJ	Dow Jones US Industrial Sector Index Fund
IYV	Dow Jones US Internet Sector Index Fund
IYR	Dow Jones US Real Estate Sector Index Fund
IYW	Dow Jones US Technology Sector Index Fund
IYZ	Dow Jones US Telecommunications Sector Index Fund
IDU	Dow Jones US Utilities Sector Index Fund
IGE	Goldman Sachs Natural Resources Index Fund
IGN	Goldman Sachs Networking Index Fund
IGW	Goldman Sachs Semiconductor Index Fund
IGV	Goldman Sachs Software Index Fund
IGM	Goldman Sachs Technology Index Fund
IBB	Goldman Sachs Biotechnology Index Fund

Table 7-2.

ETF: Select Sector SPDR Funds.

Symbol	Name
XLB	The Basic Industries Fund
XLV	The Consumer Services Select Fund
XLP	The Consumer Staples Select Fund
XLY	The Cyclical/Transportation Fund
XLE	The Energy Fund
XLF	The Financial Fund
XLI	The Industrial Fund
XLK	The Technology Fund
XLU	The Utilities Fund

See Appendix C for sources of information on ETFs.

SUMMARY: Investment product selection is an important concept that doesn't receive the attention it deserves. Keep in mind that no investment product alternative is inherently good or bad. Individual securities, money managers, and packaged products all offer investors a particular set of advantages, disadvantages, and cost structures. Whether you are making investment decisions by yourself or are working with an investment advisor, stay on top of the array of investment product alternatives available to you.

Part III

Investment Strategies

Chapter 8

Investing in Individual Bonds: An Overview

I know that bonds should be part of a diversified portfolio, so I went to the local bookstore and started reviewing the section of investing. To my dismay, I discovered that they carried 683 different books on investing and only one of them covered bonds—and it was 1,300 pages long. I don't want to become a professional bond analyst. I just need a working knowledge of bonds and how to properly invest in them. Any suggestions?

If you decide to invest in bond mutual funds rather than in individual bonds, you owe it to your financial health to understand both the vocabulary of individual bonds and how to invest in them wisely. Because there are few "user friendly" books that deal effectively with the complexity of investing in the bond market, a great deal of misinformation tends to reach the investing public.

In the chapter on asset allocation, I introduced you to bonds and referred to that introduction as the "crawling" phase in understanding the bond market. It's time to advance to the next step: the "walking" phase of understanding bonds. To do so, you need to understand the advantages, disadvantages, terminology, and mathematics of investing in individual bonds.

Advantages

1. *Control.* With individual bonds, you have more control over your portfolio—you decide, you are the boss.

> Q: *Can you exert control over your bond portfolio by wisely picking and choosing bond mutual funds instead of individual bonds?*
>
> A: *Yes. But, in no way, shape, or form can you mold your bond mutual fund portfolio in the same way you can an individual bond portfolio.*

One of the important ways you can exert control over a bond portfolio is by deciding on the quality of the individual bonds in which you'll be investing. You can try to match this level of quality by picking certain bond funds. But, keep in mind that many funds that appear to be safe give their managers the flexibility to utilize "sophisticated" strategies to maximize the fund's yield. You need to ask yourself, what happens to the high-quality bond fund portfolio if the sophisticated high-yield strategy doesn't work?[46] With an individual bond portfolio, you know your strategy and can control your investments.

2. *Economical.* Generally speaking, it is economical to invest in individual bonds. Often, either a small or no yearly management fee is charged against your individual bonds when you invest in a

---

[46] See Chapter 10 for my analysis of some "high-yield" strategies to be wary of even if you are invested in a "safe" bond fund.

buy-and-hold strategy, unlike bond mutual funds, which carry a yearly cost (an expense ratio) year after year after year (you get the picture). The costs to buy and sell individual bonds will vary from firm to firm and I will discuss these costs in detail in Chapter 9.

3. *Maturity date.* One of the most significant advantages of individual bonds is that they have a maturity date. I cannot stress strongly enough how important this is when putting together a bond portfolio. Individual bonds, if held to maturity, will pay off at their face value. If you buy a bond for $10,000, earn interest on it yearly, and hold it to its maturity, it will mature at the face value of $10,000. This kind of principal payback comes with individual bonds (open-end bond funds, for example, do not have a maturity date). Let me illustrate the importance of having a maturity date with the following exchange:

Q: *You know that stocks have given a superior rate of return over cash and bond investments, but you just can't accept the volatility of a 100 percent stock portfolio. So, you are thinking of adding some bond mutual funds to your portfolio. Will that lower your portfolio's risk profile?*

A: *Sorry to be the bearer of bad news, but there is a possibility you won't be lowering it as much as you hope because you may be substituting interest rate risk for stock market risk. If interest rates go up, your entire portfolio could still drop in value. The stock portion of your portfolio may go down and most assuredly your bond mutual fund holdings will go down (recall from Chapter 6, the inverse relationship of interest rates and bond values). Individual bonds just like bond funds will go down in value when interest rates increase, but with individual bonds you can sit tight, do nothing, and know that they will pay off your principal on maturity. Since bond mutual funds don't have a maturity date, they can't guarantee your principal.*

To further illustrate this concept, let us evaluate an oversimplified example of two investors (see Table 8-1). In this example, each investor puts $100,000 in the bond market. The first investor puts money into a triple-A rated intermediate-term U.S. Treasury and the second investor puts money into an intermediate U.S. Treasury mutual fund. Some time after the investments are made interest rates dramatically increase and both the individual bonds and the bond mutual fund drop in value by 15 percent. Both investors decide that they will not try to time the market, but will instead sit tight and continue to earn interest—after all, the value of their bonds will return eventually to $100,000, won't it? Under the conditions I just described, would you be more comfortable with the individual bond portfolio or the bond mutual fund?

Table 8-1.

Interest Rate Changes and the Return of Principal.

	Investor 1 Individual Bonds	**Investor 2** Bond Mutual Fund
Initial value	$ 100,000	$ 100,000
Dramatic increase in interest rates		
Current value	$ 85,000	$ 85,000
Will the investors get back $ 100,000?	Yes	Maybe
When will it occur?	On maturity	Not sure

This concept is so important that I will say it one more time. If interest rates increase dramatically and cause your bond portfolio to plunge in value, individual bonds offer you the comfort of having a light at the end of the tunnel. If you sit tight, collect your interest and wait, your individual bonds will mature at the $100,000 face value. The same cannot be said for the owner of a bond fund. If interest rates are stable or decline, these types of issues are less critical.

> *Q:* *What kinds of maturities are available if you invest in individual bonds?*
>
> *A:* *Almost anything you want. You can invest in short-term, intermediate-term, or long-term bonds.*

Q: *What maturity ranges constitute short term, interme-diate term, and long term?*

A: *There are no rules etched in stone, but here are some general guidelines:*

- *Short-term maturity:* Normally thought of as zero to five-years. (A six-year bond might still be short term, but that will depend on your perspective—such as your age and financial needs—and on market conditions.)
- *Intermediate-term maturity:* Seven to twelve-year range (Some consider fourteen-, fifteen-, and sixteen-year bonds as the extreme edge of intermediate term.)
- *Long-term maturity:* Fifteen years or longer. (Some argue that long term begins at twenty years or more.)

Disadvantages

1. *Building expertise.* The first disadvantage new bond investors have to overcome has to do with expertise—both lack of expertise and what I call "delusional" expertise. It takes time and effort to understand individual bonds. Some folks give up on the commitment and opt to turn the money over to a bond mutual fund manager. Others make the mistake of convincing themselves that they're bond experts just because they've read a few articles on bonds or surfed the Internet. Nothing could be further from the truth; understanding the opportunities and potential pitfalls of the bond market takes time and effort. Thoroughly educate yourself and then you'll be able to invest wisely and take advantage of this important market sector.

2. *Diversification.* If you invest in only one bond, you don't need to be a rocket scientist to figure out that you will be breaking one of my cardinal rules: diversify your investments. If the U.S. government

backs the single bond in your portfolio, safety won't be an issue. However, you'll be missing out on other important aspects of individual bond investing. For example, if you have only one bond means that you aren't investing in a variety of maturities that could stabilize and assure cash flow from your portfolio during an extended period of time.

3. *No monthly cash flow.* Many individual bonds pay their interest every six months. If you need a monthly income, you'll either be limited to certain sectors of the bond market or you will need to create a portfolio with several bonds that pay their interest on dissimilar six-month cycles. Receiving monthly cash flow is less complicated with a bond mutual fund.

4. *Dividend reinvestment.* To reinvest the income from your bonds into more bonds, you must first accumulate an amount large enough to purchase another individual bond. While this may seem obvious, it's important to understand that you cannot purchase shares or partial shares of individual bonds the way you can with a bond mutual fund. Depending on the size of your portfolio and the cash flow it generates, you could have a very long wait on your hands before reinvestment becomes possible.

5. *Movement of funds.* If you plan to move money back and forth between stocks and bonds, you should seriously evaluate whether individual bonds are right for you. The ongoing buying and selling of individual bonds can be expensive.

6. *Reaching for yield.* Investors can be seduced by the high yields of certain sectors of the bond market. Be aware that there is no such thing as a "free lunch." If a bond is paying a "high" return, then it is your job to find out what type of risk is associated with the higher return and determine if it meets your investment criteria. Interest rate risk, call risk, and credit risk are some examples of what may need to be evaluated.

Besides the specific advantages and disadvantages that I have listed, here are two additional features that need to be understood before making any final decisions before investing in certain types of bonds: call risk and a mandatory put.

Call Risk

A call date is when the bond's original issuer can call (redeem) the bond. If a bond can be called, the call date will be before the final maturity date. For example, if you were to purchase a bond in ABC Corporation Inc. that matures in the year 2020 but is callable starting in the year 2005, the corporation would be able to redeem or call the bond starting in 2005—whether you like it or not.

> *Q: If one of your bonds is called can you refuse to give it up?*
>
> *A: Refusing to give up a bond would not be wise, because the bond will no longer pay any interest.*

Investing in bonds that have call protection assures you that you will be able to keep your bonds and their interest payments even if interest rates drop dramatically. If you have a bond portfolio filled with callable bonds, you run the risk of having your portfolio paid off at an untimely point in any given interest-rate cycle.

Before investing in a bond, then, be sure to know what the call provisions are.

Mandatory Put

A mandatory put is, in essence, the opposite of a call provision. You, the investor, decide when you want to turn in your bond and "put" it back to the corporation. When you put the bond back, to the original issuer, you will be paid the bond's full face value. Because put features give investors rather than the bond issuer more control over their bonds, bonds with a mandatory put are rarely issued.

TERMINOLOGY & MATHEMATICS OF BONDS

If you plan to invest in bonds, you need to have a working knowledge of the "lingo" and the mathematics of bonds. Let me illustrate the importance of this in the following manner. You decide to start searching for some individual bonds, and you find a couple of ads in the newspaper, which describe two different bonds: (1) two-year triple-A rated bonds paying 6 percent, and (2) two-year triple-A rated bonds paying 7 percent. Of course, 7 is more than 6, and since both bonds are triple-A rated, you decide to call the investment firm in the second ad, open an account, and purchase some of the 7 percent yielding bonds. But, when your confirmation arrives in the mail, you discover your bond is going to be paying you considerably less than 7 percent. What happened? It is entirely possible for this to occur because you didn't read the fine print.

The first bond you saw was priced at **par**, was **non-callable**, and had a **coupon** of 6 percent; while the second bond was priced at a **premium**, was **callable**, had a **coupon** of 7 percent rather than 6 percent, and a **yield to call** of only 5 percent (considerably less than the anticipated 7 percent return). When evaluating bonds, it just isn't enough to ask the age-old question, "How much is it paying?"

In addition to knowing a bond's maturity, there is additional information you'll need before you can calculate how much is it paying and understand what the answer means. Here are some of the important terms:

Bond Prices

Before your can evaluate the merits of a bond offering, there are some key terms about "price" you must understand: (1) par, (2) discount, and (3) premium.

Par bond

A bond priced at its maturing face value. For example, if a bond is selling at par, it will be selling for 100 percent of its face value; sometimes, it will just be listed as priced at 100 without the percent (%) sign. If you invest $10,000 in a par bond, at maturity the face value (par) will also be $10,000. If you invest $25,000 in a par bond, at maturity the face value (par), will be $25,000.

Discount bond

A discount bond is one that sells for less than its face value, or less than par. For example, if you buy a $10,000 bond at 93 cents on the dollar, your actual cost, or investment, will be $9,300 (or priced at 93), not $10,000. With a discount bond, you not only receive the interest from the bond, but on maturity your $9,300 investment will pay off at $10,000.

Premium bond

A premium bond is one that sells for more than its face value (more than par). For example, if you buy a $10,000 bond at 105 cents on the dollar, your actual cost will be $10,500, (105) not $10,000. You will collect the bond's cash flow, and on maturity the bond will pay off at $10,000, not $10,500.

Bond Yields

Just as with bond prices, bond yields can be confusing. There are a number of different types of yields you need to understand before you can evaluate how much a bond is paying: (1) coupon yield, (2) current yield, and (3) yield to maturity.

Coupon Yield

The yearly cash flow of the bond normally listed as a percent of par. For example, if you invest $10,000 in a bond priced at par with a coupon of 6 percent, you will earn $600 per year. If the bond matures in five years, you will have received a total of $3,000 in interest from your bond ($600 x 5), and of course, your bond will mature at $10,000.

> Q: *If you invest in a discount bond for 95 cents on the dollar or $9,500 with a coupon of 6 percent, how much will your yearly cash flow be?*
> A: *It will be $600 per year because the 6 percent coupon is still based on the par value, which in this example would be $10,000, not $9,500.*

Current Yield

The coupon yield of the bond divided by the price paid for it. For example, using the same $10,000 bond, the current yield in this example will be the same as the coupon: the coupon ÷ price of the bond is represented as $600 ÷ $10,000 = 6 percent.

Yield to Maturity

Your anticipated yield to maturity is based on the following information: how much you paid for the bond, its coupon, when you purchased it, its value at maturity, and the date of maturity. The calculation also assumes that the cash flow from the bond (the coupon) is reinvested at the same yield to maturity. It gives you the best answer to the much-asked question: "How much is it paying?"

To help you better understand the preceding terms and yield calculations, I will evaluate the following three bonds:

- A bond priced at par—$10,000.00
- A bond priced at a discount—$9,578.80
- A bond priced at a premium—$10,421.20

Each bond is triple-A rated, non-callable, to be held to maturity (not traded), and matures in five years.

Example: **Par bond** $10,000 (100), coupon of 6 percent = $600 of income per year. The current yield of 6 percent comes from the bond's coupon ÷ price (6 ÷ 100). It matures at $10,000 and gives a yield to maturity of *6 percent.*

Example: **Discount bond** $9,578.80 (95.788), coupon of 5 percent = $500/year of income. Current yield of 5.22 percent comes from coupon ÷ price (5 ÷ 95.788). The bond matures at $10,000 (not $9,578.80) and gives a yield to maturity of *6 percent.*

Example: **Premium bond** $10,421.20 (104.212), coupon of 7 percent = $700/year of income. Current yield of 6.717 percent comes from coupon ÷ price (7 ÷ 104.212). It matures at $10,000 (not $10,412.20) and gives a yield to maturity of *6 percent.*

From these examples, you can see that all three bonds are calculated to give a yield to maturity of 6 percent despite their being structured differently. The yield to maturity calculation, however, is based on a few assumptions: (1) you will reinvest the cash flow (which is the coupon), and (2) the cash flow will be reinvested at the same yield to maturity (6 percent). These assumptions may be more difficult to achieve than originally calculated. (I will give some examples of this subsequently.)

Q: *If you don't trade your bonds but keep them to maturity, which bond is the best—par, premium, or discount?*

A: *Well, that depends, and here's why: you don't know what's going to happen to interest rates during the next five years. If you knew that interest rates were going to decrease, buying the discount bond would be your best choice, and the premium bond would be the worst choice because more of the total return from the premium bond is based on the high 7 percent yearly coupon.*

Example: If interest rates drop, the $700 per year in cash flow you receive from the premium bond is being reinvested at a significantly lower rate of return (not anywhere close to the 6 percent yield to maturity of the original bond calculation). On the other hand, the discount bond depends on less of its total return from the 5 percent coupon, (the $500 per year in income), because part of its total return comes from your having paid $9,578.80 for the bond and it maturing at $10,000. With discount bonds, you are earning money two ways.

Another advantage of discount bonds is that they give you some added financial returns if they are called. If you were to purchase a five-year bond today for $9,500 and it was called next week for $10,000, I suspect that you wouldn't be too upset.

Q: *What is the best bond choice if interest rates increase during the next five years?*

A: *A premium bond would be your best choice for the opposite of all the reasons I cited in my answer to the previous question: you would have more cash flow per year available for reinvestment in the new higher interest-rate environment.*

As you can see from the information on the previous pages, the answer to the question "how much is it paying?" can have a number of different meanings. Know the price of the bond, and understand all of its yield calculations before making any investment decisions.

Basis Points

A final term to add to your bond vocabulary is **basis points**. It is used to avoid some of the confusion that can occur when investors or traders describe what is happening to a bond's yield or price.

Example: If bonds are paying 5 percent and a few weeks later bond yields have gone up to 6 percent, what percentage increase has occurred? Some people will say that yields have increased 1 percent (the difference between 5 and 6), while others will say 20 percent (20 percent of 5 = 1, added to 5 gives you the new yield of 6 percent). However, an astute bond investor or bond trader would say that the rates increased by 100 basis points, which equals 1 percent. If a bond yield goes from 5 percent to 5.5 percent, how much has the yield changed: 0.5 percent, 10 percent, or 50 basis points? The answer is 50 basis points.

SUMMARY: *Many investors believe that the only complex part of their portfolio (the part that requires time and study) is the stock portion. However, there is complexity inherent in investing successfully in bonds, either individually or within a bond mutual fund. If you can get your arms around this, you'll be on your way to becoming an informed bond investor.*

Chapter 9

Individual Bond Alternatives

What do you mean, I can't buy savings bonds in my IRA accounts and savings bonds have nothing to do with investing in the bond market? I've been buying savings bonds at work for more than thirty years. What else is there to know about buying bonds? Okay, so maybe I'll just have to buy some U.S. Treasuries in my IRA account. After all, I have a Treasury direct account. What? I can't use a Treasury direct account for my IRA? I give up. I guess I have to admit that I don't know as much about individual bonds as I thought.

I will complete my discussion of individual bonds by reviewing some specific bond alternatives and by evaluating some strategies for putting together a bond portfolio.

In this chapter, I will focus on three sectors of the bond market: (1) U.S. Treasuries, (2) corporate bonds, and (3) mortgage-backed securities (MBS). Tax-free municipal bonds will be discussed in Chapter 13 (Investing Outside Your IRA). As you evaluate these different types of bonds, understand that there is no single best choice; each alternative offers investors a unique set of advantages and disadvantages.

U.S. TREASURIES

U.S. Treasuries are the safest bonds in the world. The U.S. government has never defaulted on a Treasury because it can meet its financial obligations by increasing the taxes of the citizens in the wealthiest country in the world. While this type of safety has obvious advantages, the corresponding disadvantage of this is that Treasuries pay a lower yield than other types of bonds with comparable maturities.

Besides being a safe harbor for investment capital, the importance of Treasuries towers over all other sectors of the bond market because it is the most liquid, actively traded bond market in the world and serves as the benchmark against which all other bonds are compared. The only real decision you have to make with Treasuries is about the kind of interest rate risk you are willing to assume. Quality, safety, and liquidity are not an issue. Here are the three most basic ways to invest in individual Treasuries:

1. *Treasury bills.* When originally issued, Treasury bills come in maturities of three, six, and twelve months. They are structured a little differently from other bonds in that they do not pay cash flow in the traditional way: you buy them at a discount and they mature at face value. For example, if you invest $9,500 in a Treasury bill and in one year it matures at $10,000, the $500 difference is the interest earned.

2. *Treasury notes.* Treasury notes are issued with a maturity of two to ten years and pay interest every six months. Every Treasury note you invest in will have its own particular six-month interest-rate cycle. For example, a note might pay interest on the January/July cycle or the February/ August cycle.

3. *Treasury bonds.* Treasury bonds pay interest every six months, just like Treasury notes. When the bonds are issued, they will have a maturity of ten years or more.

Which maturity of U.S. Treasuries you should invest in will depend on your risk tolerances, market outlook, and financial needs. For a review of the historical returns of Treasuries, see Chart 6-D in Chapter 6.

CORPORATE BONDS

Corporate bonds are backed and issued by corporations. Their yields depend on maturity date, call date, and rating (the higher the quality, the higher the rating, the lower the yield, and the lower the quality, the lower the rating, the higher the yield). If you invest in corporate bonds, I recommend staying with bonds rated "A" or better. While there can be exceptions, "A" or better is a good place to start.

> *Q: Why should you invest in corporate bonds rather than U.S. Treasuries?*
>
> *A: The simple answer to that question is "yield." For a comparable maturity, the corporate bond will usually pay you a higher yield than a U.S. Treasury.*

If a corporate bond offers you no yield advantage or if the advantage is only a few tenths of a percent, I suggest that you stay with Treasuries. If you are investing in bonds outside your tax-deferred accounts—such as an IRA—there may be some additional considerations for you to evaluate. (I cover these differences in detail in Chapter 13.)

MORTGAGE-BACKED SECURITIES (MBSs)

Mortgage-backed securities (MBSs), also called mortgage pass-through securities, represent an enormous sector of the U.S. bond market in the amount of billions and billions of dollars. If you're planning to invest in individual bonds or through a mutual fund, it's important to know how these bonds work. They can be more complicated than corporate or Treasury bonds, so I am dedicating more information to their discussion.

Hundreds of thousands of individuals own MBSs, and yet many of those investors have no idea what these securities are or where they come from. One reason for this is that the major purchasers of MBSs are institutions—through money managers, mutual fund managers, and retirement and pension plan managers—although often on the behalf of individuals. Treasuries come from the U.S. government, corporate bonds come from corporations; but, where do mortgage-backed securities come from? Typically, they begin with a homebuyer.

Origination of MBS Pool

A couple of happy homebuyers, I'll call George and Wanda in this example, decide that they want to buy a house. They go to a lender to take out a mortgage to buy a new home. The mortgage lender then goes to an MBS agency such as Ginnie Mae (there are others) and, after meeting certain criteria, receives a guarantee of a loan—in this case Ginnie Mae.

George and Wanda have their loan, buy their house, and they may not even know, remember, or care about something called Ginnie Mae (GNMA). Their qualifying mortgage is then "pooled" and shipped off to a securities dealer that sells off the pieces of the Ginnie Mae pools to investors.

When people such as George and Wanda make their monthly payments, a service collects interest and principal payments and passes them through to the MBS investors—hence the term **mortgage pass-through**. This process makes everybody happy: George and Wanda have a loan, the lender and the securities dealers are paid, and investors are earning a high rate of return backed by the U.S. government.

Q: *What about the happy couple, George and Wanda? Do they know that their mortgage pool has been sold off?*

A: *Probably not.*

Q: *What happens if George and Wanda get into financial difficulty and don't make the payment on their interest and principal on time?*

A: *Well, it's not a problem for the investors because the good old U.S. government guarantees the principal and interest payments of those GNMA pools.*

At this point you may be saying to yourself, "Boy oh boy, I want income from my investments; I want my investments to be safe and secure, but MBSs sound confusing, and perhaps I should consider investment alternatives."

Q: *Should you make mortgage-backed securities part of your investment portfolio?*

A: *The answer could very well be a resounding "yes."*

There are distinct advantages associated with investing in MBSs: (1) monthly cash flow rather than cash flow every six months, (2) safety (GNMAs are backed by the full faith and credit of the U.S. government), and (3) high yield (typically higher than other triple-A rated bonds).

There are, however, some major disadvantages associated with MBSs, which I will discuss as I review the following four major categories: (1) Ginnie Maes, (2) Fannie Maes, (3) Freddie Macs, and (4) CMOs. The names sound like some kind of a family gathering; but, while they are indeed related, each category has its own set of characteristics.

Ginnie Mae (GNMA)

GNMA stands for Government National Mortgage Association pass-through certificates. They are probably the best known of the MBS family. Originally created by Congress, the initial GNMA pools were issued during the early 1970s to provide cash to homebuyers. One big advantage of GNMAs is that they are backed by the full faith and credit of the U.S. government, but there is no hiding from the fact that GNMAs can be a complex investment alternative.

When investing in GNMAs, you will see some unusual terms: (1) yield to average life (not yield to maturity), (2) estimated yield (not a specific yield), and (3) the "factor" of your bond. I will define them in the course of this discussion.

> Q: *Why is there so much ambiguity and complexity associated with GNMAs?*
>
> A: *It has to do with the uniqueness of their cash flow.*

GNMA Cash Flow

GNMA yield calculations and cash flow models are not only complex, but they are also very different from other debt instruments such as Treasury or corporate bonds. The element of uncertainty in them is your not knowing exactly when your investment will pay off—and so you don't know your bond's exact cash flow. GNMAS have an average life, not a maturity date in the traditional sense that corporate and Treasury bonds do. What's key here is that GNMAs are based on mortgages.

Let us compare a GNMA investment with one in a corporate bond. In this example, you will be making two different investments: you will invest $10,000 in a triple-A rated corporate bond and $10,000 in a GNMA and then compare the cash flows of the two.

Example 1: On an 8.5" x 11" piece of paper, write "$10,000 corporate bond" in big bold letters. Underneath the $10,000, write "6.5 percent coupon," which is the yearly interest, and finally, under the 6.5 percent write "five-year maturity." The sheet of paper now represents your investment of $10,000 in a triple-A rated corporate bond with a coupon of 6.5 percent. Every six months your bond will pay you $325 in interest, which is $650 per year, and at the end of five years your bond will mature in a lump sum of $10,000. This is a simple and straightforward investment.

Example 2: Now use a second piece of 8.5" x 11" paper and write all the specifics of your GNMA on it, just as you did with the corporate bond. In this example, the GNMA also has a 6.5 percent coupon interest and a five-year average life—*not a five-year maturity but a five-year average life.* With the GNMA, you will be paid monthly interest; and as the bond matures, you will be paid back your full $10,000 in principal, just as with the corporate bond. But, here's the important difference: you will not receive the $10,000 principal payback from the GNMA in one lump sum in five years as you did with the corporate bond. Rather, you will be paid back the original $10,000 of principal from your investment in monthly pieces.

Take the 8.5" x 11" paper that represents your GNMA and start tearing off pieces the size of a silver dollar. These pieces represent your monthly principal payback. After some months, the pieces will be larger than a silver dollar and in some months they will be smaller. Over time—after getting back many pieces of the paper—you will have torn off 100 percent of the sheet, which represents the full payback of your original $10,000 investment. Even though all $10,000 will have been paid back (redeemed), you will not have had any control over the amount of principal that returned to you each month. Before investing, it is very important to understand what will happen to the average life and principal payments of your GNMA if interest rates were to increase or decrease by 1, 2, or 3 percentage points (100, 200, and 300 basis points).

> Q: *Why do changing interest rates cause the monthly principal payback amounts to change?*
>
> A: *Changes in interest rates can cause changes in individual behavior. People might be more, or less willing, to sell or refinance their homes. Any of these personal decisions can cause a change in the principal payback schedule of a given GNMA.*

The risks associated with GNMAs are related to the acceleration or the slowdown of **principal redemption**. It is these potential changes to the average life and its impact to the total yield of your investment, rather than default risk, that investors need to be concerned with before investing. Let me clarify this with the following examples.

> *Example 1:* Perhaps you own a five-year average-life GNMA paying you a 7 percent coupon and all of a sudden, interest rates drop and people start refinancing their mortgages or selling their houses and moving into bigger ones. That nice five-year average-life GNMA that was paying a great interest rate gets paid off sooner than originally planned, perhaps in two or three years, rather than an average of five. What's next? You're stuck reinvesting the proceeds (the return of your original investment) in the new lower-interest-rate environment.

Example 2: Of course rates don't always go down; so, what happens if interest rates increase dramatically? People don't usually refinance their mortgages, and they don't typically move to bigger homes with bigger mortgages. This creates an environment where the payback schedule of your GNMA could slow down. Consequently, your five-year average-life GNMA might turn into a seven-year, ten-year, or longer average life. You started out with a 7 percent yielding bond—which looked good at the time—but with increased interest rates, your 7 percent yield no longer looks so attractive. And, to top it off, your original five-year average life GNMA is now a much longer-term average life. Interest rates change, and the average life of a GNMA can change.

Remember, just as with other bonds, if you sit tight and hold your bond until it matures, you will be paid back its face value.

GNMA Face Amount and Factor

Understanding something called the "factor" of your GNMA is an important part of investing in MBSs. Here's an illustration of how the factor works.

Example: You march down to your local bank and take out a loan to buy a house for $200,000. Depending on where you live, it might be a loan for a small house or it could be a loan for the house of your dreams. This loan you take out is a fixed loan and has a standard thirty-year maturity. If you're a good citizen and make your monthly mortgage payments, you will gradually pay off the loan. As the years go by, let us assume you have paid off $50,000 of the original $200,000, leaving you with a balance of $150,000 on the original loan. That's when you decide to sell your house, and you do so, for $250,000.

Although most home loans are not assumable, for illustrative purposes and to clarify the point of this example, the buyer assumes your original loan, which now has a balance of $150,000 and also gives you a $100,000 check for the balance of the total sale price ($250,000). Now, if the new owner looked up the paperwork on your original loan, he or she would see that your original loan was for $200,000. You had paid off 25 percent of the original $200,000 leaving 75 percent of the loan intact, which equates to a factor of 0.75. The factor, then, lets you know how much of an original loan is yet to be paid off—that is, how much principal on a percentage basis is still intact.

Table 9-1 has some additional examples of how the factor and the price of the GNMA can impact the actual dollars you invest in a given MBS.

Table 9-1.

Amount Required to Invest in a Given GNMA.

Face Value (in $)	Price (in %)	Factor	Total Investment (in $)
50,000	102.75	0.4811	24,716.51
125,000	97.40	0.1800	21,915.00
25,000	100.00	1.0000	25,000.00

Because of the factor, the bond with the largest face amount ($125,000) actually resulted in the smallest amount being invested ($21,915).

GNMA: Discount, Par, and Premium Bonds

If you invest in a discount, par, or premium corporate bond that is non-callable, you will be able to calculate fairly accurately the bond's yield to maturity. On the other hand, if you invest in a discount or premium GNMA and interest rates change, the total return on your investment could be very different from the original total return your calculations showed.

Before I discuss how this would work, here are some general observations about investing in par, discount, or premium GNMAs. (See Chapter 8 to review these terms.)

1. The changes in price of discount GNMAs are more sensitive with respect to interest-rate changes than the prices of par or premium bonds.
2. The changes in price of premium GNMAs are more stable to interest-rate changes than the prices of par or discount GNMAs.
3. If interest rates go down, the rate of return on your discount GNMA bonds will probably be higher than originally stated while the rate of return on your premium GNMA will probably be lower than originally stated.
4. If interest rates go up, the rate of return on your discount GNMA bonds will probably be lower than originally stated while the rates of return on your premium GNMA will probably be higher than originally stated.

Let me explain how your rates of return can change (compared to the original calculations) under the following scenarios: (1) interest rates decrease, (2) interest rates stay the same, and (3) interest rates increase.

Example 1: What happens to the investment returns of your GNMAs if interest rates decrease? Perhaps, you buy a

GNMA at 95 cents on the dollar (a discount bond) with a five-year average life. Your investment return will come from two sources: (1) the yearly interest rate (the coupon) and (2) the difference between 95 and 100. Remember, bonds mature at 100 cents on the dollar, even though you only paid 95 cents on the dollar.

If interest rates decrease, your GNMA will probably get paid off more quickly—for instance, in a three-year average life instead of a five-year average life. Because of this accelerated pay off, you will earn the difference between 95 and 100 more rapidly, increasing your discount GNMA's overall investment return. Conversely, if you invest in a five-year average life premium bond at 105 cents on the dollar, you earn a much higher yearly coupon yield than the discount bond, but to calculate your total return, you must factor in the loss that occurs when the GNMA pays off at 100 rather than at 105. If this occurs more rapidly, say in three years rather than in five, your return will be lower than originally calculated. So, the bottom line is that under the scenario just described, the total return of your discount GNMA increases, while the total return of your premium GNMA decreases.

Example 2: What if interest rates are stable for the life of your bond? Under that kind of scenario, the actual investment returns will be very close to the original calculations. Having said that, your total return could be slightly higher with the premium GNMA. Why? Premium bonds are a little more complicated and investors are less likely to invest in them. Because of that, they are typically priced to yield a slightly higher total rate of return, than the discount or par GNMAs.

Example 3: What happens if interest rates increase? Under that scenario, the discount GNMA is a lousy choice and the premium GNMA would be your best alternative. Don't forget that a premium GNMA is priced that way because it is paying a yearly coupon rate higher than the prevailing market. If you can earn that high coupon yield for a six-, seven-, or eight-year average life rather than for the origi nal five years, your total return will be higher than the original calculation.

Types of GNMAs

GNMAs were originally created to make it possible for people to purchase single-family homes. But over the years, the program has been expanded to assist other types of homebuyers in a variety of ways. The different types of GNMA programs go by the following names: GNMA 1, GNMA 2, Midget, and Mobile-home GNMAs. These different names have to do with how the mortgage pools are created, what sector of the housing market they represent, and the maturity of the pools. The U.S. government backs each type.

Fannie Mae (FNMA)

The acronym "FNMA" stands for Federal National Mortgage Association. It is known colloquially as **Fannie Mae**. FNMA started life as a government-owned corporation, but, during 1968, it was converted to a privately held corporation that now trades on the New York Stock Exchange.

The concepts associated with a GNMA—average life, par, discount, premium, and factor—are also the essentials of how a FNMA works. The key difference is that a FNMA is not backed by the full faith and credit of the U.S. government. It has what is often referred to as U. S.

government agency status. FNMAs do, however, carry an implied triple-A rating.

Freddie Mac (FHLMC)

The Federal Home Loan Mortgage Corporation (FHLMC, or **Freddie Mac**) is also a private corporation, similar to FNMA. It is comprised of conventional mortgages on single-family loans that are not assumable. Also, just as with FNMA, Freddie Mac is not backed by the full faith and credit of the U.S. government, but has agency status and an implied triple-A rating.

CMOs (Collateralized Mortgage Obligations)

CMOs are also called REMICs, which stands for Real Estate Mortgage Investment Conduit. I prefer the acronym CMO and will use it throughout this part of the book. (I will limit my discussions here to CMOs backed by GNMAs, FNMAs, and Freddie Macs.)

Many years ago, I worked for an investment firm named Kidder Peabody, which was eventually acquired by PaineWebber. During that period of time, Kidder Peabody became the largest CMO dealer in the country. Kidder Peabody originated billions and billions of dollars of triple-A rated CMOs that were offered to investors—institutions and individuals alike. Now, I have a question for you: If so much money was invested in CMOs, why is it that most investors have never heard of them? What the heck is a CMO?

Annette Thau, in *The Bond Book*, uses the terms "diced" and "sliced" to begin her description of CMOs.[47] I love those terms because that is exactly what happens to an MBS before it is repackaged and sold to investors as a CMO. But, before we look at the specifics, I want to

---

[47] *The Bond Book* 2nd ed. by Annette Thau (New York: McGraw Hill, 2001). P.187.

describe an investment to you so you can decide if it's something you should add to your portfolio.

The investment that I will describe is safe, secure, triple-A rated, and pays a higher interest rate than Treasuries and quality corporate bonds. "Wow," you may be thinking, "sounds pretty attractive, and almost like you're describing a GNMA. But, don't forget, Dan, the big disadvantage of a GNMA is the uncertainty about its average life, so you'll have to do better than that to get my attention." Well then, let me add that not only is this investment triple-A rated and high yielding, but it also will maintain its average life as originally stated under a wide range of interest-rate changes—an obvious advantage compared to the standard Ginnie Mae.

CMOs were originally created to fulfill the needs of investors concerned with the following issues: (1) safety, (2) high yield, (3) monthly income, and (4) a higher degree of maturity or average-life certainty. I'll begin my analysis with the simplest type of CMO: the sequential CMO.

Sequential CMOs

I like to describe a sequential CMO as a neatly sliced loaf of bread. This loaf of bread represents a gigantic mortgage pool that investors can purchase. What is unique about CMOs, as compared to a plain old GNMA, is that you, the investor, can decide in which slice you want to invest.

You could for example decide to invest in the fifth slice out of a total of twenty slices. In the investment world, the slices are referred to as **tranches** (French for "slice")—maybe because buying a certain tranche sounds more sophisticated than calling up your broker and telling him or her to buy the fifth slice. Each tranche, or slice, gets paid a monthly interest rate, but when the principal payments come into this investment, the payback of principal is not prorated to all of the bondholders, as is the case with a typical GNMA. With a sequential CMO, 100 percent of the principal that is being paid back is directed to all the owners of the first tranche. Once they are paid off, the owners of the second slice get paid off, and then the third and so on. The remaining slices are also redeemed *sequentially.* You, the investor, have a tighter payback schedule associated with your triple-A rated, high-yield investment than you'd have with a GNMA.

Because of the needs of different types of investors, the sequential CMO soon evolved into different "classes," each with its own set of characteristics, advantages, and disadvantages. Some benefit from increasing interest rates while others benefit when interest rates drop. If you want to make a detailed analysis of this sector of the market, you can review Dr. Frank J. Fabozzi's 1,373-page *The Handbook of Fixed Income Securities.*[48]

I do want to briefly mention, however, a few other types of CMOs.

PAC CMOs

PACs are the **planned amortization class** of CMOs. Essentially, these bonds offer a very stable principal payback schedule, even under a very wide range of interest-rate changes. Some PAC CMOs will maintain their original average life even if interest rates increase or decrease by one, two, or three percentage points.

If you choose to evaluate or invest in a PAC, you may come across the term **busted PAC.** Be wary about investing in a PAC that has been busted. This term describes a PAC that has started paying off principal (busting the original payback schedule) faster or slower than originally planned. If you decide to invest in a CMO (even a PAC), you'll want to understand what will happen to the average life of your bond under a variety of interest-rate-change environments.

---

[48] *The Handbook of Fixed Income Securities* 6th ed. by Frank J. Fabozzi.

Companion CMOs

Companion CMOs and PAC CMOs are attached at the hip: if one is created, you'll have the other. Now, while PAC bonds are very stable, companion bonds are the tranches that accept the volatility and uncertainty that allow PACs to exist. What that means is that if there is a significant change in the original principal payback schedule of a CMO, it is directed to the companion bonds, which can have a dramatic impact on the average life of those investments. If the payback schedule overwhelms the companions, then any further payment changes will start to impact the original payback schedules of the PAC CMOs, creating the potential for a busted PAC.

Although they are usually triple-A rated and their yields can be very attractive, before investing in companion CMOs, you should have a thorough understanding of what will happen to its average under a variety of interest-rate changes, since the average life of companion bonds can be extremely volatile.

TAC CMOs

TACs are **target-amortization-class** CMOs. The simplest way to describe them is to say that they are similar to PACs, but when issued they lack the same degree of principal payback stability. They are sometimes structured to be very stable if interest rates decrease, but not as stable if rates increase.

Z Bond CMOs

Think of Z bond CMOs as zero-coupon bonds. Generally, they don't provide investors with any cash flow and usually have long-term maturities. They are purchased at a deep discount and then mature at face value

Esoteric CMOs

Interest only (IOs), principal only (POs), floaters, and inverse floaters are not for the novice CMO investor. They are esoteric investment vehicles; if you are considering these alternatives, make sure that you do your homework and consult a professional.

BUILDING YOUR BOND PORTFOLIO

It's time to use your working familiarity with the bond market and some of the alternatives within this investment sector to begin formulating your bond portfolio strategy. Here is the process and some of the basic issues you will need to address: (1) where to buy your bonds, (2) how to evaluate the yield curve, (3) how much will your bond portfolio cost, and (4) what are your portfolio strategies.

Where to Buy Your Bonds

Investing in bonds can be very different from investing in stocks. When people think of stocks and where they are traded, the names New York Stock Exchange, American Stock Exchange, or NASDAQ come to mind. While some bonds do trade on the New York Stock Exchange, most bonds are traded very differently.

Most bonds are bought and sold in something called the **over-the-counter** market, which is made up of hundreds of dealers, such as securities firms and banks. These dealers buy and sell bonds for their clients either from an inventory they maintain or from other dealers. The bonds offered could be either newly issued bonds or bonds selling in the **secondary market**.

With hundreds of bond dealers in the country selling so many bonds, how do you decide which bonds and firms fit your investment needs?

I recommend beginning with a firm that has qualified to become a **primary dealer**. Primary dealers are institutions authorized to buy and sell U.S. government securities in direct dealings with the Federal Reserve Bank of New York in its execution of Fed open market operations. The number of primary dealers in the United States changes from time to time, but historically there have been about thirty institutions with the qualifications to meet government requirements for reputation, capacity, and adequate staff and facilities. Before you set up an account and start investing in individual bonds, ask whether the firm with which you are dealing is a primary dealer. If it isn't, it can still be of service, but you'll also want to ask the following kinds of questions in order to evaluate its offerings and expertise:

- Does it have a bond research department?
- What is the size of its inventory?
- What are the fees or markups for its offerings?
- Does it have institutional expertise or does it only handle individual retail accounts?

By the way, you should also ask these questions even if the firm is a primary dealer.

Yield Curve

Before you make any decisions about which maturities to invest in, evaluate the yield curve (see Charts 9-A and 9-B). The yield curve represents, in a graph, what the yields are for bonds of different maturities. It can help you decide whether you should be investing in short-term, intermediate-term, or long-term bonds.

Chart 9-A.

Sample Yield Curve.

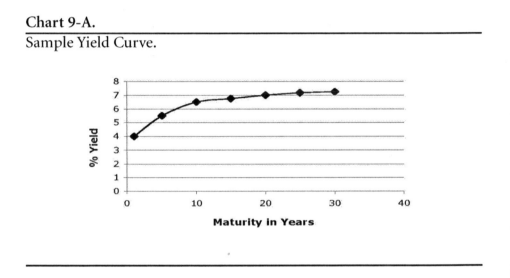

You can see in Chart 9-A that the longer the maturity, the higher the yield. However, the look and structure of a yield curve can change. When the yield curve is inverted, the yields of short-term bonds are paying more than longer-term bonds, as represented in Chart 9-B.

An inverted yield curve can occur for a number of reasons, but one of the most common is when inflation or the expectation of inflation is high. The most dramatic recent example of this was during the early 1980s, when short-term treasuries peaked at more than 16 percent, and long-term Treasuries paid more than 14 percent.

Chart 9-B.

Sample Inverted Yield Curve.

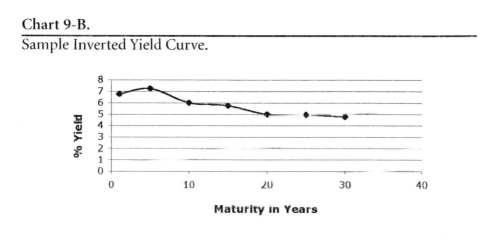

Maturity in Years

When I review a yield curve, I like to invest in what tennis players refer to as the "sweet spot"—the area where you get the most power with the least amount of effort. In the bond market, the sweet spot is where you get maximum yield and return with minimum additional risk.

If I'm going to invest farther out on the yield curve, in a longer-term maturity, I want to be compensated for the added interest-rate risk and bond volatility that comes with longer-term bonds. Here's an example of what I mean:

> *Example:* If a three-year bond is paying 5 percent and a six-year bond is paying 6 percent, I would view that as a pretty reasonable trade-off and give serious consideration to investing in the six-year, rather than the three-year, bond. For an additional three years of maturity, I will earn a rate of return that is 20 percent higher per year for the first three years. At the end of three years, my 5 percent-paying bond would have paid me a simple interest rate of return of 15

percent (5 percent x 3 years), whereas the six-year bond would have paid me a simple interest rate of 18 percent (6 percent x 3 years). At the end of three years, the first bond matures and I can reinvest it at the new current rate. If interest rates are the same or lower, obviously the original six-year bond at 6 percent was the superior choice.

Q: *If interest rates had increased in those three years, which bond would have been the better choice?*
A: *It depends, because it's hard to make up for the lost ground.*

Let me clarify my answer. When the original three-year bond paying 5 percent per year matures, you would have to invest in a new three-year bond paying 7 percent per year—a 40 percent increase—just to break even with the original six-year bond that paid 6 percent per year for the full six-year period. I have formatted this scenario in Table 9-2.

Table 9-2.

3-Year Bond at 5 percent versus 6-Year Bond at 6 percent.

Years	% 3-year bond	% 6-year bond
1	5	6
2	5	6
3	5	6
4	7*	6
5	7*	6
6	7*	6
Total Interest Earned	**36%**	**36%**

* The interest rate needed in years 4, 5, and 6, after the 3-year bond matures, to give a 6-year total simple interest rate of return of 36 percent.

After reviewing these numbers, you can see from Table 9-2 that investing in the six-year bond is the superior choice under a number of different circumstances. The exercise is one you will want to use when selecting bonds. Here is another example.

> *Example:* A five-year bond is paying 6 percent per year and a twelve-year bond is paying 6.25 percent per year. Is the added volatility and financial uncertainty during the next twelve years worth the extra 0.25 per year percent yield? Well, if you could predict interest rates, deciding which maturity to invest in would be easy. However, because no one can, the twelve-year bond might not be such a wise alternative since you won't be compensated for the risk. Again, if you could know that interest rates were going to decrease during the next several years, the longer-term bond would be the better choice. However, most bond experts have a hard time figuring out what's going to happen during the next twelve days, much less the next twelve years, so take a hard look at the yield curve when deciding on maturities for investment. Analyzing the yield curve doesn't guarantee success, but understanding it is one more way you can make yourself an informed bond investor.

Cost of Individual Bonds

Have you noticed much advertising for individual bonds in your newspaper or on TV and radio? The answer is probably no. There's a reason for that: individual bonds are very economical. Even if investors responded to the ads, opened investment accounts, and purchased the advertised bonds, it would be difficult for the firm advertising the bonds to cover its advertising costs.

Q: *What is the yearly cost to hold your bonds in an invest-*
   ment account?
A: *You shouldn't have to pay a yearly fee for most accounts.*
   It's different when you invest in bond funds, which have
   a yearly management fee.
Q: *Is there a cost to you when your bond matures?*
A: *Typically, when your bond matures or is called, there is*
   no cost.
Q: *Is there a cost when you buy an individual bond?*
A: *Yes. Buying bonds can be inexpensive, but certainly they*
   are not free. Individual bonds are usually traded on
   what is called a net basis. The fee for your investment is
   built into the price of the bond.

Example: Perhaps you invest $10,000 in a five-year bond
paying you a 6 percent coupon. You don't see a charge, but
rest assured it is there. The bond in this example has a 1
percent charge built into it (this built-in charge can vary
dramatically, depending on the type of bond and how
much is being invested). The five-year bond—if purchased
for free—would have cost you $9,900 instead of $10,000.
(The $100 built into the sale price of the bond is the com-
mission for buying the bond.) If the bond had been purchased for free (for $9,900), you still would have earned the
same coupon of 6 percent as someone who paid $10,000;
plus, you would have the bonus of an extra $100 at matu-
rity—the difference between the purchase price of $9,900
and the maturity value of $10,000.

Q: *Is there a charge for selling the bond before maturity?*
A: *Usually yes.*

When you sell bonds, you have to consider something called the **spread** (the difference between the selling and the buying price). Let us review the following example.

> *Example:* You buy a bond for $10,000. You live in a perfect world, so there's no change in interest rates or in the price of your bond. A couple of weeks later, you decide that you want to sell the bond. Your bond dealer quotes you a price of $9,900. You accept and sell. A few minutes later, your bond might be sold to another investor for say $10,000, not $9,900. This is the spread, and it can *vary widely*, depending on the bond's value, the type of bond, its maturity, market conditions, and with whom you are dealing.

As I've advised before, holding on to high-quality bonds can be both safe and economical, but trying to outguess the market and trading your bonds can be an expensive undertaking. If you decide to implement a buy-and-hold strategy, here are some strategies that can help you build your portfolio.

Bond Strategies

Bond Ladder

One of the simplest yet most powerful bond strategies is to implement a bond ladder. A simple example of a bond ladder in action is to divide your bond investments into ten different pieces. You invest each piece in a given year, say from years one to ten. The net result will be that you never have more than 10 percent of your bond account maturing in any one year. Having bonds coming due every year during a ten-year period will not only give your portfolio stability, but it can gradually increase the portfolio's average yield, even if there are no changes in interest rates. How is that possible? See Tables 9-3 and 9-4 for explanations of how that is possible.

Table 9-3.

Bond Ladder Initial Portfolio.

Maturity (in years)	Amount Invested (in $)	Yield (in %)
1	10,000	3.00
2	10,000	3.50
3	10,000	3.75
4	10,000	4.25
5	10,000	4.50
6	10,000	4.75
7	10,000	5.25
8	10,000	5.75
9	10,000	6.00
10	10,000	6.25
	Average yield	**4.70**

In Table 9-3, $10,000 is invested in each year of a one to ten-year ladder with an average bond-portfolio yield of 4.7 percent.

Each year when a $10,000 bond matures, the money is reinvested in a new ten-year bond. This maintains our ladder since the original ten-year bond is now a nine-year bond, and the original nine-year bond is now an eight-year bond and so on. What happens to our portfolio if there has been no change in interest rates and we have been reinvesting bonds for three years as they have matured?

Table 9-4.

Initial Portfolio Three Years Later.

Maturity (in years)	Amount Invested (in $)	Yield (in%)
1	10,000	4.25
2	10,000	4.50
3	10,000	4.75
4	10,000	5.25
5	10,000	5.75
6	10,000	6.00
7	10,000	6.25
8	10,000	6.25
9	10,000	6.25
10	10,000	6.25
	Average yield	**5.55**

By utilizing the strategy of a bond ladder, you can increase the average portfolio yield even if interest rates remain the same. In this example, the average yield increases from 4.7 percent to 5.55 percent. At this point, you might shrug their shoulders and say, "Big deal, the difference between 4.7 and 5.55 is only 0.85 percent." But, yes, it is a "big deal" because on closer inspection, you can see that the yield of the portfolio was increased by 18 percent (0.85 ÷ 4.7) and it was done in a remarkably simple way. A final advantage of this strategy is that generally, your average yield with a bond ladder will be higher than if you had put 100 percent of your money into short-term bonds. The bond ladder strategy is a simple yet powerful way to put together your bond portfolio.

Barbell Portfolio

If you've ever worked out with weights on a barbell, you know that there are weights on the left, weights on the right, and a bar in the middle. You are following a barbell strategy if you have bonds invested in short-term maturities for liquidity and stability, in long-term maturities for maximum yield and consistency of yield over time, and nothing in the middle (no intermediate-term bonds). This strategy isn't one of my favorites, but, under the correct market conditions, it can be worth investigating. For example, if interest rates increase after you have put together your bond portfolio, a barbell strategy would allow you to sell the short-term bonds in your portfolio with less principal risk than would occur from selling intermediate term bonds in a laddered portfolio. But, taking advantage of these types of market changes requires more aggressive management than the simpler laddered strategy.

Testing your Knowledge

You should now have a basic understanding of bond terminology and the rudiments of investing in individual bonds. Your assignment, if you decide to accept it, is to go into the marketplace and invest in the following three bonds priced at par (100):

1. A five-year U.S. government Treasury note.
2. A five-year triple-A rated non-callable corporate bond.
3. A five-year average life government guaranteed MBS such as a GNMA.

Don't trade the bonds. Instead, employ the buy-and-hold strategy, which I prefer. Which one of the three alternatives will quote you the highest yield? Place a checkmark next to your choice.

_____ Treasury bond
_____ Corporate bond
_____ MBS: for example GNMA

Over the last fifteen years I've given this assignment to hundreds, if not thousands of my students and clients. About 80 percent of the time they have placed their checkmarks alongside the triple-A rated corporate bond—which is a very logical answer. After all, GNMAs and Treasuries are backed by the full faith and credit of the U.S. government, a backing corporate bonds do not have. The default risk is greater with the corporate bonds and higher risk should ensure a higher yield. Surprisingly, the bond that usually quotes the highest-yield is not the corporate bond but the GNMA. Why? You already have the information at your fingertips.

Remember that U.S. Treasuries and corporate bonds have a specific maturity, whereas MBSs such as GNMAs have an *average life*. It's because of this average life uncertainty that GNMAs as well as other MBSs will initially quote a higher rate of return. Recall that the stated yield to average life of a GNMA is based on many variables and can change—sometimes dramatically. In an environment where interest rates drop for an extended period of time, such as what we have seen the last couple of years, it can have a profound impact on the portfolio's average life, and the total rate of return of your MBSs. Although the initial yields may be very attractive, MBSs should only be one part of a well-diversified portfolio that is consistent with your particular investment needs.

SUMMARY: Bonds can be a very important component of a diversified portfolio. Each alternative (U.S. Treasuries, corporate bonds, and mortgage-backed securities) offers the investor its own set of advantages and disadvantages. Before you can build a bond portfolio, you need to resolve and evaluate a number issues: (1) where are you going to buy your bonds,

(2) what their yield curve looks like, (3) the cost of your portfolio, and (4) the strategy you plan to employ. In the world of investing, there is no such thing as a something for nothing. If an investment is paying a higher rate of return, there must be a reason why. Your goal is to understand what that reason is and decide if it's consistent with your portfolio needs.

Chapter 10

Investing in Bond Mutual Funds

When an investment is advertised as being safe, high yielding, and backed by the U.S. government, there is a certain under-standing among investors as to the meaning of those claims. I've been earning a high monthly yield on a government bond mutual fund that I'm invested in, but I've noticed during the last couple of years that the price per share keeps dropping. Sometimes it's only a few cents per month, but it's definitely dropping. If the U.S. government backs it, how could it be going down in value?

Billions and billions of dollars are invested in bond funds, yet many of the investors that participate in these funds would be hard pressed to explain how bonds work or to accurately describe the advantages and disadvantages of owning them. When it comes to investing in and eval-uating bond funds, the first question many investors ask, unfortunately, is "How much is it paying?" without having the knowledge to accurately understand what the answer means and no understanding of how the yield is actually generated.

By the end of this chapter you will be better prepared to ask the right questions and to analyze the answers.

I'll discuss some of the key elements of bond funds and then review four categories of funds: (1) U.S. Treasury funds, (2) mortgage-backed funds (e.g. Ginnie Maes), (3) corporate bond funds, and (4) multi-Sector bond funds. Tax-free municipal bonds will be discussed in Chapter 13.

KEY ELEMENTS OF BOND FUNDS

Maturity of Bonds

I'd like you to consider whether at this moment in time, you have any interest in investing in a thirty-year bond or in a portfolio of thirty-year bonds. If your answer is "No way, are you nuts?" then you should reconsider investing in a bond fund that, as a matter of policy, invests in thirty-year bonds.

If you are thinking, "Well I can sell the bond mutual fund," I want to remind you that you can also sell your individual bonds. Or, if you are thinking, "Yeah, but individual bonds can drop in value," let me also remind you that if individual bonds drop in value because of increasing interest rates, bond mutual funds will drop too. They both move up and down in value inversely to interest rates.

The informed bond investor knows the maturity or the average life of the bonds in a fund's portfolio and the risks associated with those bonds. Do not be beguiled into believing that a bond fund has no risk and will protect your investment from a rising interest rate environment just because it is "backed" by the government.

Average Portfolio Price

Understanding whether a bond fund is investing in par, discount, or premium bonds allows you to evaluate the current yield as compared to the fund's yield to maturity or yield to average life. (See Chapters 8 and 9 for a review of these terms.) Here's an example of the importance of knowing the average portfolio price of a bond fund (it's an exaggerated example, but it makes the point). I touched on this concept in Chapter 9, but it is of such significance that an additional example is warranted.

> *Example:* If money market accounts are paying about 4 percent and 2 to 3 year CDs (certificates of deposit) at the bank are paying 4.5 percent, would you be interested in some investment alternatives. What if you noticed a two-year U.S. Treasury listed in your local newspaper that was paying 6 percent? You'd probably not only invest, but you'd brag about it to your friends.
>
> So you decide to call an investment firm and tell them that you'd like to invest $10,000 in the two-year U.S. Treasury paying 6 percent that you saw in the newspaper. But, when the confirmation arrives in the mail, you notice that something isn't quite right. Yes, it's a two-year Treasury, and, yes, it has a 6 percent "coupon," but the "price" of the bond is 103.30. It's a premium bond, and it has a yield to maturity of 4.25 percent. You go back to the newspaper listing and find that under closer inspection, that's exactly what was listed. You'd been so excited about the 6 percent coupon that you didn't read the listing carefully enough to understand the itemization of the bond's specifics.
>
> You call the investment firm and after a few choice words, you come to realize that you made an investment

decision without a complete understanding of the bond. The $10,000 bond will actually cost you $10,330 because it's a premium bond priced at 103.30. It will pay you $600 per year in interest (the coupon), but on maturity it will pay off at $10,000, not $10,300. And your yield to maturity is going to be 4.25 percent, which might be a perfectly reasonable rate of return, but nothing close to the 6 percent you thought you'd be earning. (See Chapter 8 for a review of yield to maturity).

I hope this will never happen to you, and that you will take the point of the story away with you: when you invest in an individual bond, you have the opportunity to see all the numbers—not just the coupon rate, but also the price of the bond and the yield to maturity. When you invest in a bond fund, you don't receive this kind of information on your confirmation. If a bond fund is quoting a high current yield, it can achieve that yield in a variety of ways, one alternative being to load up on premium bonds. Premium bonds (as I showed in the preceding example) will give you lots of cash flow, but if they are held to maturity, they will pay off at par (100). If lots of high coupon premium bonds are purchased in a fund and held to maturity for par (100), then you will probably see principal erosion in the fund.

This is an important concept and in some bond funds a major concern. However, I want to be very clear that just because a fund manager is buying premium bonds it does not mean he or she is a poor manager. There are many instances when premium bonds in a mutual fund may indeed be the most appropriate strategy. The key is not to fall into the trap of investing in a bond fund just because it quotes you a high current yield. Know the average price of the bond fund portfolio: is it priced at par, at a discount, or at a premium? Then weigh the information before deciding if the fund is right for you. Here is a review of some additional advantages and disadvantages of investing in bond funds:

Advantages

1. *Management.* Most bond funds are actively managed (an exception would be the typical bond index fund), so that just as with a stock fund, having a good bond fund manager looking out for your interest can be comforting and financially rewarding.
2. *Income.* Most bond funds pay interest every month. Contrast that with many types of individual bonds, which pay interest only every six months.
3. *Dividend reinvestment.* It's easy to reinvest the dividends from a bond fund. Reinvesting the dividends from alternatives such as individual bonds can be a little cumbersome.
4. *Ease of moving money.* When you decide to make changes in your portfolio, you have the option of moving your assets from one fund to another within mutual fund families at little or no charge.

Disadvantages

1. *Management.* Although many bond funds are actively managed, there is no guarantee that the bond manager will be a good manager. Over the years, some bond funds have employed a variety of techniques to quote high yields, including investing heavily in premium bonds, leveraging the fund, or adding options to the portfolio without producing a high total return. If your bond fund manager participates in strategies like these, be sure you know about it before you invest.
2. *Fees.* With a bond fund, year after year you will pay a management fee. Be sure you know exactly what you will be getting for these charges, against just buying and holding individual bonds.

3. *Interest rate risk.* Bonds have interest-rate risk because their prices go up and down inversely to changes in interest rates. An additional concern with bond funds is that unlike individual bonds, a fund doesn't have a maturity date.

4. *Principal erosion.* Principal erosion occurs when a fund's NAV (net asset value) drops over time, and this can occur even if interest rates remain stable. I would also like to stress that while this it is not a problem with all bond funds, it's an important issue bond fund investors need to consider.

> Q: *If you invest in a government bond fund that has a high yield, is triple-A rated, and there is no change in interest rates, how can there be principal erosion?*
>
> A: *There can be a variety of reasons for principal erosion. But, loading up on premium bonds is one of the most common reasons for this problem. (See the section "Average Portfolio Price" for one of the reasons principal erosion can appear in a bond fund.)*

TYPES OF BOND FUNDS

U.S. Treasury Funds

For anyone not well acquainted with the workings of the bond market, it can be comforting to invest in a 100 percent U.S. Treasury fund, often called a government fund. Having said that, it is important to understand that Treasury funds can call themselves government funds, but funds that are advertised as government funds aren't necessarily made up of only Treasuries. Therefore, before investing in a "government" fund, review the prospectus and confirm that you are investing in the correct type of fund.

Here are some of the advantages of investing in Treasury funds: (1) they are liquid (can be bought and sold daily), (2) they pay a monthly dividend, (3) the U.S. government backs the underlying securities, and (4) they are available as short-, intermediate-, or long-term maturity funds.

In light of these advantages, it's easy to think that nothing could be wrong with this type of investment, not so. If you are planning on investing in this sector of the bond fund market, I advise you to "look before your leap." Here are some of the first questions you need to ask:

Q: *Sample question: "How much does your fund pay compared to buying the individual Treasuries outright?"*

A: *Sample answer: "Our fund is paying 6.5 percent, compared to individual Treasuries that are paying 6 percent."*

Q: *Follow-up question: "How does your Treasury fund manage to pay more than what individual bonds are paying, especially considering that your fund has a yearly management fee and the individual bonds don't?"*

No matter what the response, there is a good possibility that it won't actually answer your question. I want to be very clear about the above exchange: no one creates money out of thin air. If a bond fund is paying more than the yield you could earn by purchasing the same bonds individually, you have to investigate the reasons for the discrepancy. It's not because mutual fund managers are really nice people and want to give you free money, and it's not some aberration in the market that no one other than you knows about. The section on key elements of bond funds reviewed some of the issues you need to understand, which should compel you to "look before you leap."

Mortgage-Backed Security (MBS) Funds

Investing in an MBS fund such as a GNMA fund has the same appeal to investors as investing in a U. S. Treasury fund: safety and liquidity, with the added benefit of paying a yield that is typically higher than a Treasury fund. If you decide to invest in this category of mutual funds, you'll need to ask the same questions you would ask before investing in a Treasury fund.

While the yields from MBS funds can be attractive, there are some distinct disadvantages associated with MBS funds, which are based on the characteristics of the underlying securities found in these types of investments. It's possible to invest in an MBS fund that has downside risks and not much upside potential to its price per share. For example, if interest rates increase, bond prices will drop, as will the value per share of your GNMA fund. Conversely, if interest rates go down, the value of bonds will increase as could the price per share of your GNMA fund, but perhaps not as much as anticipated. Recall from the discussion on individual bonds that as interest rates and mortgage rates drop, many homeowners have a tendency to refinance their mortgages or to sell their homes and move into a different house. When individuals pay off their mortgages (from refinancing or selling), the loans are paid off at face value, not at a premium. These types of financial maneuvering by homeowners can prevent much of an increase in the price per share of some GNMA funds, since the funds often own the very mortgages that are being paid off.

My point, once again, is that it is very difficult to evaluate a bond fund unless you understand how individual bonds work. For a refresher on individual bonds, see Chapters 8 & 9.

> *Q: Is it possible for a GNMA fund manager to avoid the
> downside risks that I have just described?*
>
> *A: That is the goal of the fund manager who invests for
> total return rather than only for high monthly yield.*

If managed for total return, a fund manager could buy discount
bonds (e.g. at 95 cents on the dollar) before interest rates drop and then
watch the portfolio's GNMAs get paid back at 100 cents on the dollar—
on an accelerated basis. The strategy would give a superior total return
to a fund being managed only for high current yield with premium
bonds. The disadvantage of this strategy is that a fund made up of discount bonds will not pay as much in monthly cash flow, and the current
yield advertised would be lower.

For these reasons, before you invest in an MBS fund such as a Ginnie
Mae fund, confirm whether the fund is managed for total return or just
for high monthly cash flow.

Corporate Bond Funds

The #1 question to ask when investing in a corporate bond fund is
"What is the rating [quality] of the bonds in the portfolio?" If the fund
is paying a very high yield but is doing it with junk bonds (low-rated
bonds), my suggestion is to run for the hills. Stay away from such
investments unless you are convinced by the reason for taking the risk.
In addition to rating, you should also—just as with the other funds—
know what the maturity and the average portfolio price of the bonds
are in the portfolio. (See Chapter 6 for a discussion of bond ratings.)

Multi-Sector Bond Funds

The goal of most multi-sector funds managed for total return is to take
advantage of changes and aberrations in the market. For example, now
might be a good time to sell all long-term bonds and put the money

into short- to intermediate-term bonds. In another example, the bond manager might believe that there is no more appreciation available in U.S. Treasuries, but that value can still be found in corporate bonds or GNMAs. These types of funds often don't advertise a "high yield" to attract investors and, as a result, can be overlooked as an attractive investment alternative.

SUMMARY: While bonds should be part of a diversified portfolio, selecting the right bond fund can require at least as much effort as selecting the right stock fund. There are many good bond funds from which to choose, so be sure that the one in which you invest is consistent with your needs. Remember, the answer to the question "How much is it paying?" won't tell you whether it's a good or bad bond fund and therefore, shouldn't guide your investment decisions.

Chapter 11

Investing in Individual Stocks

*I have purchased individual stocks based on recommenda-
tions given from investment programs on television, research
from a major investment firm, the Internet, and countless
newsletters. I've purchased twenty different stocks and all
twenty of them have gone down in value. Maybe I'm confused, but I thought the point of buying stocks was to make
money, not lose money. What am I doing wrong?*

No part of the investment world gets more attention than the stock
market. When people ask "What happened to the market today?" they
are almost universally referring to the stock market—not the bond
market, not the commodity market, but the stock market. With the
attention that it receives, it's no wonder that most media sources are
constantly on the lookout for a "hot story" that will grab the attention
of the investing public. Market stories are often either about scams
being heaped on an unsuspecting public or inspiring investment stories
that touch our hearts. You know the kind: David versus Goliath, the little guy prevailing against insurmountable odds. Among such tales,

there is none more instructive than that of the rise and fall of the Beardstown Business and Professional Women's Investment Club.

The ladies of the Beardstown Business and Professional Women's Investment Club—with whom the media fell in love—were not your usual savvy investment gurus. In fact, enjoying an average age of 70, the members defied the traditional stereotype of the successful investor. The Beardstown ladies boasted an average investment return of more than 23.4 percent per year from 1984 to 1993.

The media scrambled to feature club members in their publications and on TV so the women could share their wisdom on investing. They became the darlings of the investment world. However, the love affair soured when the media picked up on a Price Waterhouse study that demonstrated that their returns were in fact only a little more than 9 percent per year. That's right, a little more than 9 percent per year. Some revised calculations suggest that their actual returns were actually more than 9 percent but still significantly lower than originally touted. The discrepancy stemmed from the Beardstown ladies' errors in calculating returns.

Not only did the ladies not analyze their returns correctly, but they also did not include their annual dues of $4,800 in their calculations. The investing public met this discovery with predictable disappointment. After watching and listening to the Beardstown ladies, it was easy to think that anyone, with just a little effort, could invest on their own. The Beardstown story and others confirm what savvy stock investors have always known: making money in the equity markets requires time, effort, and an appreciation of the risks and rewards involved.

To keep you from assembling a stock portfolio based on pop culture and media-induced trends, here is a sampling of some of the dual principles to consider:

- Invest only in growth stocks.
- Invest only in value stocks.

- Invest only in large companies.
- Invest only in small companies.

- Earnings don't matter, it's market share that counts.
- Earnings matter, market share doesn't count.

- Dividends do matter.
- Dividends don't matter.

- Fundamental analysis is the best.
- Technical analysis is the best.

"Wait a minute," you might be thinking, "the above principles come in pairs and contradict each other. What's going on?" What's going on is that each of these principles is correct. Each one of the above strategies has been the best way to invest *at some point in time*, sometimes for several years and other times for only a few months or weeks.

What is the moral of this story? While there are many long-term winning stock strategies, do not make the mistake of buying into the investment hype of the moment and bouncing around from one investment fad to another. With that said, you also do not want to stick stubbornly to a single investment strategy. Growth investors had very good investment returns during the late 1990s, but when growth projections failed to materialize and growth stocks fell out of favor, a new mantra quickly replaced growth: value investing. It will be interesting to see how long it takes before this strategy is replaced by the latest, greatest, winning way to invest.

Because predicting the future is not one of the strengths of mere mortals (including this author), in this book I won't be predicting the stock market or giving you next year's winning sector. However, I will review some of the key elements of stock market investing that you should understand before you attempt to build a stock portfolio.

STOCK INVESTOR GUIDELINES

One of the commandments for being a successful equity investor is "know thy self." You can save a lot of time, effort, grief, and perhaps money if you come to grips with the answer to the question: "Are you an investor or are you a speculator?" While some investors have never given the question much thought, others believe that they thoroughly know their profile, even though their behavior contradicts it.

> Q: *What is an investor?*
> A: *An investor is someone who buys businesses and invests in them for the long haul—not necessarily forever, but without riding the "buy-and-sell" roller coaster every time he or she hears good or bad news about the market.*

Perhaps, you are thinking about buying a small business in your community, perhaps a dry-cleaning business. If you were a savvy investor, you would certainly first conduct a thorough analysis of the business. No doubt you would evaluate its assets, liabilities, earnings, cash flow, market share, price, competition, and amount of business over time. Only then would you reach a conclusion about whether it would be a good business to own—that indeed, it was a good business last week, it is a good business today, and it will be a good business next week and beyond. While a thorough analysis won't guarantee success, you can appreciate that it's the path successful businessmen take.

Once you become a business owner, you'd probably agree that it would be silly to try to buy and sell your new business on a weekly or monthly basis. Well, this is exactly what many investors do with their stock holdings. If there is good news and stocks are increasing, they decide that now is the time to invest in stocks. If there is bad news and stocks have dropped, they decide that now is the time to sell. This ongoing buy-and-sell strategy, based on good and bad news rather than on investing in stocks as a "business owner," is a recipe for financial disaster.

To most investors, the previous example is pretty straightforward, involving nothing more than common sense. But, before we move on, there's a second example of a business opportunity I'd like you to analyze as a potential investor.

A businessman—I'll call him Neal—is about to start a business, and he is going to let you in on the ground floor. That's right, you'll give Neal some money to buy into his project and you'll reap the rewards of its success.

> You: *What's this new business of yours, Neal?*
> Neal: *I'm going to open donut shops across America; in a very short time I'll be known as "The Donut King."*

> You: *Aren't there already lots of donut shops in the U.S.? What's going to make your shops so special?*
> Neal: *I am going to do something bold and innovative. It's actually pure genius. As a matter of policy, I'm going to give away donuts and coffee to all my customers 24/7. Is that a great idea or what? I'm convinced that as word of my free donuts and coffee spreads, people will line up for miles to get the free goodies.*

> You: *But Neal, one minor detail: how are you going to make any money? How are <u>we</u> going to make any money?*

Neal: *Well, initially, making a profit won't matter. You see, what counts is <u>market share</u>. Once I've proved that there are thousands of people entering my shops (lots of eye balls, to use an Internet buzzword), I plan to invite the biggest advertisers in the country to advertise on the walls of my donut shops. And not just on the walls, but on the napkins and the coffee cups. There's really no limit to the amount of revenue I'll be able to generate. It's so simple it's brilliant!*

Okay, so I'm pulling your leg. This is a crazy investment and no, you wouldn't invest any money in the venture. Yet that's exactly what many people did during the 1990s during the "dot.com bubble." They invested in companies that offered no possibility of profits. Many companies were only concerned with giving things away as quickly as possible to gain market share.

Be an investor, not a speculator, and add a little common sense to the mix.

Time in the Market, Not Market Timing

Another useful guideline—if you're going to be a successful stock investor—is to accept the folly of trying to time the market. If you find yourself wondering, "Shouldn't I be making some changes in my account?" or if you're thinking, "The market is dropping, shouldn't I be doing something?" I urge you to take a deep breath; then repeat three times, "I am a long-term investor, a business owner, not a market timer." If you need additional proof of the folly of market timing see Table 11-1.

Table 11-1.

Timing the Market Can Be Costly.

Period of Investment*	Average Annual Total Return (in %)	Value of $10,000 (in $)
Fully invested	3.65	11,965
Miss the 10 best days	-4.92	7,771
Miss the 20 best days	-11.01	5,582
Miss the 30 best days	-15.73	4,249
Miss the 40 best days	-19.77	3,324
Miss the 60 best days	-26.60	2,131

Source: FactSet Research Systems. Calculations provided by AIM Funds.
* S & P 500 Index, 5 years ending 6/30/02

From Table 11-1, you can see that an individual who was fully invested for five years had a positive rate of return. At the same time, being out of the market for the ten best days—during a five-year period—gave an investor a negative return. I know that the numbers are hard to believe, but they dramatically illustrate that time in the market, not timing the market, is a guideline successful investors should heed.

Keep It Simple

Over the years, I have observed that one of the tenets of successful stock market investing is to *keep it simple*. If you have ever watched the *Star Trek* television series and films, you may recall that the characters on the starship *Enterprise* like to use whiz-bang expressions like *sub-warp speed* and *gold-press latinum*. Well, they terms sure sound important, but they don't actually mean anything when they are sprinkled into the conversation. Don't be influenced by snazzy or esoteric buzzwords about stocks. If something sounds ultra-sophisticated and oh so complex, avoid it—or at the very least, do a thorough analysis of it before you decide to invest.

CATEGORIES OF STOCKS

Individual stocks can be categorized in a number of different ways. It is the category or type of stock you invest in that will often determine your overall returns and risk profile, not your specific stock picks. If you are striving for diversity, here are some of the different ways in which you can diversify your stock portfolio.

Market Capitalization

Capitalization or company size refers to a company's market value. It is an important factor in assessing the kinds of companies or categories of companies in which to invest. Many financial analysts believe that you simply cannot have a diversified portfolio without exposure to different size companies.

To figure out a stock's market "cap," take the number of shares outstanding and multiply it by the price per share.

> *Example:* If the price per share of a company is $60 and there are ten million shares outstanding, you have a market capitalization of $600 million.

The three most commonly used terms to describe the market capitalization of stocks are large cap, mid cap, and small cap.

Large-Cap Stocks

Depending on market conditions, the dollar value that constitutes a large-cap stock can vary. Currently, a company would need a market value of about $10 billion to join this elite club (some sources say it is $5 billion). Some examples include companies such as Coca Cola Company and Microsoft Corporation.

Mid-Cap Stocks

Mid-cap companies will have a market value of approximately $2 billion to $10 billion. Some examples include companies such as Barnes & Noble Inc., Coach Inc., and Dreyer's Grand Ice Cream Inc.

Small-Cap Stocks

Small-cap companies will have a market cap of approximately $500 million to $2 billion. Some examples include American Italian Pasta Company and Ann Taylor Stores. (Companies with a market cap of less than $500 million bring you into the area of micro-cap stocks, which I'd be inclined to avoid.)

Which category has had the best returns?

Which category of stocks has brought the best return is, surprisingly, not an easy question to answer. Measuring and comparing the returns of different sectors of the market can be a tricky challenge. Let me explain the dilemma.

When you invest in a stock, it's usually because you want your investment to increase in value. So, let us say that in January 2002, you invest a few thousand dollars in a stock with a market cap of $8 billion, which is a mid-cap stock. By June of that same year, the market cap of the company increases to $12 billion. Hmmm, now it's officially a large-cap stock. This same stock then proceeds to drop in value and ends the year at a market cap of $10 billion. Does that mean that your mid-cap stock was up 25 percent for the year ($8 billion in January to $10 billion at year's end), or does it mean that somebody who bought the same stock in June purchased a large-cap stock that was down almost 17 percent ($12 billion market cap to $10 billion market cap) in value for the year? Before accepting as gospel the returns of large-, mid-, and small-cap investing, be sure of the source and its credibility. Having said that, let us review Table 11-2, which shows the returns of various market sectors over time.

Table 11-2.

Sector Returns: Periods Ending July 31, 2002.

	Annualized 1 Year	Annualized 5 Year	Annualized 10 Year
Large-Cap Growth	-28.75%	-3.06%	7.83%
Large-Cap Value	-17.24	2.96	11.49
Mid-Cap Growth	-28.68	-1.62	7.96
Mid-Cap Value	-7.69	5.34	12.28
Small-Cap Growth	-30.61	-6.14	4.15
Small-Cap Value	-5.51	5.36	12.57

Large-Cap Growth is represented by the Russell 1000® Growth Index
Large-Cap Value is represented by the Russell 1000® Value Index
Mid-Cap Growth is represented by the Russell Mid-cap® Growth Index
Mid-Cap Value is represented by the Russell Mid-Cap® Value Index
Small-Cap Growth is represented by the Russell 2000® Growth Index
Small-Cap Value is represented by the Russell 2000® Value Index

Source: Russell/Mellon Analytical Services

As you can see from Table 11-2, the "best" sector depends on what time frame you are evaluating. Although the long-term returns have been good for small- and mid-cap value stocks, I must admit that I'm more comfortable (when investing in individual stocks) overweighting investments in large-cap companies. That doesn't mean you should avoid individual mid-cap and small-cap stocks. It simply means you should exercise extra caution when investing in smaller companies.

One way to do this is to invest in individual large-cap stocks, leaving the mid-cap and small-cap investments to the pros such as mutual fund mangers and money managers. It is all a matter of personal taste and risk tolerance.

Types of Stocks

A number of terms are commonly used to describe different types of stocks: (1) blue chip, (2) growth, (3) value, (4) income, (5) cyclical, and (6) defensive. Their definitions will vary from investment firm to investment firm and can change over time. What is today's value stock could become tomorrow's growth stock.

Blue Chip Stocks

Blue chip represents stable earnings and solid growth of earnings and/or dividends to investors. While there is some comfort in investing in blue-chip stocks, I cannot stress enough that putting your money into blue chip stocks does not guarantee investment success. Some examples would include companies such as Colgate-Palmolive Company and General Electric.

Growth Stocks

When the market views a company as producing growth and revenue increases that are faster than the market as a whole, the company is said to be a growth stock. During the late 1990s, many premier technology companies were viewed not only as growth but also as blue chip. A classic example of a blue chip growth stock would be Microsoft.

Value Stocks

Are you the kind of person who prefers to buy Porsche's (Porsche Group) newest sports car when it hits the auto show rooms, or would you prefer a used Volvo when it is one or two years old and perhaps 40 percent less expensive than a new model? If you prefer the second strategy, then you may have the qualifications to be a value investor. As an investor in value stocks, you will encounter the terms *low price to earning ratio, high book value, undervalued,* and *intrinsic value.* More analysis is done on the underlying business of value companies than on the year-by-year growth of the stock market as a whole.

Income Stocks

Many years ago, a clear distinction existed between dividend-paying stocks and non-dividend-paying stocks. Companies that paid a high dividend not only gave investors cash flow, but also were considered to be "safe." Some examples of this were oil, phone, and utility stocks. At the same time, non-dividend-paying stocks gave no income, but offered the opportunity for capital appreciation and were viewed as being more aggressive.

Over the years, these distinctions between dividend and non-dividend stocks have blurred. Many "safe" blue-chip companies believe that today's investors are seeking total return over dividends as a top priority. The assumption is that long-term value can be enhanced when management retains earnings and reinvests in the company for future growth and capital appreciation. Dividends, it is important to note, are normally taxed as ordinary income whereas stock appreciation is tax deferred until the stock is sold.

Cyclical Stocks

Like the weather and the seasons, you can count on certain types of stocks to experience cyclical changes. An example of a cyclical industry is the auto industry. When the economy is expanding and jobs are secure, people feel that they can do some serious spending (such as on an automobile). When the economy slows, and discretionary spending decreases, that shiny new car suddenly doesn't seem so necessary.

Defensive Stocks

No matter how bad it gets, people still need to eat and still need to take their medication; so goes the thinking about investing in defensive stocks. Of course, such stocks don't guarantee investment success. Albertson's Inc., a large national grocery store, is a defensive stock, yet its share price has languished because of razor-thin profit margins and competition from the likes of Costco Wholesale Corp., Wal-Mart Stores Inc., and others.

Since you now understand some of the ways that stocks can be categorized, I will now move on to some sample portfolio strategies.

PORTFOLIO STRATEGY

While there are a number of equity strategies that will allow you to assemble a diversified portfolio, in this section, I will concentrate on something called **sector investing.** It is a simple yet powerful way to invest in the stock market. The strategy will not only bring you diversification, it will also impose upon you the important concept of *investment discipline*. The concept helps to resolve the question, "When should I buy and when should I sell?"[49]

---

[49] Unfortunately, no definitive guidelines exist for what constitutes a given sector, and, depending on where you get your investment information, you may discover that your sources offer conflicting definitions.

Here is an example of how this strategy works. This example refers to 10 different sectors and each sector will represent 10 percent of the portfolio. The following list does not constitute specific sector recommendations, but rather is prepared to introduce you to this concept and style of investing.

- Consumer Cyclical
- Consumer Staples
- Energy
- Financial
- Health care
- Industrials
- Technology
- Basic materials
- Telecommunication
- Utilities

An additional strategy to employ in sector investing is the concept of buying your stocks in "baskets." This is how it works: if you decide to invest in the Pharmaceutical industry, pick two, three, or four pharmaceutical stocks, rather than trying to pick the single best stock. Buying stocks in baskets will give your portfolio additional diversification and allow you to share in the growth of a given industry rather than trying to figure out which individual companies are going to be the big winners.

When you're ready to choose stocks for your portfolio, there are numerous surveys, reports, and companies that can assist you with your research. Value Line, Standard and Poor's, as well as investment and brokerage firms, come to mind.

Q: *After you make the initial investments, how often should you make sector changes in your portfolio?*

A: *Perhaps every three to six months. However, some long-term investors believe that a serious evaluation is necessary only on a yearly basis.*

Q: *How much does a given sector need to change before you alter your portfolio?*

A: *That will depend on whether you utilize what I call the "fixed mix" approach or a variation of it, the "fixed mix plus."*

Fixed Mix

The fixed mix sample portfolio that I will discuss has many similarities to the Dogs of The Dow strategy I reviewed in Chapter 7. One key similarity is that you will evaluate and make changes in your portfolio only *once a year*. (You can certainly vary the timing and the number of changes to your account, but we'll stick to an annual re-evaluation in this example to keep things simple.)

You opened your portfolio with each sector representing 10 percent of the overall portfolio. At the end of the year, if one or more sectors have done well and appreciated more than the others (for example technology now represents more than 10 percent of the account), you peel off that portion, and reallocate it to other sectors. With this strategy you will begin each year with a fresh "fixed mix" of 10 percent in each sector.

Does this strategy guarantee results? Of course it doesn't, but it is a simple way to manage a portfolio and it forces you to capture some of your gains every year and reinvest the proceeds in depressed (hopefully undervalued) sectors of the market.

If you're not comfortable picking sectors and then deciding on the stocks for each sector, you can use the same strategy with the thirty stocks in the Dow Jones Industrial Average, which represents some of the largest and best-known companies in the country. In the example we use here, each stock would have a fixed mix of 3.33 percent. In Table 11-3, I have listed the thirty companies that make up the Dow Jones Industrial Average. I will admit that it would be a tad cumbersome to manage an account this way, but it could be done. If you are looking for something simpler, you could invest in various sectors of the market with ETFs. (See Chapter 7 for a review of ETFs.)

Table 11-3.

The Dow Thirty.

Alcoa	Exxon Mobil	J.P. Morgan
American Express	General Electric	McDonald's
AT & T	General Motors	Merck
Boeing	Hewlett-Packard	Microsoft
Caterpillar	Home Depot	3M
Citigroup	Honeywell	Philip Morris
Coca-Cola	IBM	Procter & Gamble
Disney	Intel	SBC Communications
DuPont	International Paper	United Technologies
Eastman Kodak	Johnson & Johnson	Wal-Mart

Fixed Mix "Plus"

Some of the concerns investors have with the plain old vanilla fixed-mix strategy are the same as the ones they have with the Dogs of The Dow unit trust strategy. There is no analysis regarding overweighting or underweighting certain sectors of the stock market. Furthermore, when you begin every year with a specific fixed mix, you might be forced every twelve months to make tiny changes in your portfolio, which can be cumbersome and expensive. Plus, you run the risk of selling off potentially big winners just because they've gone up a few percentage points more than companies in other parts of your portfolio. To address this concern, I'll discuss a variation of fixed mix called fixed-mix "plus." Here are the particulars of this sample:

1. You start with ten sectors, each sector representing 10 percent of your account (just as you do with the vanilla version of fixed mix).

2. Once a year you make management changes (just as you do with the vanilla fixed mix).

3. Here is where the key difference begins: The yearly management is handled differently than the plain vanilla fixed mix portfolio. On a yearly basis, you have the flexibility to either overweight or underweight the portfolio, rather than starting each successive year with an even 10 percent in each of the ten sectors.

4. If you implement this strategy, it is important to set guidelines on the maximum amount of exposure you will accept in any given sector (for example 15 percent). If a given sector is worth more than 15 percent of the total portfolio, you sell off that portion above the 15 percent threshold and add the proceeds to the underrepresented sectors (for example, if technology is now 17 percent, sell off 2 percent; if energy is now 8 percent, add the 2 percent to get it back to 10 percent).

5. You should also consider having guidelines on the minimum amount of exposure you will accept in any given sector (for example 5 percent). If a sector is worth less than 5 percent of the portfolio, you sell off the highest value sectors and add the proceeds to the sectors that are less than 5 percent (for example, if energy is now 3 percent and technology is your largest position with 15 percent, sell off 2 percent of technology and add it to energy).

This strategy is not an exact science, nor does it guarantee results, but you'll find that fixed-mix plus shares many of the advantages of plain old vanilla fixed-mix. And it offers the flexibility of either overweighting or underweighting certain sectors of the market yearly. You can determine which sectors you want to either overweight or underweight by following the guidelines of an advisory service, an investment firm, or by building a portfolio that mirrors the sector breakdown of the S&P 500.[50] "Me."

If you implement such a strategy, setting portfolio guidelines will keep you from making emotional decisions or getting carried away with an analyst's "can't miss" recommendations. Remember, the ceiling that will cap out a given sector might be 15 percent, while the floor you will not allow a sector to fall below might be 5 percent.

> **Q:** *What is your thinking about starting a portfolio that is overweighted and underweighted in various sectors rather than starting with a fixed mix?*
>
> **A:** *There is nothing wrong with that strategy. It does, however, require some additional analysis and research.*

Sector investing is a powerful yet simple way to manage an individual stock portfolio. Your personal risk tolerance, investment costs, market outlook, and taxes when applicable will determine which strategy makes the most sense for you.

---

[50] For a current sector breakdown of the S&P 500 Index, you can visit their web site at www.spglobal.com/indexmain500_data.html.

COSTS

There are hundreds, if not thousands, of companies that will trade stocks for you. Each offers its own pricing schedule and of course advertises to investors why it's the best. Regardless of which investment company you choose, the costs to buy and sell individual stocks can essentially be broken down into two major categories: charge per transaction and wrap account.

Charge per Transaction

With a charge-per-transaction account you pay as you go. If you buy a stock today, you will pay a commission. If you sell a stock next week, you will pay a commission. If you never sell any of your stocks, you will not pay any commissions although some firms are now charging a yearly account fee for what they deem an "inactive" account.

If you decide to implement this type of investment account, you'll have some basic decisions to make, beginning with whether to place your trades with a discount or a full-service investment firm.

Discount Firm

The commission costs on stock trades typically will be less expensive at discount investment firms than at full-service investment firms. Unfortunately, the commission cost alone will not give you the total cost of your transaction. You must also be aware of your execution costs. What are execution costs? Execution costs are determined by how and when the executing firm transacts your trade. How long does it take them to execute a trade and are pricing opportunities missed? Is the brokerage firm searching all possible places to get the best execution or is it simply dumping your order with another firm for execution. Execution costs are rarely discussed or advertised even though they can be a significant part of your total transaction costs.

If you have successfully been doing research by yourself, then making decisions and getting good executions, and you are happy with the results, then yes, you can save money by trading stocks at a discount firm. But, even though individual commission trades may be inexpensive, overtrading an account (that is, buying and selling regularly) can become very expensive, regardless of where you place your trades.

Full-Service Firms:

Are there any reasons to deal with a full-service firm? The answer is very simple: it depends. Let me illustrate what I mean with the following two full-service alternatives. In the first example, you will be dealing with a full-service advisor named Richard and in the second example your full-service advisor will be Fred. You meet with each of these individuals and come away with the following information.

> *Example 1:* Richard is very clear that with him, (1) your investment costs will be significantly more expensive than with a discount firm, (2) his service will be lousy, (3) his investment ideas are terrible, and (4) he will not have your best interests in mind when he gives you his investment recommendations.

Now, given the choice of investing with a discount firm or of investing with good old Richard, whom will you pick? The answer is clear: the discount firm. In defense of Richard, it must be said that at least he was honest about what to expect. Now, let us review your meeting with Fred.

> *Example 2:* Fred also is very honest about what you can receive when dealing with him. He will (1) match or beat any trading charges advertised by discount brokers, (2) deliver outstanding service (according to his clients), (3) have great

investment ideas that will flat out make you money, and last but not least, (4) always have your best interests in mind when making investment recommendations.

So are you going to deal with the discount firm or with Fred? Once again, the answer is clear: you'll want to deal with Fred because you can't say no to maximum service, insightful advice, and the cheapest price in town.

After you've done your analysis and compared the different investment firms that might handle your account, it comes down to this:

- What are your investment portfolio needs?
- Who or what, will best meet those portfolio needs?
- What are you willing to pay to have your needs met?

Different investors have different needs. You could line up a hundred people, ask them about their portfolio needs, and get hundreds of different answers. Smart investors know what their financial needs are and evaluate whom or what will best satisfy those needs and at what price. Examples of portfolio needs might include, but not be limited to the following issues:

- Advice or no advice
- Research or no research
- Service or no service
- Financial planning or no financial planning
- Asset-allocation models or no such analysis
- Access to a full range of investment alternatives, or will a limited range be adequate for your needs

Wrap Account

An alternative to the charge-per-transaction account is a relatively new choice called a wrap account. It has always been a concern of the investing public that an inherent conflict of interest exists when the buying and selling of securities in an investor's account is paying someone's salary. After all, the more you buy and sell, the more that someone gets paid.

To address those concerns and to move themselves to a more service-oriented business model, many full-service investment firms now offer wrap accounts. Certain restrictions can apply, and the structure of these accounts can vary by firm, but wrap accounts basically work as follows. You pay no commission to buy and no commission to sell any of your securities. For example, you could buy twenty different stocks today and not pay a commission on the transactions. You could then decide to sell ten of those stocks next week and reinvest the money in ten other stocks, and once again there would be no commissions to buy or sell.

No cost to buy and no cost to sell, how do the firms make any money? Investment firms allow this because you will pay a yearly all-encompassing wrap (or management) fee that allows you to make changes within your account without incurring commission costs. The wrap costs to you can vary from a few tenths of a percent per year to 2 percent per year or more, depending on the size of your account and the structure of your investment portfolio. Are there any other costs besides the wrap that I should be aware of? Yes! Once again you must be aware of your execution costs (as previously discussed) and understand how your trades will be handled even if there are no commission costs for the transactions.

Deciding if a wrap account is right for you will depend on your investment needs, portfolio profile, and service desired.

SUMMARY: To succeed at investing in individual stocks, you will have to think like a business owner—not as a speculator—and recognize that time in the market rather than timing the market is a key component to being successful. To diversify with individual stocks requires a conscious effort based on a plan and a strategy. Sector investing is one such strategy that offers simplicity, diversification, and discipline as some of its strong tenets.

Chapter 12

Investing in Stock Mutual Funds

I bought a magazine the other day because it listed the "Ten Best Funds" in which to invest. I was all set to invest my retirement accounts and my lump-sum distribution until I noticed three other magazines with their "Ten Best Funds" list. What concerns me is that not one fund was repeated in any of the top ten lists. How can each list be the ranking of the ten best funds, yet be totally different? It looks like this isn't going to be as easy as I thought.

There is no "top ten" list that I or *anyone* else can offer you that will lead you to the promised land of financial security. If you were to invest your retirement accounts or lump-sum distribution in a mutual fund you read about in this book without investigating whether it had undergone any internal changes in the interim, you would have no way of knowing if the fund was still consistent with your financial needs. So, you see the potential financial pitfalls in making investment decisions on a particular "to buy list" based solely on any author's use of current information at the time of writing.

For that reason, rather than recommend a list of stock (equity) mutual funds, I will offer you something more important: the investment tools to help you navigate the process of evaluating, assembling, and managing a mutual fund portfolio now and in the future. As the saying goes, "Give a man a fish and he will eat for a day, teach a man how to fish and he will eat forever." I want to teach you how to fish.

BEFORE YOU INVEST

It's hard to resist investing in stock mutual funds, especially once you become aware of their long-term investment results compared to such alternatives as bonds or money market accounts. But, as you begin to put together your mutual fund portfolio, be aware that many mutual fund investors have had less impressive results than the funds in which they invested.

Table 12-1 displays some of the dramatic differences between investors, their rates of return, and the major indices to which they are compared.

Table 12-1.

Market vs. Investor Returns.

Jan. 1, 1984 to Dec. 31, 2000	Annualized Return (in %)
S&P 500 Index	16.29
Long-term bonds	11.83
T-bills	5.82
Average fixed-income investor	6.08
Average equity investor	5.32
Inflation (CPI)	3.23

Source: Dalbar Financial

The gap between what many investors actually earned and what the major indices earned (in the same period of time) is so large that the image of the Grand Canyon comes to mind. Why the huge discrepancy? Here are some reasons why many investors under-perform: (1) rear-view mirror investing, (2) short-term perspective, (3) improper asset allocation, and (4) lack of diversity.

Rear-View Mirror Investing

It can be very exciting to make a new investment in a mutual fund that was up 30 to 40 percent last year or that has averaged 20 percent per year for the last five years. All the fund has to do to make you wealthy is repeat its performance for the next however many years. So, on the basis of its *historical* investment returns, you take out your checkbook and prepare to throw money into this fund you've just discovered. After all, if it were not such a good investment, would so many financial publications be discussing it?

At this point, I hope you're saying to yourself: "Investing like that is pretty silly. Surely people don't make mutual fund purchases based on last year's winners." I'm going to let you in on a little secret. Last year's best-performing funds are the ones that get advertised the most; the underperformers, which can often be ripe for a turnaround, get very little attention or press. With the heavy advertising that promotes last year's winners, can you guess which funds bring in the most new assets—last year's losers or last year's winners? Be very careful about investing in last year's winners.

Short-Term Perspective

On a short-term basis, even great investments can go down in value. If you are fortunate enough to find an equity mutual fund that averages 12 percent per year for the next ten years, I can assure you that it will not be a nice neat positive return of 1 percent per month for 120 months. If you are going to invest in the stock (equity) markets, you must have a long-term perspective and an investment time horizon that extends beyond next quarter's earnings reports.

Improper Asset Allocation and Lack of Diversity

Another reason for poor investment results is that many investors do not properly allocate or diversify their investments. Proper asset allocation and diversity will not only give your portfolio more stability, but it will also allow you to be more patient with your investments. If your bonds are up in value 10 percent, your growth mutual funds down 15 percent, and your value mutual funds up 12 percent, you simply will be less likely to panic and make changes in your account.

The alternative is to concentrate your money in a single sector, such as "hot" growth funds. Investors who are concentrated in only one sector of the mutual fund market can have—if they're guessing right—tremendous upside potential. But, remember that concentrated portfolios can be volatile and create an environment where it's easy to make emotional decisions about when to buy or sell your holdings.

Now that you're aware of some of the reasons why mutual fund investors underperform, you're ready for the next step in putting together your portfolio: developing a mutual fund strategy. You will recognize some standard investment terms to direct your strategies, but be aware that various advisory services such as Morningstar, Lipper, and Wiesenberger rank and describe funds differently (see Appendix C). As a result of the potential ambiguity that this creates, be sure that you always (1) evaluate mutual funds by their names, (2) evaluate funds by their prospectus, and (3) review the specific stocks in which the funds are investing (since they may be different from what the name of the fund implies).

INITIAL DECISIONS

As you begin to implement your mutual fund game plan, you must initially make some critical decisions:

- What percentage of your mutual fund investments should you place in growth mutual funds, value mutual funds, or a blend of the two?
- What percentage of your portfolio should you place in mutual funds that invest in large-, mid-, and small-cap funds?
- What percentage of your portfolio should be placed in international investments?

Table 12-2 is a useful tool for analyzing the breakdown for your mutual fund portfolio.

Table 12-2.

Style of Investing.

Value	Blend	Growth	
%	%	%	**Large cap**
%	%	%	**Medium cap**
%	%	%	**Small cap**

The information in Table 12-2 is particularly important because of the following statement:

Your investment returns from a mutual fund are determined largely by the fund's management style, rather than by your ability to pick a winning fund.

I want to make sure that there is no misunderstanding about the above statement. Let me clarify this data in the following manner: if you are invested in large-cap value funds and that sector of the market does exceptionally well, you have a good chance of earning a positive rate of return on your investments—not because of your brilliant mutual fund choices, but because you were in that market sector. Conversely, if you are overweighted in technology and it does poorly, your tech-funds will probably go down in value—not because you chose bad funds, but rather because you were in that sector of the market. Unfortunately, many investors spend an inordinate amount of time analyzing specific mutual funds, thereby jeopardizing the returns and the stability of their portfolio by not focusing on the overall structure of their investments.

Growth vs. Value

I introduced the concept of "growth vs. value" in Chapter 11. I'm continuing that discussion here because the concept is of such significance. While some advisors readily accept the idea of growth versus value, others say that no such distinctions can be made—that it is all just a matter of semantics. No doubt, the debate will continue for a number of years. Chart 12-A gives some additional insight to this discussion and, in my opinion, reveals that different styles of investing exist and that the results of those styles have varied over time. For that reason, I feel that a combination of growth and value not only can give investors capital growth over time, but also can help to reduce portfolio risk.

Chart 12-A.

Large-Cap Growth vs. Value: 1987 to June 30, 2002.

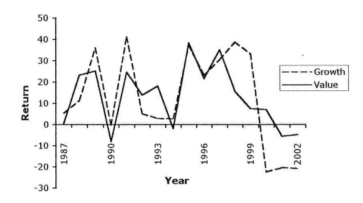

Dash Line: Russell 1000® Growth Index
Solid Line: Russell 1000® Value Index

Source: Phoenix Investment Partners, a member of the Phoenix Companies, Inc.

After reviewing the data in Chart 12-A, perhaps you're thinking, "Why shouldn't I put my money into growth funds when they're going up and doing well, and then switch out of them at the top of the market and move to underpriced value funds?" In a perfect world that is exactly what you would do. But, timing the market and making perfect financial transactions are impossible, unless of course you can figure out some way to gaze into the future. Here are some of the types of mutual funds that would be needed to construct a diversified portfolio.

Growth Mutual Funds

Growth mutual fund managers evaluate and invest in stocks that (based on the manager's analysis) are increasing their profits, sales, and/or earnings faster than the market as a whole and are expected to maintain or accelerate those trends. While growth mutual funds offer investors the potential for tremendous capital appreciation, the risk to your principal, is always lurking on the horizon.

During the late 1990s, many "growth" companies were consumed by revenue growth and failed to focus on earnings growth. The mantra was "Get market share at all cost." Making a profit didn't fit into the new paradigm. There was a new world order. After a few years of that kind of financial hot air, the markets rediscovered that earnings do matter, always have, and I dare say, always will.

If you decide to invest in growth mutual funds, understand that not all growth funds are created equally. This sector of the market has several subcategories, which include but are not limited to the following alternatives:

1. *Conservative growth funds.* Comprised of companies perceived to be growing in a conservative, consistent fashion. These include funds that invest in companies such as Pepsi Cola, Pfizer and General Electric.
2. *Growth and income funds.* Comprised of companies that are perceived to be growing conservatively, but that often also include an income-generating component (dividend-paying stocks, bonds, convertible bonds, and other securities). These include funds that invest in stocks such as Duke Energy Corp., Exxon Mobil Corp.
3. *Aggressive growth funds.* Comprised of fast-growing, cutting-edge companies (in the judgment of the mutual fund manager) that will continue to grow rapidly. (Remember, aggressive investments that offer greater upside potential can be expected to bring more risks.) Sorry, but I won't be giving any examples in this particular sector of the market. Just too much volatility, especially since today's aggressive growth company could be tomorrow's catastrophe.

Value Mutual Funds

"Boring" and "out of favor" sometimes come to mind when thinking about value mutual funds and the types of stocks in which they invest. Many investors hold the misconception that value managers invest only in low-priced stocks or shares that have dropped precipitously in value. Not so. Just because a stock has dropped in price doesn't mean the company now represents value. Value managers look for value in relation to a company's earnings, growth, peer group, and potential appreciation. Simply put, value managers look to buy companies that are selling as undervalued assets compared to their true worth, which the rest of the investing public will some day discover.

While the concept of growth and value should form an important part of the foundation of your mutual fund portfolio, there are other important types of mutual funds with which you will want to become acquainted: (1) international and global funds, (2) sector funds, (3) asset-allocation funds, and (4) index funds

International and Global Funds

Historically, having a little international exposure not only increased investment returns, but also helped to lower overall portfolio volatility.

> Q: *What is the difference between a global fund and an international fund?*
>
> A: *Global funds invest in companies whose headquarters are based anyplace in the world, while international funds invest in companies based outside of the United States.*

This difference looks pretty clear on paper, but from a practical point of view, does it mean anything? As a result of the unprecedented amount of "globalization" that has occurred during the last few decades, it has become more difficult to know whether you're invested in an international fund, a global fund, or a global fund with an investment focus on companies based in the United States. The drawback of this ambiguity is that if you don't choose wisely, you may not give your portfolio the balance you are seeking.

Country and Regional Funds

A sub-category of international and global funds includes country and region-specific funds. Examples include funds that invest only in Mexico, South America, or Europe.

There can be some advantages to this type of investment focus, but overly focused mutual funds are often obligated to invest in a given region of the market, even if that region is no longer attractive. If you plan to invest in a region- or country-specific fund, be diligent in evaluating its prospectus, its level of diversification, and its investment restrictions and requirements.

Sector-Specific Funds

Examples of specialized sectors include: REITS (Real Estate Investment Trusts), health care, technology, energy, utilities, and precious metals. Sector-specific funds have many of the same advantages and disadvantages of country or region-specific funds. For example, they are very focused and often are obligated to invest in a given sector of the market even if that sector is no longer desirable. Some sector funds can be incredibly volatile and during the last few years, they have fallen from favor among some investors.

Asset-Allocation Funds

Asset-allocation funds come in a number of flavors. Some of these types of funds move assets back and forth only from a single index such as the S&P 500 to another sector of the market such as cash. Other funds strive to offer you the whole range of investment vehicles in one package. Their strategy is to invest simultaneously in the three major sectors of the market (cash, bonds, and stocks), and then to alter the allocation by moving money from asset class to asset class as market conditions change. It's a strategy that looks good on paper, but actual investment results have been mixed.

Index Funds

Over the last five to ten years, the popularity of investing in index funds has grown so dramatically that some of the largest funds in the country are now index funds. Their appeal is that they are usually economical and their returns have been as good or better than many managed mutual funds.

Unfortunately, many investors don't realize that "diversified" index funds won't protect you from a market decline or that they aren't as broadly diversified as once believed. Because of the way that most index funds are constructed, it is very easy for one of its sectors to become overweighted. An example of this is the Standard & Poor's 500.

The popular Standard & Poor's 500 Index fund is a weighted index based on the market cap of each of the stocks in it. Therefore, some large market-value stocks can make up 2, 3, or 4 percent of the index or more, with smaller companies representing only a fraction of that amount. During 1999, the S&P 500 was up almost 20 percent, a great rate of return. However, if you look a little deeper, you will discover that a large percentage of the return came from a handful of companies: America Online (AOL), Cisco Systems (CSCO), Dell Computer (DELL), EMC Corporation (EMC), General Electric (GE), International Business Machines Corporation (IBM), Lucent Technology Inc Tech. (LU), Microsoft Corporation (MSFT), and Wal-Mart (WMT).

Q: *Does it make sense for you to place your entire financial well-being in an investment that can become so
concentrated and overweighted in one sector of the
market, such as technology?*

A: *No. It defeats one of the tenets of mutual fund investing,
which is diversity by style and sector.*

There is nothing wrong with investing in index funds, but you do
need to make sure that they are only one part of an overall balanced
portfolio. For some confirmation of how volatile the stocks in an index
fund can be, look at Table 12-3 for the highs and lows between January
1, 2000 and December 31, 2001 of some of the high performing stocks
of 1999 cited.

Table 12-3.
Stock Highs and Lows Jan. 1, 2000 to Dec. 31, 2001.

Name of Stock	High	Low
CSCO	82.00	11.04
EMC	102.64	10.01
LU	73.26	5.00
AOL	83.375	27.4
GE	60.50	28.5

Another problem with investing in index funds is that the investing
public loves a winner, which sets off a certain cycle: the need to invest in
a winner begets a better return for a given index, which begets more
press coverage, which begets more money flowing to the index.

Consider what happened during the late 1990s to the Dow Jones
Industrial Average. When the Dow's investment returns started lagging

behind those of the S&P 500, many investors openly discussed whether we needed to pay attention to the Dow. The S&P 500 was viewed as better representing the stock market and for many investors it became the index of choice. The same thing—to a lesser degree—happened to the S&P 500 when the returns of the NASDAQ Composite began to outshine it, making the NASDAQ the "new" index darling of the late 1990s. By the way, the NASDAQ Composite had a high of a little more than 5000 during 2000, and, a low of just less than 1390 during 2001, which was a drop of more than 70 percent (5132 to 1387.06 = 72.98 percent drop). Don't make the mistake of getting swept up in the hype of the current year's hot new index.

Capitalization

Capitalization or company size, sometimes referred to as a company's market value, is another important way in which you can and should diversify your mutual fund portfolio. Please understand that the market capitalization to which I am referring has nothing to do with the size of the mutual fund itself, but rather the size of the companies in which the mutual fund is investing.[51]

While most funds can be categorized as small-, mid-, or large-cap, it is also possible to invest in "blended funds." By design, blended funds move investments from small cap to mid cap to large cap, and from growth to value, depending on where opportunities lie. I am not a fan of market timing, but having these types of mutual funds in your portfolio can add an element of diversification that would otherwise be difficult to achieve.

Once you have decided to diversify your account in small-, mid-, and large-cap mutual funds, the obvious question is what percentage of your equity mutual fund investments should be placed in each category?

---

[51] See Chapter 11 for a refresher on what constitutes small-, mid-, and large-cap stocks.

While there are no set rules for what percentage of your money should be placed in each category, most experts think that the more aggressive you are, the more you should place in small- to mid-cap funds while the more conservative you are, the more you should place in large-cap funds. Here are some guidelines to get you started.

- Large-cap funds: 60 to 80 percent
- Mid-cap funds: 20 to 40 percent
- Small-cap funds: 0 to 20 percent

You may also want to compare the contents of your portfolio against the current breakdown of the S&P 500.[52]

BUYING DECISIONS

Once you have decided on an overall strategy for your mutual fund portfolio, you must then make some "buying" decisions: (1) where you will buy your funds, (2) how many funds you will invest in, and (3) what will be the timing of your purchases. Since costs are an important part of your buying decisions, I will cover them in detail in a later section. Let me begin this discussion by reviewing where you can buy your funds.

Purchase Directly

You do not need to purchase mutual funds through a broker, a financial planner, or an investment counselor. You can contact a mutual fund company directly to set up an account and invest to your heart's content. This can be an attractive alternative when investing in true no-load funds, but it doesn't make a lot of sense if you are investing in load

---

[52] See Appendix C for their web address.

funds. Why? If you invest in a load fund directly, you will pay the same charges, fees, and commissions as if you were investing with an investment advisor. If you choose to pay the load, it makes sense to at least do it through a professional, who will be involved in managing and servicing your account.

When dealing directly with a mutual fund, all of your statements and trade confirmations will come to you from the mutual fund company. A potential disadvantage of this style of investing is that if you are dealing directly with several firms, you will be receiving statements from each mutual fund family when perhaps a consolidated analysis of your holdings is preferred. As a result of these issues, many individuals are turning to mutual fund supermarkets through either discount or full-service firms.

Mutual Fund Supermarkets

When people think of a supermarket, a certain mental image comes to mind: lots of variety, convenience, and a generous return policy. Mutual fund supermarkets offer many of the same advantages as your local grocery store supermarket: tremendous variety and the convenience of buying just about everything you want at one location. Because of these powerful advantages, mutual fund assets invested in this manner have dramatically increased during the last several years. Unfortunately, unlike a grocery store, if you don't like your mutual fund most mutual fund supermarkets do not offer generous return policies.

How Many Funds

After you have decided where you will purchase your mutual funds, the next step will be to decide how many funds you will need. While there are no specific rules about how many funds you should have, it should be driven by factors such as your age, risk tolerance, net worth, and financial needs. The objective is to asset allocate your portfolio so that you have representation in the sectors of the market I have discussed. Having one to two funds in each of these categories may be more than adequate.

The Timing of Your Investments

The preparation that leads up to assembling an investment portfolio is a little like planning for a marriage. You can think about it, you can talk about it, but at the end of the day it's not enough to talk the talk—you have to walk the walk. It is an interesting phenomenon, one minute you are single and the next minute you are married. What causes you, in the eyes of the law, to make this transformation? It is when you utter two simple words: I DO! After careful thought and consideration, you are now ready for the "I do" phase of putting together your mutual fund portfolio. It is time to take the final step. It is time to make the transformation from planning to doing and commit your money to a mutual fund portfolio. You can consummate this transformation with two basic strategies: lump-sum investing or dollar cost averaging.

Lump-sum investing is straightforward; you have an amount of money to invest (e.g., $50,000), there's no timing the market, no waiting for things to be just right, you just make the investment.

The alternative to lump-sum investing is dollar cost averaging. It works as follows: you start by dividing an amount of money (e.g., the same $50,000), into a certain number of equal parts (e.g. $50,000 ÷ 5 = $10,000 per part). Then, you invest the fixed amount ($10,000) each month for five months. Rain or shine, good or bad, you stick to the plan and religiously invest the fixed dollar amount for the pre-determined time frame. (See Table 12-4 to review how the strategy works.)

Table 12-4.

Dollar Cost Averaging.

Periodic Amount (in $)	Cumulative Amount (in $)	Price per Share (in $)	# Shares Purchased
10,000	10,000	5.00	2,000
10,000	20,000	8.00	1,250
10,000	30,000	5.00	2,000
10,000	40,000	2.00	5,000
10,000	50,000	5.00	2,000

Average Price per Share	*$ 5.00*
Average Cost per Share	*$ 4.08*

It is interesting to follow the math in Table 12-4. Even though the price/share has gone up and down by an equal dollar amount, your average cost/share is lower than the average price/share.

Here's another example to illustrate the power of dollar cost averaging. What would have happened if an investor had employed this investing strategy in the Dow Jones Industrial Average, during the Great Depression between December 31, 1928, and December 31, 1937? We'll say that our investor decided to invest the same fixed dollar amount at the close of each year for ten years during the worst economic time this country has ever known. Look for the surprise answer in Table 12-5.

Table 12-5.

Great Depression Dollar Cost Averaging.

Trade Date	Closing Price	Periodic Amount	Cumulative Amount	# Shares Purchased	Cumulative Shares
12/31/28	300.00	$1,000	$1,000	3.33	3.33
12/31/29	248.48	$1,000	$2,000	4.02	7.36
12/31/30	164.58	$1,000	$3,000	6.08	13.43
12/31/31	77.90	$1,000	$4,000	12.84	26.27
12/31/32	59.93	$1,000	$5,000	16.69	42.96
12/31/33	99.90	$1,000	$6,000	10.01	52.97
12/31/34	104.04	$1,000	$7,000	9.61	62.58
12/31/35	144.13	$1,000	$8,000	6.94	69.52
12/31/36	179.90	$1,000	$9,000	5.56	75.08
12/31/37	120.85	$1,000	$10,000	8.27	83.35

Total Investment $10,000.00

Value 12/31/37 $10,072.87

I think that the information in Table 12-5 is amazing. An investor deploying the dollar cost averaging strategy during the Great Depression would have earned a positive rate of return. Of course, I've taken the liberty of making a tremendous number of assumptions: I haven't included transaction costs, I assumed that our investor was getting the closing value for the last day of the year, and of course, our investor would have needed the resources and the courage to invest. After all was said and done, our investor earned $72.87. Not bad considering that this positive rate of return occurred even though the Dow was at 300 at the end of 1928 and 120.85 at the end of 1937, a drop of almost 60 percent.

So which strategy is better: lump-sum investing or dollar cost averaging? You can find recommendations for both. The alternative that gives the best return will depend on the time frame of the dollar cost averaging, the specific period during which the investing was done, and the sector of the market in which you invested. Having said that, many investors—especially in uncertain times—are more comfortable emotionally with dollar cost averaging.

COSTS

The costs to invest in mutual funds will vary widely. It will depend on which mutual funds you purchase, where you purchase them, and whether or not you opt for professional assistance in managing your portfolio.

Regardless of the funds in which you invest and how you choose to invest, no mutual funds are free. Unfortunately, many investors think that no load means no cost. Nothing could be further from the truth. All mutual funds carry an expense ratio. These costs cover management of the fund, operations, 12b-1 fees (if applicable), and perhaps administrative costs. Moreover, internal trading costs incurred by managers in the buying and selling of securities in the fund are additional fees that are often not included in the expense ratio.

Knowing the trading costs of a fund is important because it's possible for a mutual fund to have a very low expense ratio and yet have a very high overall total cost because of excessive trading in the portfolio. If you are purchasing funds based on the cost or the load, remember to evaluate the trading cost before making any final investment decisions. Let us now review the different ways you can pay for your mutual funds: (1) A-, B-, and C-share funds, (2) no-load funds and, (3) no-load funds with a wrap.[53]

---

[53] There are subcategories to each of these pricing alternatives. The important issue is to understand the concepts that I am about to discuss.

A Shares (Front-End Load)

Cost to Buy

There was a time when, if you wanted to invest in a mutual fund, you not only had to pay a load, but often the initial load was somewhere in the neighborhood of 6, 7, or even 8.5 percent. Plus, each additional purchase had its own front-end load attached to it at the time of purchase. You'd invest $10,000 and right off the top you'd be paying as much as $850 in the form of a commission. These funds remind me of the comedian from "Laugh-In" who had the famous line "Sock it to me baby." It goes without saying that even when investors had few pricing alternatives, they were still not happy with that kind of a charge. Because of those concerns, the mutual fund industry responded with some ingenious ways to lower your costs and get you to invest more of your money.

Break Points. A break point is a volume discount. It works something like this:

- If you invest from $0 to $10,000, there is a 6 percent sales charge.
- If you invest from $10,001 to $50,000, the sales charge drops to 4 percent.
- If you invest from $50,001 to $100,000, the sales charge drops to 3 percent.

You can see that as the amount of the investment increases, the percentage of the front-end charges drop. Today breakpoints vary by fund, but most A-shares front-end load charges are in the neighborhood of 4.75 percent or less.

Rights of Accumulation. A second way to get a price break on your front-end load is called rights of accumulation. Basically all this does is give you volume pricing based on the total dollar amount you have invested in all of the mutual funds in a given family of funds. For example, if you have $25,000 in the ABC Growth Fund, $25,000 in the ABC Value Fund, and $50,000 in the ABC Bond Fund, your pricing schedule will be based on a $100,000 total investment.

Letter of Intent. A third way to get a break on the front-end load is with a letter of intent. Yes, it's an actual letter to which you sign your name. In a nutshell, what it tells the mutual fund company is that you might only be investing a certain amount today—for example, $10,000—but within the next so many months you plan to invest more, for a total of $50,000. In this way, you get the discount commission cost based on $50,000, even though you are investing a lesser amount. If you don't fulfill your obligation to invest the full $50,000, the mutual fund company will retroactively charge you the fee based on your initial $10,000 investment.

Cost to Sell

While A-share mutual funds charge you a front-end load to buy, there are no sales charges or commissions to sell them. There is no selling charge for the simple reason that you already paid the load when you purchased the fund.

Expense Ratio

Let me be very clear about the following statement: different mutual funds can have different expense ratios. These costs can vary widely from fund to fund, and the types of charges included in the expense ratio can vary as well. A relatively new addition to the expense ratio is something called a 12b-1 fee. These types of fees are often used to compensate the firms or individuals that are selling the funds. Some mutual funds have no 12b-1 costs while A-share mutual funds typically have 12b-1 charges of about .25 percent per year. Unfortunately, a mutual fund's total expense ratio can be difficult to track down unless you make a concerted effort to uncover it. The reason for this is that they report net returns after their expenses.

> *Example:* If a fund earns a total return of 11 percent for the year and has an expense ratio of 1.5 percent, your net total reported will be 9.5 percent (11 − 1.5 = 9.5).

As you can well imagine, because of the front-end load, 12b-1 fees, and the alternatives now available, the popularity of A shares has waned over the years.

B Shares (Back-End Load)

Cost to Buy

B-share mutual funds were introduced several years ago to fight the stigma of paying a front-end load. If you invest $10,000, the entire amount goes to work for you with no deduction in the form of a load, which obviously is a distinct advantage for the investor over A shares.

Cost to Sell

There can be a charge to sell B-share mutual funds. The charges are on a sliding scale and might look like this: 5, 4, 3, 2, 1, and 0 percent. In other words, the charge to sell starts at 5 percent and then goes down by 1 percent per year until it eventually gets to zero. If you sell the shares the first year, your costs will be 5 percent; the second year, 4 percent; the third year, 3 percent; and so on. This declining sales charge makes it possible to invest in B-shares without paying a front-end load and also to sell them with no load. Plus as a general rule, only your investments are subject to these sales charges. Capital gains or dividends can be taken out at any time and not be subject to the back-end charge.

Expense Ratio

B shares offer some distinct advantages over their older sibling, the A shares. However, the expense ratio is a major disadvantage of the B shares. The internal costs of B shares will be about 0.5 to 0.75 percent per year higher than the internal expense ratio of A shares. These differences are usually based on the higher 12b-1 fees found in B shares. Over time, this higher internal cost can accumulate and be as expensive as paying the A-share front-end load.

It is interesting to note that the higher expense ratio of the B shares usually lasts only for six to seven years. At some point, their internal costs are lowered and become the same as those for the A shares.

C Shares (Level Load)

Cost to Buy

The C-share mutual fund is one of the new mutual fund creations brought to us from the minds on Wall Street. Just as with B shares, the front-end load is zero. If you invest $10,000, all of your money is invested and goes to work for you—so far so good.

Cost to Sell

As a general rule, if you sell your C-share mutual fund during the first twelve months that you own it, there will be a charge of only 1 percent—which is obviously less expensive than selling B shares during the first year. Starting the thirteenth month, if you sell the fund, the sales charge drops to zero, whereas B shares have a sliding-scale back-end charge for several years. C shares are sounding better and better. Is there anything wrong with C shares?

Expense Ratio

The expense ratio, which includes the 12b-1 fees are basically the same for both B and C shares, except for a single twist. You will recall that the internal costs of B shares, converts to the less expensive internal costs of A shares after six to seven years. This conversion to the A share internal costs doesn't occur with C shares (there are a few exceptions).

> Q: *A, B, or C: Which is best? Which is the most expensive? Which is the least expensive?*
>
> A: *The answer to each question is "it depends." That is, it depends on how long you hold the mutual fund and on your strategy for managing your mutual fund portfolio.*

Let me explain my answer. If you had put half of your money into an A-share mutual fund and half of your money in the exact same fund but under the C-share pricing structure, initially the A shares would have been significantly more expensive, because with the A shares you paid a front-end load while the C shares had no front-end load. However, depending on your holding period it is possible for the C shares to become the more expensive of the two. Don't forget that all mutual funds have a yearly expense ratio. Eventually, the higher internal costs of C shares will accumulate to the point where they will overtake and became more expensive than the initial load you paid with the A shares.[54] So now, which was better? Here are two additional scenarios.

---

[54] Remember, the internal cost of the C-shares will be about 0.5 to 0.75 percent higher each year than the A-shares. You don't see this cost unless you dig through the prospectus, but rest assured it's there.

Example 1: In this scenario, your mutual fund investments in the A and C shares turn out to be a disappointment and after a couple of years, you decide to go into a different mutual fund. In this case, the C share is clearly the superior choice because you didn't have to pay a front-end load and a year later you didn't have to pay a back-end load to sell. There was a higher internal expense ratio with the C shares, but not enough to make up for the front-end load you paid with the A shares.

Example 2: In this second scenario, you pick a fantastic, world-beating, winning fund that averages 20 percent per year for ten years. Will you be happy with your A-shares investment, even though you paid a front-end load? I think the answer is "probably." Will you be happy with your C-shares purchase? "Probably." The total costs would have been higher with the C shares because the higher expense ratio during ten years would have been more than the initial front-end load you paid with the A shares, but you will most likely still be happy with both alternatives.

The bottom line is that the C shares offer the most flexibility. They allow you to make changes in your account (after a twelve month holding period) without incurring a front-end or back-end load.[55] If C shares are held for an extended period of time, they will be more expensive than A shares.

---

[55] *Caution: Beware of the advisor that recommends the B-shares, since there is no load to buy, then rationalizes, in a few years, why you should sell your holdings and go into a different B-share fund. It may be the correct strategy, but more likely than not, it's being done to generate commissions to the advisor.*

No-Load Funds

Some major advantages of true no-load mutual funds are that they don't impose any sales charges when you buy or sell their funds, they often have lower management fees than load funds, and they usually have little to no 12b-1 fees. Not only can this be cost-effective, but it also gives you the flexibility to make changes in your portfolio, even if you have owned the fund for a short period of time. Unfortunately, some mutual fund families have begun imposing restrictions and penalties on the unlimited buying and selling of their funds, even if, officially, there is no load to make the changes. One of the reasons for these new restrictions was the appearance during the last few years of a cottage industry that shows you how to time the market by regularly buying and selling no-load funds. That kind of constant movement can cause a royal headache for the no-load mutual fund manager. Consequently, some funds are now restricting unlimited trading. If you plan to invest in no-load funds and time the market, make sure that you understand the fund's restrictions on this type of activity

No-Load vs. A, B, and C Shares

If you are a 100 percent do-it-yourself kind of investor and you are willing to spend time analyzing funds, following funds, and putting together an asset-allocation model, you will save money with true no-load funds. However, if saving money is your top priority, investing in no-load mutual funds may not be your least expensive alternative. For example, you may want to consider individual bonds rather than no-load bond funds, as well as exchange-traded funds (ETFs) rather than no-load stock funds. Of course, each of these alternatives offers investors their own set of advantages and disadvantages, which you might want to review before deciding on a course of action.[56]

---

[56] See Chapters 7, 8, and 10 for the differences between these various investment vehicles.

No-load Funds with a Wrap

A recent creation in the world of mutual fund investing is the no-load mutual fund portfolio with a wrap, which is now being offered by a number of investment advisors and mutual fund families.

You will recall that with a wrap account, there are no sales charges for transactions; but there is a yearly management fee of approximately 1 to 2 percent per year on the assets under management (this is in addition to the mutual funds internal expense ratio).

An interesting commentary on this type of investment alternative is that not only are full-service investment firms offering these investments, but many no-load mutual fund families are now offering these services as well. They are now offering these types of programs, even though it would seem to defeat one of the tenets of no-load fund investing: saving money. The need for this service was created because many investors are suffering from information overload. Many investors (and no-load fund families) are coming to the conclusion that evaluating thousands of mutual funds, creating an asset-allocation model, and monitoring an account requires professional assistance.

Before implementing this type of program, it's important to confirm that the firm handling your account has access to a number of different mutual fund families, rather than being restricted to only their own company-sponsored mutual funds.

SUMMARY: Choosing equity mutual funds is a process that must be kept independent of last year's winners and this year's hot sector. It begins by deciding how conservative or aggressive you want to be. The next step involves preparing an analysis and determining how much should be invested in growth and value funds, in domestic and international funds, and last but not least, deciding on the amounts that should be placed in large-cap, mid-cap, and small-cap funds. The goal of a well-diversified mutual fund portfolio should be to earn consistent returns over time.

Deciding where to buy mutual funds should be based largely on whether an investor requires professional assistance in assembling a portfolio or decides to tackle the task alone.

Chapter 13

Investing Outside Your IRA

It's enough to give an investor a migraine. First, I had to deal with being pushed into early retirement. Then I had to learn all the rules and regulations that only apply to people receiving a qualified lump-sum distribution. Once I got my money, I had to figure out how to put together a portfolio and now I discover that investments that are appropriate in an IRA may not be so hot outside of an IRA. Where do we keep the Excedrin?

Investments in an IRA account grow and compound on a tax-deferred basis. It doesn't matter if the growth is from income, dividends, or capital gains; there is no tax liability until distributions from the account begin. But, when you invest outside of a tax-deferred account, not only must you pay attention to taxes, but the higher your tax rate, the more important this issue becomes.

While taxes alone shouldn't govern your investment decisions outside of your IRA accounts, their impact on your portfolio's returns should have a place in the equation. The following example illustrates the power of tax-deferred growth and the destructive nature of yearly taxation. I will evaluate the stock portfolios of two investors under the following assumptions:

- Each investor earns 12 percent per year.
- No dividends are earned, only capital appreciation.
- Both investors are in a combined state and federal tax bracket of 35 percent.
- Both investors start with $10,000.
- I am also assuming no transaction costs.

The first investor employs a buy-and-hold strategy, while the second investor turns over 100 percent of his or her portfolio each year. What happens to the value of their respective accounts during a five-, ten-, and twenty-year period of time? See Table 13-1 for the results.

Table 13-1.

Taxable vs. Tax-Deferred Growth Outside an IRA Account.

	Investor #1	Investor #2
Initial Investment	$10,000	$10,000
Return/year	12%	12%
Combined State and Federal Tax Rate	35%	35%
Investment Strategy	Buy & Hold	Market Timing
Value in 5 years	$17,623	$14,558
Value in 10 years	$31,058	$21,193
Value in 20 years	$96,463	$44,913

While these are exaggerated examples (investor #2 has been paying taxes all along while investor #1 will eventually pay taxes when the stocks are sold), they clearly demonstrate the negative consequences of taxes when investing outside of your IRA account. They also illustrates that the "best" investment in an IRA might not be the "best" choice outside of one. A brief review of the major asset classes follows. It will assist you in determining if your strategy inside of your IRA will also be appropriate outside of your IRA.

BONDS OUTSIDE AN IRA

Municipal Bonds

Municipal bonds pay investors tax-free interest and are issued by state and local governments. The money raised is used to pay for municipal projects, which include, but are not limited to, improving schools, streets, sewers, and other public works. Just as with other sectors of the bond market, you can invest in short-, intermediate-, and long-term municipal bonds.[57] Like other sectors of the bond market, they are rated for their credit worthiness; the credit quality of an offering will vary, depending on the municipality and the underlying project.[58]

Why Buy Municipal Bonds

Tax-free municipal bonds are popular with investors because of the simple fact that the federal government doesn't tax the income earned. Also, depending on where you live and where the bonds were issued, the income may also be free from state and local taxes. The higher your

---

[57] Do not purchase municipal bonds inside of an IRA account. All distributions that come out of IRA accounts are taxed as ordinary income.

[58] See Chapter 6 for my discussion of rating services.

income, the higher your tax rate, and the more valuable the tax-free income from municipal bonds becomes. Because of that, you will need to know your tax bracket and how to calculate the taxable equivalent yield before you decide if municipal bonds are right for you. The formula for the calculation is as follows:

Tax exempt yield ÷ (1 - tax bracket)
= Taxable equivalent yield

Example: If you are earning a 4 percent tax-free rate of return and your tax bracket is 40 percent, what is the taxable-equivalent yield?

4 ÷ (1 - .40) = taxable equivalent yield (6.667 percent).

Table 13-2 displays what tax-free yields are worth based on your tax bracket:

Table 13-2.

Tax Free Yields vs. Taxable Yields.

Tax Bracket	10.0%	27.0%	30.0%	35.0%	38.5%
Tax-Exempt Yields	**Taxable Yield Equivalents**				
3.0%	3.33%	4.11%	4.29%	4.62%	4.88%
3.5%	3.89%	4.79%	5.00%	5.38%	5.69%
4.0%	4.44%	5.48%	5.71%	6.15%	6.50%
4.5%	5.00%	6.16%	6.43%	6.92%	7.32%
5.0%	5.56%	6.85%	7.14%	7.69%	8.13%
5.5%	6.11%	7.53%	7.86%	8.46%	8.94%
6.0%	6.67%	8.22%	8.57%	9.23%	9.76%

Over the years, there have been a number of changes in the laws that have made municipal bonds a less attractive investment for institutions. Because of that, the tax-free municipal bond market is one of the few bond markets that is dominated by individual rather than institutional investors. As a result of this, investment firms and municipalities have added features to the bonds to enhance their attractiveness to the investing public. One of the most popular of those features is municipal bond insurance.

Bond Insurance

A number of firms insure municipal bonds; two of the best known firms are **MBIA** (Municipal Bond Insurance Association) and **AMBAC** (American Municipal Bond Assurance Co.). Although bonds typically receive a triple-A rating after being insured, many of the underlying municipalities would be highly rated on their own without the insurance. This is because insurance firms don't insure any old municipal bond, even when a municipality is willing to pay for the insurance. The insurance companies initiate a thoughtful due diligence process to evaluate all bonds before they agree to apply insurance.

One final thought about investing in bonds that are triple-A rated and insured: insurance on a bond protects it from default. It does not, however, insure against or prevent the changes in bond values that can occur when interest rates fluctuate.

GO vs. Revenue Bonds

I sometimes think that there are as many different municipal bonds in the United States as there are stars in the sky. While they go by a variety of names, you can lump most of them into two broad categories: **GO bonds** (general obligation) and **revenue bonds**.

- **GO bonds:** carry the full-faith, credit, and taxing authority of the issuer.
- **Revenue bonds:** income is generated from the revenues of the municipal project. An example of this would be tolls collected on a toll bridge.

Q: *Which is better: A GO or a revenue bond?*
A: *Some advisors would strongly argue that general obligation bonds are better because the underlying issuer can raise taxes to pay off the bond.*

Of course, if the answer to the preceding question were as simple as that, most, if not all, GO bonds would have a triple-A rating. After all, if a municipality needs more money for its bond, it can just raise taxes. However, consider that increasing taxes is not easy, subject as it is to financial as well as political considerations. For that reason, perhaps revenue bonds are better, especially if they are based on a needed municipal structure, such as a bridge. Raising the toll on a bridge crossing might be a prudent alternative to shutting it down and forcing drivers (also known to politicians as "voters") to travel on alternative routes. So, the question of "which is better," just depends on the offering.

As you evaluate whether to invest in GO or revenue bonds, do your homework, deal with someone who understands this market, and make sure that the firm you are dealing with has a large inventory of municipal bond offerings. This will give you a better chance of finding the bonds that are appropriate for your needs.

Pre-Refunded Municipal Bonds

Pre-refunded municipal bonds are specialized, not well known, and often misunderstood. They usually have a short-term maturity, pay a large coupon rate, and sell for a premium.[59] What makes them unique is that they are guaranteed by U.S. Treasuries and therefore represent the pinnacle of safety to municipal bond investors. Once a bond becomes pre-refunded by U.S. Treasuries, it is no longer subject to the credit worthiness of the original issuing municipality.

Pre-refunded bonds usually come about when a municipality has a bond issue that is paying a high interest rate, but because of call features, can't be redeemed and paid off. Under those circumstances, one alternative—if the municipality wants to lower its interest costs—is to refinance the original high-yielding bond at a lower interest rate.

The basic procedure is as follows: (1) a new lower-yielding municipal bond offering is sold to the investing public, (2) the proceeds from the new bond offering are then used to purchase U.S. Treasuries, which are then placed in an **escrow account**, and (3) from that point on the principal and the interest from the Treasuries will guarantee the principal and the interest of the original municipal bond.

---

[59] For a refresher on coupon and premium see Chapter 8

For instance, if you had purchased some municipal bonds issued by Hollywood, California, and those bonds became pre-refunded, the safety and credit worthiness of those bonds would no longer be backed by the city of Hollywood, but rather by U.S. Treasuries. Even if Hollywood fell into the ocean, you'd have no need to be financially concerned: the bonds are pre-refunded and U.S. Treasuries guarantee your investment. If this happened, there might be fewer movies the following summer, but at least you would have your money, which you could spend on other forms of entertainment.

Tax-Free Bond Funds

No discussion on tax-free bonds would be complete without reviewing tax-free bond funds. If you understand the basics of investing in taxable bond funds then you should have a good understanding of tax-free bond funds. They share many of the same features, advantages, and disadvantages. And with both types of bond funds, you can invest in them directly or through an investment advisor.

The most unique difference between tax-free bond funds and other taxable bond funds is the obvious tax-free status of the income. Depending on the state in which you live, and in which municipal fund you invest, the income could be free from both state and federal income tax. That being said, it's possible to invest in one of those types of funds and still be zapped occasionally with a taxable distribution. How is that possible? The reason is that if any capital gains distributions are paid from the fund, there could be a tax liability on those distributions. If that occurs, it doesn't mean that the fund is being mismanaged; it's simply a part of tax-free bond fund investing.

One last item of significance: tax-free bond funds have no place in tax-deferred accounts such as IRAs. All distributions from IRA accounts are considered taxable income, even if the income originated from a tax-free municipal bond fund.

Taxable Bonds

All bond returns are tax-deferred *inside* an IRA account. Some subtle considerations come into play, however, when investing in and comparing taxable bonds—i.e. U.S. Treasuries, mortgage backed-securities (MBSs), and corporate bonds— outside an IRA.

> Q: *How do U.S. Treasuries compare to alternatives such as corporate bonds or MBSs (Ginnie Maes, Fannie Maes, Freddie Macs, and CMOs) outside an IRA?*
>
> A: *A key difference is that you pay no state tax on the income earned from your investments in U.S. Treasuries, whereas you would with corporate bonds and MBSs.*

Corporate bonds and MBSs normally pay investors a higher rate of return than a Treasury with a similar maturity. But, such a yield advantage can be wiped out because the income from them is taxed by the state in which you reside, while the Treasury bond yield is not. You'll want to factor these state-tax differences into any final decisions you make about bonds.

> Q: *How about investing in MBSs outside your IRA?*
>
> A: *Corporate bonds and U.S. Treasuries have a fixed maturity date. MBSs don't have one in the traditional sense, but instead have an average life.*

The significance of an average life is that on a monthly basis, MBSs will pay you both interest and principal. Keeping track of your Ginnie Mae principal payments can be a little cumbersome outside an IRA, so you'll want to take care not to spend your principal thinking that it is income.

I am not suggesting that you avoid MBSs outside of your IRA. Just keep in mind that they carry an added layer of complexity when invested in taxable accounts.

GROWTH INVESTMENTS OUTSIDE AN IRA

In previous chapters, I discussed growth strategies and the advantages and disadvantages of investing in individual stocks, money managers, and packaged products. In this section, I will touch upon a few of the most important issues inherent in investments outside your IRA.

Individual Stocks

Investing in individual stocks outside an IRA can be very tax efficient: there is no tax liability on their capital growth until they are sold. If you are a conservative buy-and-hold investor, individual stocks may have some advantages to offer you over such alternatives as mutual funds. You may recall that you have no control over the mutual funds capital gains distributions, which can have an adverse effect on your tax planning.

Money Managers

When you invest with a money manager outside an IRA, you start with your own new cost basis. You choose your money manager, empower the firm to make investments with your money on your behalf, and you don't have to worry about an embedded capital-gain tax liability, which can occur with mutual funds.

> *Example:* If your manager buys you Mighty Widgets Inc. for $50 per share, then that is your cost basis. You don't need to be concerned about the purchase price or the cost

basis for other clients, through the same money manager, who own Mighty Widgets Inc. The reason for this is that you will have your own individual account rather than a "pooled" account, which would have occurred if you had used a mutual fund.

All things being equal, the above-mentioned advantage over mutual funds might make this the more attractive choice outside your IRA, even if you prefer mutual funds within your IRA account.

Mutual Funds

While mutual funds can be an attractive investment choice within an IRA, some of their features diminish their value outside an IRA. Of course, everyone's situation is unique, so I am not recommending that you avoid mutual funds outside an IRA. However, even if they do become your investment of choice in your IRA, evaluate them against investment alternatives in an otherwise taxable environment.

There are three basic ways a mutual fund can generate income and capital gains:

1. *Dividend income.* If a mutual fund manager invests in a number of stocks that all pay big, fat, juicy dividends, which are passed along to the investors as dividend income, the income is taxed as ordinary income, whether you take the distributions or reinvest them in the fund.
2. *Capital appreciation.* You can earn a rate of return from your mutual fund from capital appreciation. For example, if you invest in a fund, pay $22 per share, and the price per share increases to $27 per share, you have made a nice return of $5 per share. The best part is that there is no tax liability until you sell the fund.

3. *Embedded capital gains.* Embedded capital gains are a complex feature of mutual funds and they have been a bone of contention for many mutual fund investors. (See Chapter 7 for a review the of embedded capital gains.)

SINGLE PREMIUM DEFERRED ANNUITIES SPDA

A **single premium deferred annuity** is basically a tax-deferred savings account that you hold with an insurance company. Tax-deferred doesn't mean tax free; it means that as the money grows and compounds, there is no tax liability. The tax liability occurs only when you take distributions from the deferred annuity.

You can invest in deferred annuities through insurance agents, investment firms, brokers, financial planners, certain banks, and some savings and loans. However, at the end of the day, the company that is actually issuing the deferred annuity will be an insurance company or the insurance arm of a company.

Regardless of where you buy your deferred annuity, you will need to know its rating. I would stick with only highly rated companies and deal with investment firms that have access to a number of different annuity offerings, rather than dealing with the types of firms that have access only to a single internal company product. If you decide to invest in an annuity, understand that two broad category alternatives are available: fixed and variable. Each category has its own set of advantages and disadvantages.

Fixed Annuity

Fixed annuities offer investors the following advantages: (1) they are safe, (2) they have a fixed rate of return, (3) there is no risk to principal, (4) the earnings are tax-deferred, and (5) they usually pay very competitive rates—often higher than money market accounts, CDs, or bonds of comparable maturity. The fixed rates on these types of investments can be locked in for a few months or for several years.

So far so good; but, what could be wrong with an investment like this? Why not take all your cash and money market investments and transfer them into this higher-yielding, principal guaranteed alternative? That probably wouldn't be a wise choice because of the fees, penalties, commissions, and other charges. Most deferred annuities have very stiff penalties for early withdrawals. These penalties can vary by annuity and can also be based on your age. You will want a complete understanding of ALL penalties and charges before investing.

One last item of concern: beware of the teaser rate. This occurs when a high initial rate is quoted to lure you in, without your realizing that after the initial time frame, your deferred annuity will be renewed at the new going rate, which could be significantly lower.

> Q: *What if you feel that the rate is no longer competitive and you can earn more in alternative investments? Can you take your money out and go somewhere else?*
>
> A: *Yes. But, don't forget that you will usually be socked with some substantial penalties for early withdrawal.*

Variable Annuity

The simplest way to begin the description of a variable annuity is to say that it is very similar to an equity (stock) mutual fund. Variable annuities have many of the same advantages as mutual funds: diversity, the ability to move your assets around, professional management, and so on. There are, however, some key differences: the income and growth on variable annuities is tax deferred and some variable annuities will guarantee your principal. The words "guarantee" and "stock market" don't usually appear in the same sentence, so I'll explain what I mean with the following example.

Example: You invest $100,000 in a variable annuity and over time, the fund grows to $200,000. The new value of $200,000 becomes the guaranteed floor. In other words, if your account then drops in value from $200,000 to $150,000, you will know that your account is guaranteed for the full $200,000 value. There is, however, usually a strict criterion that you are required to fulfill to guarantee the full $200,000 value: *you must die.* If your account is liquidated while you are alive, you typically will not have these types of principal guarantees. The principal guarantee can be comforting to your heirs, but usually it won't benefit you while you're alive.

The basic disadvantages of variable annuities are as follows: (1) variable annuities can impose substantial penalties for early withdrawal, (2) internal costs are typically higher than those in a plain vanilla mutual fund, (3) there are usually a limited number of investment choices, and (4) upon death, your heirs will not get a stepped up cost basis on the appreciation—which is possible with individual stocks and mutual funds.

Q: *Should you place a tax-deferred investment like this in a tax-deferred account such as an IRA?*

A: *As a general rule no! There is no reason to pay the extra fees associated with deferred annuities, and restrict yourself to their limited offerings, unless you are attracted to the principal-guarantee death benefit or some other unique features.*

SUMMARY: *When investing outside of tax-deferred accounts such as IRAs, an additional key point to consider is how your portfolio will be taxed. The best investments in an IRA account may not be your best choices outside of an IRA account. Diversify your accounts, strive for consistency over time, and try to make your investments as tax efficient as possible.*

Chapter 14

Constructing & Monitoring Your Portfolio

Bonds, stocks, mutual funds, money managers, ETFs, unit trusts and so on, where should I begin? Combining all of this information into a properly constructed portfolio seemed overwhelming. Then it dawned on me: building an investment portfolio is like building a house. Having the right tools and materials at your disposal isn't enough. You need a plan, a strategy, and a course of action before you can get the job done.

So, let us begin our course of action by asking a key question. If you are receiving a lump-sum distribution, which is the most important: (1) understanding the rules and regulations of lump-sum distributions, (2) mastering the mechanics of setting up your IRA rollover properly, (3) constructing your portfolio correctly, or (4) monitoring your portfolio after you have made your initial investments? The answer is that all of them are critical to your financial health. Unfortunately, finding information about all of these critical issues in one place can be difficult at best, and next to impossible at worst. While there are many fine books, which discuss investment strategies, retirement planning, and portfolio analysis, few books focus on the wide range of needs of the lump-sum recipient.

In Part I, I discussed the changing face of retirement and the rules and regulations that you need to understand in order to manage your retirement accounts. In Part II, I reviewed how to build a portfolio blueprint through the process of financial planning, asset allocation, diversification, and investment-product selection. In Part III, I evaluated various investment alternatives and strategies. I will now conclude this chapter and this book by walking you through the process of constructing and monitoring a sample portfolio.

PORTFOLIO CONSTRUCTION

For this scenario, I will assume that you are a lump-sum recipient in your mid-to-late 50s, and the value of your account is $500,000. You are going to roll over your distribution, and you want to put together a portfolio that will give some income (that can be reinvested or taken out if needed) and generate a little growth to combat inflation.

After preparing an analysis from a commercially available program or from an investment firm, you agree to put 50 percent of the $500,000 account into bonds and 50 percent into growth. (I am not including any cash investments in this analysis because in this example, cash will be part of your investments outside of your IRA). You now have the big picture: your asset-allocation model. Now what? From the thousands of choices at your disposal, how do you decide which are the right ones for your portfolio? Gathering up a number of brochures and evaluating every alternative open to you would be a daunting task. Here is the process I would recommend, beginning with the bond portion.

Sample Bond Portfolio

The First Challenge

Do you want your bond investments to be in individual bonds, money managers, or in some type of packaged product such as mutual funds or unit trusts?

> *The First Solution.* After reviewing the advantages and disadvantages of each alternative (covered in earlier chapters) and after understanding your different investment product alternatives, you decide in this example to go with individual bonds.

The Second Challenge

What types of individual bonds will you invest in: municipal bonds, U.S. Treasury bonds, corporate bonds, or mortgage-backed securities such as Ginnie Maes?

> *The Second Solution.* You immediately eliminate municipal bonds as a viable alternative because you know from reading previous chapters that (1) tax-free bonds pay a lower yield than other bond alternatives, (2) they offer no tax-free advantages in an IRA account, where everything grows tax-deferred, and (3) all distributions from an IRA rollover are taxable, even if the earnings come from tax-free municipal bonds.
>
> How about Treasuries? Yes, they're safe and very liquid, but in this scenario, your emergency cash needs can be met with assets outside of your IRA. Treasuries don't pay as much as corporate bonds, and the state tax exemption of the Treasury's earnings are of no value inside of an IRA account, so you decide to eliminate them from this exercise.

What about corporate bonds or mortgage-backed securities such as Ginnie Maes? The quoted estimated yield of a Ginnie Mae is higher than a comparable maturity corporate bond, so perhaps you don't need to consider corporate bonds and, instead, should put all of your bond investments into Ginnie Maes. After all, they are not only high yielding, but the U.S. government backs them. While Ginnie Maes seem very appealing and could be your bond alternative of choice, putting all of your bond investments in this one category would probably be a mistake. Remember, corporate bonds have a specific maturity, while Ginnie Maes have an average life. Because you cannot control the payback schedule of your Ginnie Mae, you can't control the average life of your Ginnie Mae. If interest rates drop, your entire Ginnie Mae bond portfolio might be redeemed within a short time, and you'd be stuck having to reinvest your entire bond portfolio in a new lower-interest-rate environment. What's an investor to do?

After careful analysis, you determine (this is just a sample portfolio) that you'll invest two-thirds of the bond portfolio in Ginnie Maes, and one-third in corporate bonds. This strategy will give you a higher total return under a stable interest rate environment than a 100 percent high quality corporate bond portfolio. Furthermore, having some corporate bonds will help to stabilize your account and maintain cash flow even if there is a dramatic shift in interest rates.

The Third Challenge

Because one-third of your portfolio will be in corporate bonds, you now need to make some important decisions about the ratings and credit quality of the corporate bonds in which you'll be investing and the call features of the bonds.

The Third Solution. I'd stick with bonds that have a rating of "A" or better. Also, depending on the maturity (if longer term), I would consider upgrading to double A or better. I would address the concern of callable bonds by striving to build a bond portfolio of either non-callable bonds, or of bonds that have good call protection.

The Fourth Challenge

Once you have decided on the types of bonds in which you will invest, you'll now need to look at the yield curve to determine the bond maturities that make sense for your stage in life and risk tolerances. (See Chart 14-A for the analysis of the yield curve.)

Chart 14-A.

Sample Yield Curve.

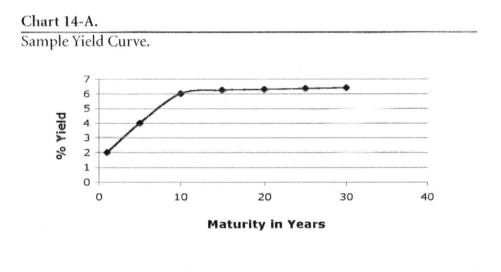

The Fourth Solution. Your yield-curve analysis tells you that it makes sense to take advantage of a laddered portfolio, with maturities of three to twelve years. This type of a portfolio will give you a higher return than just being in short-term bonds, will be more stable than investing in long-term bonds, and will give you flexibility, since bonds will mature at face value on a yearly basis.

The Last Challenge

You have one more decision to make before you can start investing: should you invest in discount, par, or premium bonds?

> *The Last Solution.* In this scenario, you learn that market analysis and research suggests that interest rates should continue to be stable or might drop a little. You therefore decide to invest in discount Ginnie Maes and par corporate bonds.[60] Both bonds will give good monthly cash flow, plus if interest rates drop, your discount Ginnie Maes could be paid off early at the full price of par. This early pay off at par will give you a higher rate of return than originally calculated.

Congratulations! You have followed a set of guidelines and have created your sample bond portfolio in a logical and informed manner.

Sample Equity Portfolio

It's now time to put together the equity portion of your portfolio. A word of warning before we get started: Once you have constructed your equity portfolio, you should be able to explain your strategy or game plan to neighbors, friends, or anybody else who will listen. You may not want to tell a soul about your finances, but you should understand your portfolio well enough so that it can be explained. If you own stocks but have no idea what the company does, then you need to ask yourself why in the world you have that investment. The same goes for your mutual funds and money managers.

---

[60] For a review of these terms, see Chapter 8.

The First Challenge

The first question to ask yourself is the one you asked in assembling your bond portfolio: Do you want to invest in individual stocks, money managers, or in packaged products such as mutual funds or unit trusts.

> *The First Solution.* Based on your needs, your interest in the stock market, and the advantages and disadvantages of each investment product alternative, you decide to put $150,000 in individual stocks and $100,000 in a portfolio of equity mutual funds.

The Second Challenge

So, how do you assemble your stock portfolio and how do you put together your mutual fund portfolio? There are so many choices, and of course every "expert" has an opinion on the "best" strategy.

> *The Second Solution: Individual Stocks.* In this example, you decide to go with a relatively simple strategy called sector investing. (You can review this strategy in Chapter 11.) You opt for the fixed mix "plus" alternative and plan to take advantage of the ten sectors I covered in Chapter 11.
>
> In order to pick and analyze stocks in each of the ten sectors, you order up Value Line's stock analysis, compare its recommendations to Standard & Poor's research, and for final confirmation compare their recommendations to the research of a major investment firm. Based on your stock market analysis, you decide on a few stocks (baskets) in each of the ten sectors, overweighting a few of them (say in technology). You decide not to have more than a 15 percent weighting in a given sector, and you also decide to underweight a few (say transportation), determining that you will always have at least 5 percent in any given underweighted sector.

These guidelines will not only give you an overall strategy, but they will also impose investor discipline on your investments. When something looks too good to be true, you won't allow your emotions to rule your portfolio and risk becoming dangerously overweighted in any given market sector.

The Second Solution: Mutual Funds. You recognize that now is not the stage of your life in which to get overly aggressive, and you don't want to complicate your carefully orchestrated retirement. Therefore, you choose a 50/50 split between value and growth, and decide to divide the market cap of your mutual fund investments in the following manner: large caps 70 percent, mid caps 20 percent, and small caps 10 percent. (For a review of these terms go to Chapter 11.) Now that you have the overall mutual fund strategy, you can then review specific mutual fund alternatives using an advisor or by utilizing one of the services listed in the appendix.

There you have it! You have now put together the guidelines for your equity portfolio, in the same logical manner as you constructed your bond portfolio. From Chart 14-B, you can see how this sample portfolio is allocated:

You have assembled your asset-allocation model, made investment product decisions, and diversified your account. Do you just forget about your accounts after having put so much care, time, and effort into their initial creation? Of course not! You have on-going portfolio management, and in the remainder of this chapter, I will discuss how to meet that lifetime challenge.

Chart 14-B.

Sample Asset-Allocation Portfolio.

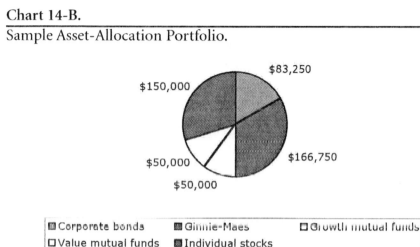

▥ Corporate bonds	▥ Ginnie-Maes	☐ Growth mutual funds
☐ Value mutual funds	▥ Individual stocks	

MONITORING YOUR PORTFOLIO

Account Statements

Most investment firms will prepare either a monthly or quarterly statement of your account that shows the percentage invested in cash, bonds, mutual funds, equities, and other securities. In addition to your holdings, you should always see any activity, which is taking place in your account: buying, selling, dividends being paid, and transfers in or out of your accounts. You'll need this information to confirm that trades are being carried out correctly. If inappropriate trading is going on in your account, you'll want to know about it as quickly as possible.

Quarterly Reviews

Every three to six months, you should subject your accounts to an investment check-up, which you can do by yourself or with an advisor. A quarterly review can confirm that you're on track with your investments and with your investment needs. I do suggest, however, that you not use the quarterly review as an excuse to "turn over the applecart" and reconfigure your portfolio every ninety days.

Annual Reviews

Annually, you should perform a detailed portfolio review. At your annual review, you should reevaluate your goals and confirm that your portfolio is consistent with your investment needs and risk tolerance.

The review will also confirm whether or not your original investment product alternatives are still appropriate for your investment needs—should you be in individual securities, money managers, or in packaged products such as mutual funds.

Life's Major Events

Besides the standard reviews you undertake monthly, quarterly, and yearly, you will also want to take a serious look at your accounts during life's major events:

- Death in the family
- Marriage of children
- Divorce
- Beneficiaries reaching legal age
- Changes in your health or that of loved ones
- Your grown kids moving back in with you (yikes)

Altered Risk Tolerance

Most likely, when you are 75, you'll have a different perspective on life than when you were 55. The change will be normal and may bring with it the decision not to maintain your existing portfolio asset allocation throughout your retirement years.

Dramatic Market Changes

Co-existing with the relentless march of time will be changes in market conditions, which can bring both opportunities and pitfalls to your portfolio.

> *Example:* Let us assume that you put 50 percent of your account into cash and bonds and invest the remaining 50 percent in equities, such as stocks or stock mutual funds. Let us also assume that after you make your investments, the stock market starts dramatically increasing in value. In fact, stock market returns are so good that a year from now only 35 percent of your account is in cash and bonds, with the remaining 65 percent being in stocks and mutual funds. What should you do?

In this kind of situation, a little prudence would be in order. Now would be a time to consider rebalancing your portfolio, staying mindful of such considerations as taxes, which can be a part of any portfolio or investment changes.

Ongoing Portfolio Rebalancing

Why in the world would an investor want to sell off one of their winning sectors such as Information Technology and rebalance those assets into a losing sector such as Utilities? Very simply, it is because markets change and no investment vehicle or sector of the market will be in the spotlight forever.

From Chart 14-C, you can see how dramatic these changes have been. Of course, hindsight is 20/20, but here's an opportunity to focus on one exaggerated example of how beneficial rebalancing a portfolio can be. During 1999, the Information Technology sector was the best performing sector and had a return of 78.4 percent; during 1999 the Utility sector was the second to the worst sector and had a return of minus 12.8 percent. Now, assume for the moment that you had rebalanced your account during 1999 and had taken some of the profits that had been earned in the Information Technology sector and had added some of those gains to your Utility sector holdings. What would have happened? Well, in the year 2000 the Utility sector was up 51.7 percent, and the Information Technology sector was down 41.0 percent.

Yes, Information Technology was down again in 2000, which means that your remaining holding in this sector would have been down, however, don't forget that you had captured a large part of the gains from 1999 and had added some of that money to the Utility sector, which was then up dramatically in 2000. Rebalancing does not guarantee results, but this example and others like it should help you to understand that rebalancing your portfolio from time to time has the potential to provide you with more consistent investment returns and additional portfolio stability.

Rebalancing a portfolio can occur in many ways and it should include answers to some of the following questions: (1) what percentage of your portfolio should be in cash, bonds, and equities, (2) what types and maturities of bonds should you have, (3) what percentage of your portfolio should be in small-, mid-, and large capitalization stocks, (4) what percentage of your portfolio should be in domestic versus international equities, (5) what percentage of your portfolio should be in various sectors of the market such as Utilities, Technology, Healthcare and so forth, and (6) will these changes be consistent with your original goals, risk tolerances, and asset allocation model. The answer to number six is particularly important, especially if there have been no substantive changes in your finances or personal circumstances. If you do all of this, you will be on your way to prudently managing your investments.

Chart 14-C.

Sector Leadership Changes from Year to Year.

1995	1996	1997	1998	1999	2000	2001
Health Care 54.5%	Info Technology 43.3%	Financials 45.4%	Info Technology 77.6%	Info Technology 78.4%	Utilities 51.7%	Consumer Dis-Cretionary 2.0%
Financials 49.6%	Financials 31.9%	Health Care 41.7%	Telecomm. Services 49.3%	Consumer Dis-Cretionary 24.1%	Health Care 35.5%	Materials 1.0%
Info Technology 38.8%	Consumer Staples 23.2%	Telecomm. Services 37.1%	Health Care 42.3%	Materials 23.0%	Financials 23.4%	Industrials -7.0%
Telecomm. Services 37.3%	Industrials 22.7%	Consumer Dis-Cretionary 32.3%	Consumer Dis-Cretionary 39.6%	Industrials 19.9%	Consumer Staples 14.5%	Consumer Staples -8.3%
Consumer Staples 36.2%	Energy 21.7%	Consumer Staples 30.5%	Consumer Staples 13.9%	Telecomm. Services 17.4%	Energy 13.2%	Financials -10.5%
Industrials 35.9%	Health Care 18.8%	Info Technology 28.1%	Utilities 10.0%	Energy 16.0%	Industrials 4.5%	Energy -12.3%
Energy 26.0%	Materials 13.4%	Industrials 25.0%	Financials 9.6%	Financials 2.3%	Materials -17.7%	Health Care -12.9%
Utilities 25.2%	Consumer Dis-Cretionary 10.5%	Energy 22.0%	Industrials 9.3%	Health Care -11.6%	Consumer Dis-Cretionary -20.7%	Telecomm. Services -13.7%
Consumer Dis-Cretionary 18.2%	Utilities 0.2%	Utilities 18.4%	Energy -2.0%	Utilities -12.8%	Telecomm. Services -39.7%	Info Technology -26.0%
Materials 17.3%	Telecomm. Services -2.2%	Materials 6.3%	Materials -8.0%	Consumer Staples -16.6%	Info Technology -41.0%	Utilities -32.5%

The above table is for informational purposes only and is not meant to represent the performance of any specific product. These sectors are not available for direct investment. Past performance is not indicative of future results.

Source: Phoenix Investment Partners, a member of The Phoenix Companies, Inc.

SUMMARY: I have covered a great deal of material in the preceding chapters. It is my hope and expectation that you now will have a clearer understanding of how to manage your investments and/or retirement accounts, and how to evaluate your options if you are receiving a lump-sum distribution from a qualified retirement plan. There is so much information out there that it's easy to lose sight of the big "picture": the overall strategic decisions you need to make to insure your financial security. Beware of getting bogged down in the minutiae and distractions that will cause you to lose track of your overall plans and goals. I will close with the following story about Sherlock Holmes and Dr. Watson that illustrates the point better than I could ever explain or articulate.

Sherlock Holmes and Dr. Watson go camping and pitch their tent under the stars. During the night, Holmes wakes his companion and says: "Watson, look up at the stars and tell me what you deduce."

Watson says: "I see millions of stars, and even if a few of those have planets, it's quite likely there are some planets like Earth out there, there might also be life."

Holmes replies: "Watson, you idiot. Somebody stole our tent."

GOOD LUCK WITH YOUR RETIREMENT PLANNING AND YOUR LUMP-SUM DISTRIBUTION.

Appendix A—Sample Questionnaires

Personal Profile
Client

Mr./Ms. Last Name	First Name	MI

Address

City   State   Zip

( )
Home Phone

( )
Work Phone

Social Security   Date of Birth

Gender   ☐ Male   ☐ Female
Marital Status   ☐ Married   ☐ Single
US Citizen   ☐ Yes   ☐ No

Spouse | Partner

Mr./Ms. Last Name	First Name	MI

Address

City	State	Zip

( )
Home Phone

( )
Work Phone

Social Security

Date of Birth

Gender	☐ Male	☐ Female
Marital Status	☐ Married	☐ Single
US Citizen	☐ Yes	☐ No

Retirement Profile

Retirement Age

Enter your desired retirement age. If you're already retired, please enter your current age.

Client's desired retirement age	**Spouse	Partner's desired retirement age**

Life Expectancy

Enter the life expectancy you would like to use to calculate your retirement period.

Client's life expectancy	**Spouse	Partner's life expectancy**

Expected Annual Inflation Rate

Expected annual rate of inflation _____ %

Tax Information

Effective Federal Tax Rate _____ %

Effective State Tax Rate _____ %

Assets	Client	Spouse | Partner	Joint
Money markets	$	$	$
CD/Savings	$	$	$
Credit Union	$	$	$
Other Cash/cash equivalents	$	$	$
Individual stocks	$	$	$
Equity mutual funds	$	$	$
International equities	$	$	$
Taxable bonds	$	$	$
Tax free bonds	$	$	$
Taxable bond funds	$	$	$
Tax free bond funds	$	$	$
International bonds	$	$	$
IRA accounts	$	$	$
Pension plans	$	$	$
Defined contribution plans	$	$	$
Direct Investments/Limited Partnerships	$	$	$
Receivables (notes/mortgages)	$	$	$
Residence	$	$	$
Rental property	$	$	$
Vacation home	$	$	$
Business interest	$	$	$
Life insurance cash value	$	$	$
Other	$	$	$

Liabilities	Client	Spouse | Partner	Joint
Loans	$	$	$
Credit card debt	$	$	$
Home debt	$	$	$
Other mortgage debt	$	$	$
Margin debt	$	$	$
Auto debt	$	$	$
Other debt	$	$	$

Net Worth

	Client	Spouse | Partner	Joint
Assets minus liabilities	$	$	$

Sources of Income

	Client	Spouse | Partner	Joint
Assets minus liabilities	$	$	$
Pensions	$	$	$
Social Security	$	$	$
Ira Accounts (value of account x expected rate of return)	$	$	$
Retirement Accounts (value of account x expected rate of return)	$	$	$
Brokerage Accounts (value of account x expected rate of return)	$	$	$
Savings Accounts (value of account x expected rate of return)	$	$	$

Expenses

Housing

Mortgage/rent	$ _____
Taxes	$ _____
Utilities	$ _____
Maintenance	$ _____
Other housing	$ _____
Home improvement	$ _____
Home insurance	$ _____

Taxes

Federal income	$ _____
State income	$ _____
Local	$ _____
Other	$ _____

Automobile

Monthly payments	$ _____
Insurance	$ _____
Maintenance	$ _____

Personal Expenses

Clothing	$ _____
Personal debt	$ _____
Food	$ _____
Childcare/housekeeping	$ _____
Medical	$ _____
Travel/entertainment	$ _____
Memberships/dues	$ _____

Education

Self	$ _____
Family Members	$ _____

Other

Charitable giving	$ _____
Other	$ _____

Total

	$ _____

Appendix B—Glossary

1099R
Report of single-sum total distribution as well as periodic annuities, pension payments, other partial distributions, distribution of excess deferrals or excess contributions from certain plans (*e.g.*, 401(k)) and withdrawals by certain unemployed individuals to pay medical expenses.

accrued interest
Interest that is due on a bond or other fixed income security since the last interest payment was made.

actuary
A mathematician employed by a company to calculate premiums, reserves, dividends, and pension and annuity rates, using risk factors obtained from tables based on both the company's history of insurance claims and other industry and general statistical data.

adjusted gross income
The amount used in the calculation of an individual's income tax liability; one's income after certain adjustments are made, but before standardized and itemized deductions and personal exemptions are made.

AGI
see *adjusted gross income*

alpha
A coefficient that measures risk-adjusted performance, considering the risk due to the specific security rather than the overall market. A large alpha indicates that the stock or mutual fund is expected to perform better than would be predicted given its beta (volatility).

American Municipal Bond Assurance Corporation
A corporation that offers insurance policies on municipal bond offering.

AMBAC
see *American Municipal Bond Assurance Corporation*

annuitant
A person who is entitled to receive benefits from an annuity.

annuity
A constant stream of income for a single or joint lifetime, or for a certain period of time.

appreciation
The increase in value of an asset.

asset allocation
Dividing investments among different asset classes, such as cash, bonds, and equities.

back-loaded
A feature of some mutual funds in which an investor pays a redemption charge when withdrawing money from an investment.

basis point
One hundredth of a percent. Used to measure changes in or differences between yields or interest rates.

beta
A quantitative measure of the volatility of a given stock, mutual fund, or portfolio, relative to the overall market, usually the S&P 500. A beta above 1 is more volatile than the overall market, while a beta below 1 is less volatile.

bonds
A debt instrument issued with the purpose of raising capital by borrowing. A bond is generally a promise to repay the principal along with interest on a specified date (maturity).

busted PAC
A PAC that has started paying off principal faster or slower than originally planned, thereby "busting" the original payback schedule.

buy-and-hold strategy
An investment strategy in which no active buying and selling of stocks occurs from the time the portfolio is created until the end of the investment horizon.

callable
Able to be redeemed before maturity.

capital appreciation
An increase in the market price of an investment or asset.

capital loss
A decrease in the market price of an investment or asset.

cash equivalents
Investments of such high liquidity and safety that they are virtually as good as cash.

CD
see *Certificate of Deposit*

Certificate of Deposit
Short- or medium-term, interest-bearing, FDIC-insured instruments offered by banks and savings and loans.

cliff vesting
A type of vesting in which no vesting occurs until the employee fulfills the service requirements.

CMO
see *Collateralized Mortgage Obligation*

Collateralized Mortgage Obligation
A mortgage-backed, bond that separates mortgage pools into different maturity classes, called tranches.

constructive receipt
This is a transaction whereby a lump-sum distribution is made payable directly to the lump-sum holder rather than to the firm handling the account.

cost basis
Purchase price, including commissions and other expenses, used to determine capital gains and capital losses for tax purposes.

coupon
The interest rate on a fixed income security, determined upon issuance, and expressed as a percentage of par.

coupon yield
The interest rate stated on a bond, note or other fixed income security, expressed as a percentage of the principal (face value).

credit quality
A rating of a bond that indicates an issuer's ability to make timely payments of interest and principal to bondholders.

credit risk
A change in the value of a security due to a change in its credit rating.

current yield
The annual rate of return on an investment, expressed as a percentage. For bonds and notes, it is the coupon rate divided by the market price. For securities, it is the annual dividends divided by its price.

defined benefit plan
A company retirement plan, such as a pension plan, in which a qualifying employee receives a specific amount based on salary history and years of service, and in which the employer bears the investment risk for the plan.

defined contribution plan
A company retirement plan, such as a 401(k) or 403(b), in which the employee elects to defer some amount of his/her salary into the plan and bears the investment risk.

designated beneficiaries
Beneficiaries who are either single or joint individuals, or certain qualifying trusts.

discount bond
A bond selling for less than its par.

dividend-paying stocks
Stocks that produce income.

due diligence
The process of investigation into the details of a potential investment,
such as an examination of operations and management and the verifi-
cation of material facts.

Efficient Frontier
A concept based on modern portfolio theory. An overall investment
strategy that seeks to construct an optimal portfolio by considering the
relationship between risk and return, especially as measured by alpha,
beta, and R-squared. This theory recommends that the risk of a particular stock should not be looked at on a stand-alone basis, but rather in
relation to how that particular stock's price varies in relation to the variation in price of the market portfolio The theory goes on to state that
given an investor's preferred level of risk, a particular portfolio can be
constructed that maximizes expected return of that level of risk.

Fannie Mae
A congressionally chartered corporation that buys mortgages, pools
them, and sells them as mortgage-backed securities to investors on the
open market. Monthly principal and interest payments are guaranteed
by FNMA but not by the U.S. government.

FHLMC
Abbreviation for Federal Home Loan Mortgage Corporation; see *Freddie Mac.*

five-year rule
A rule stating that under certain conditions, all IRA account assets must be distributed before the end of the fifth year following the death of the owner of the IRA.

fixed rate
A predetermined rate of return of a security during a given period of time.

flight to quality
Flow of funds from riskier to safer investments, such as to high quality bonds, in times of marketplace uncertainty or fear.

floating rate
An interest rate that is adjusted periodically. It is usually based on a standard market rate outside the control of the bank or savings institution, such as the prevailing Treasury bill or the prime interest rate. These rates may have a specified floor and/or ceiling, called a cap or a collar, which limit the adjustment.

Freddie Mac
Government-chartered corporation that buys qualified mortgage loans from the financial institutions that originate them, securitizes the loans, and distributes the securities through the dealer community. Not backed by the U.S. government.

FNMA
Abbreviation for Federal National Mortgage Association; see *Fannie Mae*.

Ginnie Mae
A government-owned agency that buys mortgages from lending institutions, securitizes them, and then sells them to investors. Guaranteed by the full faith and credit of the U.S. government.

GNMA
Abbreviation for Government National Mortgage Association; see *Ginnie Mae*.

graduated vesting
A type of vesting that gradually increases over time.

interest rate risk
A type of investment risk that impacts fixed income investments.

investment product selection
Deciding whether to place stock and/or bond investments in individual securities, money managers, packaged products (e.g. mutual funds and unit trusts), or a combination of these alternatives.

IRA rollover
A tax-deferred option to receiving lump-sum distributions.

laddered portfolio
A bond portfolio in which the investments mature in different years.

liquidity
The ability of an investment to be converted to cash on a timely basis.

living trust
A trust created for the trustor and administered by another party while the trustor is still alive.

lump-sum distribution
The distribution or payment, from a qualified plan within a single tax year, of a plan participant's entire balance to the participant.

market risk
A type of investment risk that involves changes to your principal.

market timing
A strategy based on buying or selling securities in anticipation of changes in market or economic conditions.

MBIA
see *Municipal Bond Insurance Association*

Modern Portfolio Theory
Nobel prize winning theory by Harry Markowitz at the University of Chicago that gave rise to the portfolio optimization principle known as the "Efficient Frontier."

money manager
A professional responsible for the portfolio of an individual or institutional investor, such as a mutual fund, pension fund, profit-sharing plan, bank trust department, or insurance company.

money market accounts
A savings account offered by banks and credit unions, insured by the FDIC and requiring a high minimum balance.

mortgage pass-through
A pool of residential mortgage loans. All payments of principal and interest are passed through to investors each month. Issued by Ginnie Mae, Freddie Mac and others.

Municipal Bond Insurance Association
A group of insurance companies that insure payment of principal and interest on certain bonds.

municipal bonds
Bonds issued by a state, city, or local government to finance operations or special projects.

NAV
see *Net Asset Value*

net asset value
The dollar value of a single mutual fund share, based on the value of the underlying assets of the fund minus its liabilities, divided by the number of shares outstanding.

non-callable
Not able to be redeemed before maturity.

non-designated beneficiaries
Non-living beneficiaries such as charities, universities, and foundations.

non-dividend paying stocks
Stocks that do not produce income but offer the opportunity for capital appreciation.

non-qualified employee plan
An employer's plan that does not meet the requirements of the Internal Revenue Service's code for qualified employee plans.

open-end mutual funds
Investment management companies that issue and redeem mutual fund shares on an ongoing basis.

over-funded
Having a positive surplus such that assets exceed liabilities.

over-the-counter market
The market for securities transactions conducted through a communications network connecting dealers in stocks and bonds.

packaged product
A packaged investment alternative governed by the SEC that includes mutual funds and unit trusts.

par
The face value of a bond, usually equal to 100.

par bond
A bond priced at its maturing face value.

planned amortization class
A CMO bond class that stipulates cash flow contributions to a sinking fund. A PAC directs principal payments to the sinking fund on a priority basis in accordance with a predetermined payment schedule, with prior claim to the cash flows before other CMO classes.

portfolio optimization
Creating an investment portfolio to achieve the highest return with the lowest overall risk.

premium bond
A bond selling for more than its face value.

primary dealer
A designation given by the Federal Reserve System to commercial banks or broker/dealers who meet specific criteria, including capital requirements and participation in Treasury auctions.

principal redemption
The timetable governing the payout schedule of an investment.

purchasing power risk
A type of investment risk caused by inflation that may impact the purchasing power of income.

QDRO
See *Qualified Domestic Relations Order*

Qualified Domestic Relations Order
A judgment or order relating to the payment of child support, alimony, or marital property rights to a spouse, former spouse, child, or other dependent.

qualified employee plan
An employer's stock, bonus, pension, or profit-sharing plan that benefits employees and beneficiaries and meets Internal Revenue Code requirements.

RBD
See *required beginning date*

RMD
See *required mandatory distributions*

Real Estate Mortgage Investment Conduit
A mortgage-backed bond that separates mortgage pools into different maturity and risk classes.

REMIC
See *Real Estate Mortgage Investment Conduit*

required beginning date
The deadline by which an IRA owner must take his or her first Required Minimum Distribution. The RBD is April 1 after the year in which the IRA owner turns age 70.5.

required mandatory distributions
Calculated by dividing account balance by the applicable distribution period.

required minimum distribution
The minimum dollar an IRA owner must withdraw each year beginning when he or she reaches age 70.5, as required by the IRS.

retirement cash-flow analysis
The process of evaluating if a person's retirement cash flow projections are sufficient to cover their retirement cash flow needs.

R-SQR

A measurement of how closely a portfolio's performance correlates with the performance of a benchmark index, such as the S&P 500, and thus a measurement of what portion of its performance can be explained by the performance of the overall market or index.

SEC

See *Securities and Exchange Commission*

secondary market

A market in which an investor purchases a security from another investor rather than the issuer, subsequent to the original issuance in the primary market.

sector

A distinct subset of a market or industry whose components share similar characteristics.

sector investing

Investing in a particular sector such as health care, financial services or technologies. A way to invest in a specific industry related opportunities without exposure to one particular company.

Securities and Exchange Commission (SEC)

The SEC is the primary federal regulatory agency for the Securities industry and is responsible to promote full disclosure and to protect investors against fraudulent and manipulative practices in the securities markets.

single premium deferred annuity

A tax-deferred savings account held with an insurance company.

spread
The difference between the selling and buying price.

standard deviation
A statistical analysis that tells you how tightly all the various examples are clustered around the mean in a set of data.

target-amortization-class
A class of CMOs that are similar to PACs, but lack the same degree of principal payback stability. They are sometimes structured to be very stable if interest rates decrease, but they don't offer the same stability if rates increase.

testamentary trust
A trust created within a will that does not take effect until the death of the grantor.

trading
The buying and selling of stocks.

tranches
One of several related securities offered at the same time. Tranches from the same offering usually have different risk, reward, and/or maturity characteristics.

trustee
An individual or organization that holds or manages and invests assets for the benefit of another.

U.S. Treasuries
Negotiable U.S. government debt obligations that are exempt from state and local taxes: Treasury Bills, Treasury Notes, and Treasury Bonds.

vesting
The amount of time a person must work before he or she can earn benefits that cannot be forfeited.

Wilshire 5000
A market-value weighted index that includes all NYSE and AMEX stocks and the most active over-the-counter stocks.

yield to average life
A yield analysis most commonly seen with mortgage-backed securities. Similar to yield to maturity, but yield to average life takes into account the unique time weighted interest and principal payback characteristics of mortgage-backed securities.

yield to call
A yield that is very similar to yield to maturity, however, it is calculated using the call data instead of the maturity date and the call price instead of the maturity value.

yield to maturity
The rate of return yielded by a debt security that is held to maturity when interest payments, purchase price, length of maturity, and the investor's capital gain or loss on the security are taken into account.

Z Bond CMOs
A type of CMO that does not provide investors with any cash flow and usually has a long-term maturity. They are purchased at a deep discount and then mature at face value.

Appendix C—Lump-Sum Resources

Here are some sources of information I have used.

Books

Financial Dictionary
Barron's Finance & Investment Handbook, 4th ed.
(New York: Barron's, 1995)

Closed End Funds
Thomas J. Herzfeld, *Herzfeld's Guide to Closed-End Funds* (New York: McGraw Hill, 1993)

Open-End Mutual Funds
James P. O'Shaughnessy, *Invest Like the Best*
(New York: McGraw Hill, 1994)

Bonds
Annette Thau, *The Bond Book* 2nd ed.,
(New York: McGraw Hill, 2001)

Individual Stocks
Benjamin Graham, *The Intelligent Investor*, 4th ed.,
(New York: Harper and Row, 1973)

Retirement Benefits
Natalie B. Choate, *Life and Death Planning for Retirement Benefits*
4th ed.,
(Boston: Ataxplan Publications, 2002)

Mutual Funds

The following three companies offer a number of services that
analyze, recommend, and rank mutual funds.

* Morningstar: www.morningstar.com
* Lipper (a Reuters company): www.lipperweb.com
* Wiesenberger Inc.: www.wiesenberger.com

Web Pages for Individual Stocks & ETFs

Value Line (www.valueline.com):
Best known for its individual stock research, the company has
branched out during recent years into other areas such as mutual
fund and annuity research. It ranks stocks by safety and timeli-
ness on a scale of one to five, with one being the best and five
being the worst.

Standard & Poor's (www.standardandpoors.com):
Probably best known for the index that bears its name (the S&P
500), this company's website offers a wealth of information for
individual and professional investors alike.

American Stock Exchange (www.amex.com):
For information about exchange-traded funds (ETFs), this web
site is a great place to start.

Zack's Investment Research (www.zacks.com):
Zack's main service is a stock ranking system, which is now available to the investing public (after fifteen+ years of being available only to professional investors and Wall Street insiders). The company also has relationships with hundreds of brokerage firms and has partnered with them to make their research available to Zack's clients.

Edgar (www.scc.gov):
Official website of the U.S. Securities and Exchange Commission.

Multex Investor (www.multexinvestor.com):
This is a comprehensive site that covers funds, stocks, bonds, and personal finances.

Barclays Global Investors (www.ishares.com):
This site is dedicated to information on ETFs. Investors and advisors will find this web page useful.

www.nasdaq.com:
Just like the American Stock Exchange, this web page has a tremendous amount of data on ETFs.

Miscellaneous

Ed Sloat's IRA Advisor (www.irahelp.com):
Mr. Sloat is a CPA who specializes in the needs of lump-sum recipients and in IRA rollovers. You can get loads of tax data from this web site. A very informative newsletter is also available.

Frontier Analytics (www.frontieranalytics.com):
There are a number of portfolio management software programs that are available through this firm, including Allocation Master, which I have found to be very useful.

Ibbotson Associates (www.ibbotson.com):
Founded in 1977 by Professor Roger Ibbotson, this firm is a leading authority on asset allocation. They have a number of products to help individual and investment professionals manage investment assets.

If you have questions or would like to reach me, you can contact me at dan.flores@ubs.com or DLFLORES1@earthlink.net

Index

0-595-29790-0

Printed in the United States
15822LVS00004B/61-78